The Spectre of Sound

The Spectre of Sound

Music in Film and Television

K. J. Donnelly

 Publishing

First published in 2005 by the
British Film Institute
21 Stephen Street, London W1T 1LN

The British Film Institute promotes greater understanding of,
and access to, film and moving image culture in the UK.

Cover design: ketchup
Cover images: (front) Robert Blake as Mystery Man, *Lost Highway* (David Lynch, 1997);
(back) Jack Nicholson as Jack Torrance, *The Shining* (Stanley Kubrick, 1980).

Set by Fakenham Photosetting, Fakenham, Norfolk

Printed in the UK by Cromwell Press, Trowbridge, Wiltshire

British Library Cataloguing-in-Publication Data
A catalogue record for this book is available from the British Library.

ISBN 1–84457–025–8 (hbk)
ISBN 1–84457–026–6 (pbk)

Contents

Acknowledgments

This book has had a long gestation period. Thanks are due to institutional support from Staffordshire University and from the University of Wales, Aberystwyth. Thanks are due to Andrew Lockett, Sophie Contento and Tom Cabot at BFI publishing. Sincere thanks also go to anyone who has ever helped or supported me, while very special thanks go to Joan Donnelly and Mandy Marler.

The chapter 'Music on Television 2: Pop Music's Colonisation of Television' includes material published in 'Tracking British Television: Pop Music as Stock Soundtrack to the Small Screen' in *Popular Music*, vol. 21 no.3, 2002.

Dedicated to Robert Emmet Donnelly.

'Music has charms to soothe a savage beast, to soften rocks, or bend a knotted oak.'
William Congreve, *The Mourning Bride*, 1697

'To establish aesthetic principles of cinema music is as dubious an enterprise as to write its history.'
Hanns Eisler and Theodor Adorno, *Composing for the Films*, 1947

'Hear angel trumpets and devil trombones. You are invited!'
Alex in *A Clockwork Orange* (Stanley Kubrick, 1971)

Chapter 1

Overview – 'Birdie Sings, Music Sings'

The vast majority of us already know much about film music, even if we never take any notice of it. We can recognise musical clichés, the jaunty tune that appears during a happy scene, the sombre dirge that accompanies a funereal situation. These have become internalised in us to the point that we never really think about them. Yet music on film and television increasingly has become a subject of general interest and of commerce. Now it is possible to buy CDs of old theme tunes and old film scores that have never before been available, while many films and television programmes include the release of musical recordings as an essential part of their production. Apparently, soundtrack album sales increased threefold during the 1990s.[1] This is even more remarkable, as it has taken place against a background of consistently falling record sales overall. While I am interested in film music – and to a lesser degree its close cousin television music – as soundtrack CDs, existing outside films as cultural items and commodities in their own right, I am most interested in screen music as a unique phenomenon 'inside' films and television. It is the only element of film that emanates from outside the film's diegetic world, its 'reality'. As such, it can seem like an artificial element, a vestige from the past or a sop to the MTV generation's desire to watch pop videos in the middle of films.

This book's central concern is with film and television music as scores (also known as underscores, background music, incidental music, non-diegetic music) rather than as featured music performed on screen.[2] It focuses on how music works as a subtle medium of manipulation, which, while not consciously registered, undoubtedly exerts a considerable influence on film and television audiences. I am interested in music's apparent but consistently underrated role of invoking emotion in the viewer, where it becomes the carrier of the audience's primary reactions and emotional frailty. Consequently, I am concerned with how film music constitutes a system of control based on its ability to affect audiences in a significant manner,[3] and to assent to or validate their emotional reactions.[4] Sound and music have been central components of behaviour-control techniques and experiments, and deserve a sustained study of the aesthetics and effects of music applied to moving images.

This would be a massive project; more sustained than I intend to offer here. I am an aesthetic historian who is interested principally in the way that film and television music is all-pervading and aims to control the audience in its psychological processes, its symbolic undercurrents and through its status as one of the most potent forms of non-verbal communication.

As music can appear ephemeral, emotional and irrational, attempts to account for what it does and how are invariably unsatisfactory. It is far easier to talk about its mechanics and 'rules' of construction than deal with its 'psychic life', as a living organism that touches the emotions of its listeners. As Caryl Flinn rightly notes, 'The problem facing film music scholars is how to talk concretely and specifically about the effects generated by a signifying system that is so abstract.'[5] I am not simply interested in describing the music and film, delineating how they were composed, shot and put together. Someone else can outline that process if they so desire. I am concerned with the fact that the combination of music and the moving image is always more than the sum of its parts. It is never merely the vital aspects of the shots and the music; they become a totally different genus when unified. It matters to me how film music works and why it is effective, and how far it can be interpreted as an ethos or aesthetic that is based primarily on the notion of effect. This study will be historically inspired, looking at music accompanying the moving image as an object that has transformed over time, although I will be concerned primarily with the phenomenon of film music, a more unchanging aspect of the overall mechanism.[6] A notable aspect of this is its central role in manifesting and maintaining the authority of film narration, while being a paramount device for attempting to control and discipline the audience in a most subtle manner. Yet while film music traditionally has been conceived as part of narration, working for film narrative, in some ways it would be better to see it as part of the film's repository of special effects.

I hope this book will go some way towards allowing a re-conception of cinema and television as sonic media. Developments in film sound over the past few decades have extended film music's spatial distance from other sounds, thereby giving it more prominence, a sense of unity and, most importantly, integrity. Increasingly, this has rendered the diegetic/non-diegetic divide irrelevant, in that music now often occupies a distinct space of its own anyway. In addition to this, technological and aesthetic developments have resulted in the 'musicalising' of sound more generally. Sound designers use musical instruments (synthesizers, samplers) and equipment, and now rethink sound design less in terms of a 'realistic' sound mimesis, and more as an aesthetic possibility – therefore, in more musical terms. This is hardly surprising, as music is all about organised sound, as exemplified by avant-garde music of the mid- and late 20th century. The fact that music predates established sound design meant that it had a whole technical language available for use in film, including ideas and aesthetics as well as hardware.

Some readers may have difficulty with my approaches to film and television, and to music in this book. This is preferable, however, to the sort of indifference that regularly greets safe scholarly works of data. This book is not, for instance, an appreciation of great film music, a sociological analysis of film music, a close look at the construction of music that has appeared in or been written for films, a production history, an account of context and reception or a description of the notes and how they were played. Whole areas of film music are left out of this book. Instead, it provides a 'long shot', allowing the sort of synoptic view unavailable to detailed analysis, rather than the predominant 'close-up' of many preceding film music studies. It is a rumination, an investigation of some of the elusive and fascinating aspects of screen music. Its grounding is in the concrete aesthetic facets of music in relation to the screen (and the screen in relation to music). Some of the investigations may be 'incomplete' or partial – however, this does not aim to be a full account, but rather intends to touch on many, but not all, areas of film music, in a manner that will stimulate rather than foreclose debate.

Aesthetic Power

In an episode of *The Twilight Zone* entitled 'A Piano in the House' (1962, CBS), Barry Morse plays a misanthropic theatre critic who buys a player piano for his wife. As it plays different pieces of music (such as Debussy's *Clair de lune* and Brahms's *Lullaby*), people begin to act unusually and reveal their true feelings, their demeanours changed by the particular character of the music. While screen music is perhaps not quite this persuasive, unquestionably it aspires to be so. There are correspondences with the way that television advertisements endeavour to influence us, changing our behaviour and regulating us to suit their purposes. As a form of control, this is not a pyrrhic, heavy-handed Orwellian Big Brother, but simply a desire to induce particular audience behaviour. At least, this is usually the case. Certainly, screen culture is equally aware of music's power. In the opening episode (entitled 'Arrival') of the cult British television serial, *The Prisoner* (1966–7, ITC), there is a moment that self-consciously foregrounds the process of screen music, commenting both on the phenomenon and convention of incidental music. A large hatch opens, allowing Number Six (Patrick McGoohan) to see his 'new home' for the first time. As he enters the apartment, some saccharine orchestral music starts, quietly at first, as he reads a welcome note and peruses a map that provides no information about the possibility of escape from 'the Village'. Ths could easily be the sort of non-diegetic background 'filler' music that audiences have been accustomed to hearing when a sequence is devoid of dialogue.[7] However, slowly it begins to dawn on us, the audience, that Number Six can hear the music too.[8] The music takes on a more anempathetic character,[9] trying to drown the concerned state of the only character on screen with a soup of sweet strings that persists and begins to grow in volume. Clearly becoming more perturbed by the music, Number Six begins searching for its point of origin. After a brief search, he locates the speaker that appears to be the diegetic source of the music. He lifts it above his head, smashes it on the floor and then stamps on it, breaking it into pieces. The music persists, unaffected by his attack. It clearly has its origin elsewhere. We, the audience, are as confused as

Number Six. A maid enters the flat and he shouts at her, 'Where's it coming from? How do you stop it?' When she replies that she does not know, he interrupts her with the demand, 'Who runs this place?' This sequence demonstrates our ambiguous and uncertain relationship with screen music. *The Prisoner* has dramatised our position as the audience, illustrating our assumptions about background music, its insinuation into our minds, and our inability to understand why and from whence it attempts to control us. This emblematises screen music as control, and as an integral element of the oblique focus of the whole television series on control, power, mind games, disciplining and surveillance.[10]

There can be no doubt that music is a powerful force that attempts to configure its hearers. Tia DeNora notes that music 'serves to organize its users'[11] and that

> music may imply and, in some cases, elicit associated modes of conduct. To be in control, then, of the soundtrack of social action is to provide a framework for the organization of social agency, a framework for how people perceive (consciously or subconsciously) potential avenues of conduct. This perception is often converted into conduct *per se*.[12]

This could almost be a description of film music: the social aspects of music's power are redoubled in the cinema. Royal S. Brown notes that we cannot ignore the manipulative aspect of film music,[13] while French film director Jean-Luc Godard has promoted the notion that all music in film is manipulative. His own films frequently have had a very particular attitude towards music. In *Vivre sa vie* (1962), for example, Godard cuts up Michel Legrand's neo-classical musical cues, thus preventing their purposeful development or tonal resolution.[14] Godard preferred to have a finished score before the film was completed, so that he could cut excerpts of the music in and out of the film, as, for example, in *Pierrot le fou* (1965),[15] where Antoine Duhamel wrote themes blind that were then manipulated by the film director. As the embodiment of his attitude towards music's 'deception', in one sequence Godard made Duhamel appear in the open playing a piano next to the film's action. When the camera turns to show him, audiences are left in no doubt about Godard's point.

Screen music is a controlling device, in that it wishes to influence behaviour, shaping audience reaction to the film or television programme in which it appears. Furthermore, this influence is extended through a process of formalising the world and then using subliminal 'pointing up' to ensure a particular view of it. As Philip Tagg wrote:

> the unwanted modification of our behaviour as listeners – our manipulation by music, so to speak – is far more likely to occur if we remain unaware, not just of the mere fact *that* we respond competently to music on an everyday basis but also how that competence is used to influence our emotional judgment of phenomena associated with the music . . .[16]

Screen music is pervasive and might be construed as insidious. It masks the way it works, functioning subliminally. It is the interface between heaven and earth, and the sublime and the banal, and is accordingly powerful. According to Theodor Adorno, music 'trains the unconscious for conditioned reflexes'.[17] For him, music is not only a simulacrum for social organisation but crucially is also absolutely formative of social consciousness.

Sound and music have been regularly used as components of psychological warfare and brainwashing techniques. These tend to utilise sound's capabilities in a fundamental and highly effective manner, including, most commonly, sensory deprivatory torture, involving absolute silence, or an overwhelming amount of sound.[18] During the Korean War, US prisoners of war were subjected to brainwashing techniques by the Chinese that included forcing them to sing Communist songs.[19] Pierre Bourdieu has written of 'symbolic power' as a misrecognised form of power. It appears invincible and can only be exercised 'with the complicity of those who do not want to know they are subject to it'.[20] This may explain why film music can influence our attitudes to the screen in the same way that environmental music can change people's behaviour. A television documentary demonstrated how the decision by the Tyne and Wear Metro to start playing classical music at railway stations in the evenings had deterred vandalism. The programme-makers went on to film their own experiment by playing Brahms's *Lullaby* at a wall frequented by graffitists in south London, with largely the same results.[21] Subtle ambient music such as this, bearing notable similarities to the character and context of film music, demonstrates the hidden power of music. This is not political power, however, but an embodiment of the sort of cultural power that is in evidence in art/entertainment, and perhaps most in evidence when music accompanies screen activity.

Michel Foucault's concept of power working through a process of 'disciplining' might be relevant for conceptualising some aspects of the way that film music works. He defines this as 'techniques for assuring the ordering of human multiplicities'.[22] This is a knowledge-power that functions to normalise judgment and ideas about things, and as such is a 'gentle' form of coercion rather than an outright physical oppression that helps to keep social laws unbroken. Similarly, the power of film music is not simplistic 'effect' as a transitive equation or operation, yet nevertheless it encourages us to emote and to think what it wants us to think. Its desire is to make us the unproblematic consumers described by Claudia Gorbman, who likens it to a younger and more obviously manipulative relation, 'Muzak',[23] and other background music played in social and retail situations.

The Heart Strings: Emotion

The majority of psychologists are convinced that music has a powerful, primal and affective impact, as well as a strong therapeutic potential. According to the *Concise Dictionary of Psychology*:

> Research has found that certain feelings – joy, sadness, love, longing and calm – are elicited by music . . . The fast tempo seems to be the most powerful element in creating excitement. The expressiveness of music seems to be due less to melodies than to rhythm and tempo . . . they

evoke a creative or aesthetic response as well as different mood. Music is also credited with extending the attention span, reducing stress, facilitating self-expression, stimulating associations and imagery and helping the process of memorising.[24]

Yet the vast majority of both film and music theory tends to downgrade desire, thus failing to address film music's essential character and primary role in eliciting emotional responses in the audience and in providing consent for the audience's emotional responses.

A strong allegory of film and a credible perspective on film music is depicted in the film *A Clockwork Orange* (1971). Delinquent Alex (Malcolm McDowell) is sent for 'the Ludovico treatment', which consists of aversion therapy involving the screening of film images of violence accompanied by drug treatment, with the aim of associating violence with debilitating nausea. This is textbook Pavlovian 'classical conditioning', where two different experiences are unified mentally through repeated association. However, the white-coated scientists appear to think the film's accompanying music (the final movement of Beethoven's Ninth Symphony) is irrelevant to their process. The music, it appears, has not been carefully chosen; it is simply an 'unfortunate' association, as the scientist points out. Of course, Alex's association of the music with feelings of nausea turns out to be *crucially* important for the film. Pavlov emphasised the importance of secondary stimuli, and aversion therapists no doubt would have been aware of a secondary stimulus as powerful as music.[25] Behaviourists might well argue that film viewing/hearing scenarios can relate to conditioning in much the same way as the treatment Alex receives.

Music in films might be thought of as working in much the same way as the buzzer in Pavlov's famous experiment with dogs. Whereas the buzzer became a device that elicited a reaction (salivation), music in films functions within the cinematic context as a device for the eliciting of emotion and mental reaction in the audience. It shares with Pavlov's buzzer the fact that they are both sonic signifiers. For the dog, it signifies the imminence of dinner, while for the audience in a film theatre, film music signifies directly the preferred reaction to the on-screen action. Much like the dog, we, the audience, have learned how to react. We have learned that a swelling bank of sweet strings literally 'tugs at our heart strings', while we have also learned that a 'stinger' (a sudden blast of music) in a horror film means we should react directly to the shocking action on the screen before us. However, both of these examples also suggest the possibility of a physical reaction to the music (in association with the image). The explosive blast of the stinger can literally mean a shrinking away from its origin (as well as the screen), while romantic strings can bolster our emotional reaction – we may become tearful or feel a lump in our throat. While it may be argued that these reactions are fully dependent upon the narrative and identificatory processes of films themselves, an emotional reaction, although unspecific to music on its own, is most definitely a reality, and the effect of music with film amplifies reaction exponentially.

The fact that music is often seen as working in a subconscious manner in films (I would suggest that, more precisely, it works in a manner that plays across the line of consciousness and subconsciousness) only substantiates further the notion that music has a direct and significant *effect* upon its cinema audience.[26] According to Claudia Gorbman:

> Film music is . . . the hypnotist that lulls us into a hyperreceptive state, in order that we receive and identify with the movie's fantasy. . . . Film music is like the medium of a dream, forgotten in the waking state; but this medium is itself not neutral. It embodies and disseminates meaning, all the more powerful in not actively being noticed.[27]

In fact, as we know the musical clichés so well, we do not need or attempt to process fully the music mentally. Perception of music in the cinema is imperative. The title of Claudia Gorbman's book, *Unheard Melodies*, points to one of the most significant aspects of non-diegetic film music. According to classical Hollywood composer David Raksin:

> The purpose of film music is not to be noticed for itself. Its greatest usefulness is the way in which it performs its role without an intervening conscious act of perception. It is most telling when the music registers upon us in a quiet way, where we don't know it's actually happening.[28]

In her experiments, Annabel Cohen extrapolates this to deduce that audiences are not usually conscious of musical accompaniment for film, concluding that they failed to notice when music was missing from a film/slide presentation.[29] Such induction merely confirms long-held notions that film music is not registered by audiences.[30] Film composer Lalo Schifrin described how 'everybody congratulated me for the music I wrote for the famous chase sequence [in *Bullitt* (1968)]. However, this was the effect of an audio-visual mirage, since there was no background music during the chase, only sound effects.'[31] However, we might notice music more if we become less involved with the film as a whole. In a piece of audience research on David Cronenberg's *Crash* (1996), Martin Barker, Jane Arthurs and Ramaswami Harindranath found that some of the interviewees who were negative towards the film commented favourably about the film's music. In other words, they *noticed* the music, because they chose not to notice other aspects of the film: 'Dismissing the film on *moral* grounds leaves space for complimenting it on individual qualities. In [the interviewee] Derek's case – and he is not alone in this – the music was the striking element.'[32] Or perhaps those who appreciate film music are able to *distance* themselves from the screen activities to some degree. Musicians may well be able to focus on (to be aware of) the music more than non-musicians, but people who are less 'bound up' with narrative and character may well find themselves more *conscious* of the music – whereas others deal with music in an unconscious or semi-conscious manner, and are thus in a situation where it is most effective, according to the absolute terms in which it was conceived.

Sound and music can be, and often are, dealt with in an unconscious or semi-conscious manner. They can also be 'processed' by our brains in the most extraordinary ways. A good example of this is the 'Cocktail Party Effect', where we are able to hear our name spoken from the other side of a room amid a cacophony of voices. This is the same as our ability to 'phase out' certain noise while asleep (such as passing cars, etc.) and embodies the subconscious ways we tend to process sound. I was once in an Indian restaurant where Christmas carols were being played on a tape in the background. I did not notice that they were Christmas carols until well into the evening, although I had registered that it was the normal sort of sitar-led music that one might expect in an Indian restaurant. What this suggests is that first, expectations play a large role, and second, timbre (musical tone colour) dominates in unconscious or accompaniment scenarios (perceived as a sheen of sound, a wall of background noise), despite the fact that the unheard melodies on this occasion were so extraordinarily well known and happened to be the defining structural aspect of the music.

Haunting Melodies: Supernatural and Phantoms

Archaeologists have found that there is a correlation between sites of strong echo and the existence of ancient cave paintings. Echo was thought to embody spirit voices, and some have speculated that certain Neolithic structures not only allowed for sound to be heard through the body as a mystical resonance, but that some of them also exploited infrasound (sound beneath the range of human hearing).[33] These locations, such as Newgrange in Ireland and Camster Round in Scotland, might have used musical sound from drums and voices to create standing waves that could then be seen with the help of dust and smoke. Such passage tombs could have functioned as 'Helmholtz resonators',[34] creating a 'sound and light phantasmagoria' that retained and bolstered power for the religious elite.[35] These spaces might have constituted sound as a spirit force, as an apparition not only of mystical sound but also of *visible* sound. As this illustrates, sound has the capability of being a magical and enigmatic force, embodied most obviously in music.

Since the advent of synchronised sound, non-diegetic music has graced films as a spectral presence, one that sits uncomfortably with the mimetic 'realism' of the on-screen world constructed in mainstream cinema. Years before Eisler and Adorno wrote in 1947 about the 'ghostly effect' of the moving image without music,[36] music had marked a numinous and enchanting presence in the cinema. In recent years, the metaphor of the ghost figure has been fairly prominent in studies of culture, yet this notion of the paranormal is particularly suited to describing and conceptualising non-diegetic music in films, which has an origin outside the diegetic world of the film it inhabits, as well as helping to account for its strange effect on audiences.

Joseph Lanza noted that in 1932, 'Audiences, still new to the sound film, were known to deride a phantom symphony of violins, harps, and horns coming out of thin air whenever characters were in distress or succumbing to a kiss.'[37] Indeed, the celestial voices of film music do resemble a phantom in several significant ways. They are ephemeral, they are not 'substantial' or do not constitute part of what audiences cognise as important in the film, and have an effect that is not apparent. In addition, it is possible that they have an ulterior motive – film music regularly aims to control audiences and cause a direct emotional reaction. Film music appears supernaturally, and has something of a supernatural character more generally. It can, at times, 'burst through' from the 'other side', rather like the oppressive musical drones that accompany the spectral fog-bound sailors in John Carpenter's *The Fog* (1980). These phantoms appear from nowhere, enveloped in the cloak of fog and in the mysterious deep immersing drones of Carpenter's analogue synthesizers. Like a spectre, film music is disembodied and denies the logic of the rest of the diegetic film world. Non-diegetic film music is a seemingly 'irrational' element in the context of the film's construction of a 'rational' diegetic world on screen. It is not simply reducible to simplifying semiotic analysis or communicational discourse analysis. Royal S. Brown notes that music's emotional aspect is perceived as a manifestation of the irrational,[38] while Roy Prendergast states: 'Music has a way of bypassing the human's normal, rational defense mechanisms. . . . We tend to react to music whether we desire to or not and if we don't wish to be moved by it, we resent its presence for making us begin to lose control of our rational, "sophisticated" defences.'[39] While music's emotional effect seems irrational, this 'irrational' association is redoubled in film by its appearance 'irrationally' from nowhere in relation to the on-screen action. Film music's emotional and seemingly insubstantial presence in films highlights its important manipulative function.

Film music not only seems to have an insistent irrational edge, but it also concretises this through its power to manifest the supernatural. In Hitchcock's *Rebecca* (1940), Franz Waxman's melodic theme for the dead Rebecca, which dominates the main titles, reappears throughout the film. Upon the mention of her name or something related to her, we hear the theme, which has the effect of fleshing out her ghostly presence. However, when the nameless narrator (the new Mrs DeWinter, played by Joan Fontaine) first sees the interior of the beach chalet, Rebecca's musical theme appears without any verbal reference to her. Only later do we learn that it was a place she frequented. The 'Rebecca' theme is played on an eerie harmonium as we are shown her room and her monographed books, and during a dialogue about her between the narrator and Mrs Danvers. The music directly creates a spectral presence of the dead woman in the diegesis, almost making the film into a straightforward ghost story.

At certain times – and in its most apparent form – screen music appears as a supernatural manifestation of the audio in audiovisual as pure effect. Simultaneously, it manifests a supernatural, metaphysical level in the film. It is positioned at the apex of the film as an emotional medium that desires audience response within certain narrow, well-defined boundaries.

Film Music Function
Writing in the 1940s, Eisler and Adorno registered the jibe aimed at film music of 'Birdie sings, music sings!'[40] This not only poked fun at the very modest, even mundane functions of film music, but also pointed to how it follows and illustrates film

action pleonastically and with recourse to constant cliché. Silent-film music habitually reused perennial melodies like *Hearts and Flowers*, and the classical Hollywood cinema standardised film scores even further, in terms of production, sound and function. This 'Classical film score'[41] might be seen as distinct musical architecture, particularly in its enveloping 'wall-to-wall'[42] aspect, which attempted to homogenise film music space and thus the very social space of the cinema itself.

Musical scores for the screen can vary from the most basic functionality (often the case with television music) to aesthetic objects that add significantly to or even transcend the context in which they appear. Composer Ernest Gold noted what he called 'the faucet form of movie scoring – you turn it on and you turn it off'.[43] Here, the music simply appears, disappears, rises and recedes in line with a notable action on screen or turn in the dialogue, illustrating just how basic and prosaic background music can be, where it appears fleetingly as a complement for on-screen action only to disappear moments later – such a formulaic approach to scoring films is no surprise in the light of the way that classical Hollywood cinema, the heyday of the 'studio system', was run precisely as a production line, leading to what Eisler and Adorno call the 'tendency to neutralization' in film music.[44] The same Fordist logic that informed the production of cans of beans dictated the organisation of musical production, and the consequent standardisation of film (and film music) product. In a way, it is remarkable that a system like this produced such an array of outstanding background music, when in most cases it was easier to duplicate formulas, paying little attention to music that was generally conceived as almost wholly disposable and momentary. The cultural prominence of the films involved and their net effect of standardising film practices and expectations has made the modes of film music developed by classical Hollywood cinema the font of most other audiovisual practices.

Noel Carroll, Jeff Smith and Roy Prendergast all quote a newspaper article in which respected concert-hall composer Aaron Copland posited the following five categories of film music function: 'creating atmosphere, highlighting the psychological states of characters; providing neutral background filler, building a sense of continuity; sustaining tension and then rounding it off with a sense of closure'.[45] Royal S. Brown notes that (non-diegetic) film music functions on at least three levels: as a 'wallpaper soporific' to allay fears of the dark or silence and to hide noises elsewhere, as an 'aesthetic counterbalance to the iconic/representational nature of the cinematic signs', and as a 'cogenerator of narrative affect'.[46] This latter function is emphasised by Michel Chion, who alights on an additional purpose: the 'added value' of sound, which is able to structure or frame the other aspects of the film, and which he deems of paramount importance.[47] The arrival of recorded sound liberated film music as an aesthetic object within films. No longer was it simply cobbled together popular melodies or basic tunes, where the audience thought of the absent words as a commentary on the action on screen.[48] In many cases, silent-film music was nearly continuous and loud,[49] as it did not have to compete with other sounds, whereas sound cinema forced the music to be surreptitious, to weave in and out of other sounds and then, intermittently, take its chance to rush to the fore. Such stealth and subtlety provide for film music something of its notable nature. Generally speaking, though, music in both sound and silent film enacts a dialectic between matching action (performing as narration, as sound effect) and as general ambience (freer from the 'rest of the film').

Film music tends to be used in distinct units, usually the equivalent of the 'cues' written by film music composers to fit specific sequences, although sometimes they may predate the film. These are repeatedly based around film music schematas, which are like linguistic sentences or visual codes in films and television, representing stock situations: for example, 'car chase', 'love scene', 'scene transition', etc. Indeed, such generic music dominates much mainstream cinema in terms of function, where certain types of music, with certain musical argots, comprise music from action sequence cues to diegetic party music.[50] Nicholas Cook notes that television advertisements often exploit wide-ranging genres of musical language, for example, employing music 'in a kind of stripped-down rock style. (By "stripped-down" I mean the music embodies the features necessary for the recognition of genre, but otherwise has little or no distinctive musical content.)'[51] Such general style presents coded ambience or information about character milieu. More extensively, film music furnishes a distinct ambience for films, and something of a tension exists between general and specific functions.

In fact, there is a notable dichotomy between screen music processes more generally. On the one hand, there is music that is written to fit the film, and on the other, music that is written before the film and cut in as accompaniment to the images.[52] Classical Hollywood was premised upon a system where musical scores would be written for each film after shooting and editing, being constructed to precise timings and the exigencies of the final cut of the film. While this system is still dominant, more recently it has been partially displaced by a practice that exploits pre-existing music as an inspiration for the film, cutting the film footage to fit its structure accordingly. A notable example of this would be films that use pop songs as non-diegetic music, such as Quentin Tarantino's *Reservoir Dogs* (1992) or *Pulp Fiction* (1995). It could even include James Horner's rendering of the song theme from *Titanic* (1997), 'My Heart Will Go On', as a piano solo accompanied by images of Jack sketching the naked reclining Rose. While the vast majority of the film has had music written to precise timings in order to fit the final product, on some occasions the music was less of a secondary consideration. Often music will be cut or compressed to fit the visual edit. In such cases, albums can offer a different experience – providing a space for music that is often compromised by the film's various editors. While it is still the norm for sound to be cut to the requirements of image, now more than ever film is often cut to the music's requirements. 'Synch points' are explicit instances of dynamic convergence between film and music, and often denote significant moments. At their most obvious, they manifest 'stingers', the brief blasts of sound that emphasise action in thriller and horror films, but their proliferation suggests that screen music should no longer be conceived as simply the 'accompaniment' to the unerring primacy of the image.

Film music works through its own logic and (more importantly) through its logic of interaction with other stylistic aspects of film. Cross-rhythm and counter-point are notable attractions in music, and indeed a similar aspect exists in the relationship between film and music, most notably cross-rhythm between time in the music and time in the film (pulse, scheme, pace, etc.), and 'cross-rhythm' (in terms of an interplay/contradiction) between spaces of music and the space of the diegesis. This 'contrapuntal aspect' occurs when music and film interact, each having an impact on the other.[53] We can notice space and pulse interacting, or at least harnessed in tandem for effect. When music is added to film, it can exploit its propensity to play off two spaces (the space of the screen and the space of the music's recording) and two rhythms (musical pulse and the kinetic activity/editing on screen). Film and music have different floor plans of logic and aesthetics. Sometimes they converge. Sometimes they work off each other in a seamless manner. At other times, destructive feedback occurs, allowing for the possibility that the aesthetic object (the film composite) may break down in its workings. This, of course, is a rarity in mainstream film. However, we should note that film music's aesthetic effects are transient and insubstantial, not easily quantified or explained, or even easily conceptualised by the majority of cinemagoers.

Context: Non-Diegetic Status

The positioning of music at certain points in films tends by and large to be conventional – something that could have been (and indeed often has been) done by editing technicians without any significant access to the 'artistic vision' of the film or the film's music. Film music's sound is often unremarkable too. It is usually defined by convention, broadly in terms of sound, rhythm, harmony, melody and structure. What is remarkable about film music is its context, its place in the system of film. The fact that it is simultaneously an element of the film and outside the illusory film world on screen, added to which it addresses a captive audience, is the font of film music's seductive and structural power and influence.

Its non-diegetic status – that it emanates from outside the illusionistic world on screen – is what has given film music its remarkable role and position in films. It is a most notable anomaly in the system, being the only significant element of films that does not come from, or work for, the illusionistic, mimetic screen world that dominates narrative cinema. This non-diegetic position of film music has, in recent years, broken out of its confinement, and now much in the way of diegetic music is able to carry the characteristics of non-diegetic music. Indeed, Franz Waxman's fully diegetic music for Hitchcock's *Rear Window* (1954) is an early demonstration of how music need not be non-diegetic to retain its subtle power.[54] Indeed, film music might be seen primarily as a *context* rather than anything else. In the first place, the cinema viewing situation makes audiences particularly susceptible to musical effects.[55] Second, film music is not usually perceived in a conscious manner, at least not consistently. Third, underscores are 'outside' of the illusionistic diegetic system of films. In this way, they are a unique element of the film's system, and perhaps consequently more problematic for analysis. The film's style and narration (in mainstream narrative films) work hard to convince us that we are experiencing something approximating 'reality'. For music in film, the cinema context, allied to music with a non-diegetic status, adds up to a radical position. By radical, I mean a position of some influence and power, existing slightly beyond the constraints of the film as purely a communicational object. The fact that film music is habitually non-diegetic, thus 'not-real' in relation to the diegesis, gives it something of a supernatural character, where it is closer to 'the voice of God', the transcendent or the supernatural.

One crucial aspect is the way that non-diegetic music is able to offer an immersion, a kind of 'wrap-around sound' that envelops the audience, bathing it in affect.[56] Low frequencies are fundamental to this – they carry further and fill space more effectively, while it is also harder to identify their spatial origin precisely. Medieval churches have exploited musical immersion through the extended reverberation and amplification of low frequencies. Theo van Leeuwen suggests that in such spaces, 'Perspective and hierarchization disappear. The individual no longer feels separate from the crowd, but becomes fully integrated and immersed in the environment.'[57] We should take note that film music comprises exponentially more in the way of lower frequencies than the rest of the film's sound, and that film sound bridges the distance between the screen and audience, touching us physically as airbound vibration. Sequences without diegetic sound allow non-diegetic music not simply to come to the fore, but to obliterate other sounds and prove the power of film music. See, for instance, *Donnie Darko* (2001), in which a scene of young girls dancing on a stage is intercut with a fire in the school. The sequence starts with the girls dancing to diegetic music (Duran Duran's 'Notorious'), but then diegetic sound recedes and music dominates the scene overwhelming all other sounds.[58] A further example of using songs in this manner is John Woo's *Face/Off* (1997), where the climactic shoot-out has no gunshot sounds, but replaces them with a version of 'Somewhere over the Rainbow' that is being played on a child's headphones.

Some commentators choose to downgrade the diegetic/non-diegetic divide. Yet this divide has been crucial for the construction of the mimetic world on screen, where the non-diegetic aspects are minimalised and marginalised. It is this divide that has made film music special, providing it with its own space. Although in recent years, the logic and space accorded to non-diegetic music now can include diegetic music as well, adding up to a space of loud, separate and affecting music. A fine example is the conclusion of *Manhunter* (1986) where Iron Butterfly's 'In-a-Gadda-Da-Vida' is nominally diegetic, being played on a record player. However, the quality of sound (clear, enveloping) and the way that the music is not elided by the cuts in the image track are defiant characteristics of non-diegetic music. In fact, the sound perspective does not follow the requirements of the diegesis but is precisely the same as that of non-diegetic music. This development serves to emphasise screen music as a particular discursive position, underlined by the increased separation of music and other sounds in multi-speaker cinema sound systems and home-cinema set-ups.

A piece of music used in a film will normally have far more impact than when heard outside that context, irrespective of whether it has been written for the film or not. In fact, I am constantly amazed at how good a mediocre song can sound when allied to images in a film. Correspondingly, CDs of incidental film music can often seem to lack something without their image counterparts.[59] The context of the music is crucial, and is the cradle of its power. Of course, such music can work outside the film, but its full potential is realised only in the space of the cinema. In this respect, Noel Coward's famous adage about the potency of cheap music is particularly pertinent to music in film and television. The potency of music can be redoubled in film. According to Annabel Cohen, 'Without music, images seem prosaic, mundane, even lifeless; with music, however, the world of film comes alive.'[60] It is difficult to disagree.[61] Even the most banal songs can appear infinitely better when accompanying something on screen, while almost reciprocally, much film music can sound banal and lifeless outside of its film context. On the other hand, some music can prove to be outstanding in its own right, and while this book focuses on the context of film, it will also attempt to illustrate some of the impressive diversity and wealth of film music more generally.

The logic of this book follows developments in screen music from the cinema to television and to popular music beyond. Chapter 2 is concerned with those moments in film when music rises up and shows itself to be a remarkable agent of power. The chapter concentrates on *Lost Highway* (1997), a particularly naked example of a film in which music is not only allowed to grasp the film by the throat at various junctures, but also where music's ghostly implications cannot quite be subsumed under or assimilated into the film's narrative. Chapter 3 focuses on the music of *The Shining* (1980), some of which is very dissonant, modernist concert-hall music, which seems to have found a suitable home in the horror film. The irony here is that while one area of classical music from the last century onwards increasingly tried to invoke images through the use of sound, film music from the 1920s and after stole copiously from classical music and more recently there has been a return to appropriating classical music for certain moments in film underscores – but it is hardly the sort of music used in *The Shining*. Chapter 4 is primarily concerned with ethnicity and film music, where music becomes 'accented'. It examines how music in films can be used to represent people of different ethnic groups, while retaining a notion of the power involved in certain social groups and institutions assuming the right to represent others. It focuses on 'English', 'Irish' and 'American' film music. Chapter 5 concentrates on the genre film, specifically the horror film. I contend that horror film music, in its extremity and direct aim at effect, exemplifies the way that film music works more generally. Film genres, the horror genre perhaps more obviously than most, comprise whole mental frameworks, including 'rules', philosophies and notions of the limits and possibilities of the film genre as a world in itself that we can understand. The horror genre perhaps displays the most distinctive music, as well as having some of the most clear musical conventions. The next two chapters look at the development of screen music in another medium (television) and the changes wrought on it by the infusion of styles and modes of pop music. Chapter 6 looks at how the form of film music has developed on television and how other traditions of musical accompaniment also have fed into music on television. It is possible to see television music as a further evolutionary stage of film music, and although it is a more prosaic arena, it nevertheless retains many of film music's disciplinary and controlling functions. Chapter 7 explores the use of pop music as incidental music on television, while Chapter 8 discusses the significant infusions film music has absorbed in recent years from the pop music world. It scrutinises the concrete establishment of the pop music-inspired soundtracks as arguably a new phenomenon in films, and also looks to their nature of existence half-inside and half-outside films. These cross-fertilisations have moved apace in recent years, creating an almost autonomous area, spurred on, no doubt, by the burgeoning soundtrack CD market and a concomitant pressure upon musicians to make music that will stand up on its own and be marketable outside the film.

The 'film music' I discuss in this book is a phenomenon that has emerged since the advent of sound cinema and recorded music. Originally simply a 'score' ensconced in the film, its modes have colonised elsewhere, both inside and outside of movies, while soundtracks thrive outside the cinema, and pop music and other musical forms have been manipulated to fit the film context, all on the back of the powerful position of non-diegetic music. Cinema's power is apparent to the most naïve cinemagoer, and I believe it vital that this should be addressed. All but the most jaded are charmed by the cinema, and it is film music's part in its power to startle and amaze, to touch our deepest emotions that inspires this book.

Notes

1 Jeff Smith, 'Selling My Heart: Music and Cross-Promotion in *Titanic*' in Kevin S. Sandler and Gaylyn Studlar, eds., *Titanic: Anatomy of a Blockbuster* (New Brunswick, NJ: Rutgers University Press, 1999), p. 47.

2 William H. Rosar makes a strong argument that the term 'film music' should be reserved for the description of music that derives from a specific compositional practice, namely the (Hollywood) tradition of film scoring. For me, this is problematic, as such a restrictive use of the term is not at present in circulation in the film industry, where film music often means what he calls 'music in films'. 'Film Music – What's in a Name?' *Journal of Film Music*, vol. 1, no. 1, 2002, pp. 13–16.

3 Underscoring effectively shapes a viewer's sense of structure, specifically closure in episodes, thus affecting the overall impression of the film. W. F. Thompson, F. A. Russo and D. Sinclair, 'Effects of Underscoring on Closure in Filmed Events', in *Psychomusicology*, vol. 13, Spring/Fall 1994, p. 25.

4 S. D. Lipscomb and R. A. Kendall concluded that their study demonstrated 'evidence of the powerful effect a musical soundtrack has on the motion picture experience'. 'Perceptual Judgment of the Relationship between Musical and Visual Components in Film', *Psychomusicology*, vol. 13, Spring/Fall 1994, p. 92.

5 Caryl Flinn, *Strains of Utopia: Gender, Nostalgia and Hollywood Film Music* (Princeton: Princeton University Press, 1992), p. 7.

6 Of course, viewing films in the cinema and on a television set presents radically different contexts, which differ in the volume of sound, size of screen and the amount of concentration encouraged by the environment. Television can only indicate a fraction of the effective potential of cinema.

7 The piece is 'Moon Lullaby' by Mark Lubbock, from the Chappell Recorded Music Library.

8 Similarly, at the conclusion of *School for Scoundrels* (1960), Potter (Alistair Sim) addresses the camera and pleads for the soaring romantic incidental music to stop.

9 According to Michel Chion, anempathetic music redoubles its effect through its indifference to the action (while baring the mechanical character of film). *Audio-Vision: Sound on Screen*, edited and translated by Claudia Gorbman (New York: Columbia University Press, 1994), pp. 8–9.

10 Music has a notable place in other episodes. A placard reading 'Music says it all' appears in the shop, while in the episode 'Hammer into Anvil', Number Six implies that a Bizet record has hidden information, which his frustrated adversary, Number Two, tries in vain to decode through listening to the music.

11 Tia DeNora, *Music in Everyday Life* (Cambridge: Cambridge University Press, 2000), p. 7.

12 Ibid., p. 17.

13 Royal S. Brown, *Overtones and Undertones: Reading Film Music* (Berkeley and Los Angeles: University of California Press, 1994), p. 110.

14 Claudia Gorbman, *Unheard Melodies: Narrative Film Music* (London: BFI, 1987), p. 14.

15 Brown, *Overtones and Undertones*, p. 201.

16 Philip Tagg, 'TV Music: Quick Fixes, Semiotics and the Democratic Right to Know', paper presented at the Stockholm 'Music and Manipulation' conference in 1999, available on website <www.tagg.org/texts.html> (accessed 20 April 2003), p. 2.

17 T. W. Adorno, *Introduction to the Sociology of Music* (New York: Seabury, 1976), p. 53.

18 One form of sonic torture involves bombarding prisoners with white noise.

19 Denise Winn, *The Manipulated Mind: Brainwashing, Conditioning and Indoctrination* (London: Octagon Press, 1983), p. 8.

20 Pierre Bourdieu, *Language and Symbolic Power*, edited by John B. Thompson, translated by Gino Raymond and Matthew Adamson (Oxford: Polity, 1991), p. 170.

21 *Beware: Vandals on the Rampage*, tx. ITV (Carlton) at 10.00 p.m., on Tuesday 3 October 2000.

22 Michel Foucault, *Discipline and Punish: The Birth of the Prison* (New York: Vintage, 1995), p. 218.

23 Gorbman, *Unheard Melodies*, pp. 56–9.

24 Dan Motet, 'Music Therapy' in R. J. Corsini and A. J. Auerbach, eds., *Concise Encyclopedia of Psychology* (London: John Wiley, 1996), p. 557.

25 Recasting classical conditioning in terms of advertising: 'In practical terms, classical conditioning implies that pairing a product (conditioned stimulus) with a linked piece of music (unconditioned stimulus) should produce an association between the two, and therefore liking for the product (a conditioned response).' Adrian C. North and David J. Hargreaves, 'Music and Consumer Behaviour' in Adrian C. North and David J. Hargreaves, eds., *The Social Psychology of Music* (Oxford: Oxford University Press, 1999), p. 269.

26 While this perspective seems to bear the trace of earlier (and on the whole now unfashionable) film theory, specifically the reductive and hypostatised 'spectator theory' of the

1970s, which simply postulated a covert effect from the cinema screen onto the passive, mindless spectator.

27 Claudia Gorbman, 'Scoring the Indian: Music in the Liberal Western' in Georgina Born and David Hesmondhalgh, eds., *Western Music and Its Others: Difference, Representation and Appropriation in Music* (Berkeley: University of California Press, 2000), p. 234.

28 Quoted in George Burt, *The Art of Film Music* (Boston, MA: Northeastern University Press, 1994), p. 5.

29 Annabel J. Cohen, 'Film Music: Perspectives from Cognitive Psychology' in James Buhler, Caryl Flinn and David Neumeyer, eds., *Music and Cinema* (Hanover, NH: Wesleyan University Press, 2000), p. 366.

30 S. D. Lipsomb and R. A. Kendall found that perception of the same sequence changed markedly when different musical accompaniment was used. 'Perceptual Judgment', p. 92.

31 Lalo Schifrin, quoted in *Cinema Sounds* (*Sight and Sound/The Wire* Supplement) (London, 1993), p. 3.

32 Martin Barker, Jane Arthurs and Ramaswami Harindranath, *The Crash Controversy: Censorship Campaigns and Film Reception* (London: Wallflower, 2001), p. 118.

33 Robert G. Jahn, Paul Devereux amd Michael Ibison, 'Acoustic Resonances of Assorted Ancient Structures', *Journal of the Acoustic Society of America*, vol. 99, no. 2, February 1996, pp. 649–58; Paul Devereux, *Places of Power: Measuring the Secret Energy of Ancient Sites* (London: Blandford, 1999); Robert G. Jahn and Paul Devereux, 'Preliminary Investigations and Cognitive Considerations of the Acoustical Resonances of Selected Archaeological Sites', *Antiquity*, no. 70, 1996, pp. 665–6.

34 The most obvious example of a Helmholtz resonator is a bottle that resonates on its resonant pitch when air is blown across its opening at the neck. In recording studios, versions of this phenomenon are called 'bass traps' and can be used to reduce bass responses.

35 Aaron Watson, 'Hearing Again the Sound of the Neolithic', *British Archaeology*, no. 23, 1997, p. 6; Aaron Watson and David Keating, 'Architecture of Sound: An Acoustic Analysis of Megalithic Monuments in Prehistoric Britain', *Antiquity*, no. 73, 1999, pp. 325–36.

36 Hanns Eisler and Theodor Adorno, *Composing for the Films* (London: Athlone Press, 1994 [1947]), p. 75.

37 Joseph Lanza, *Elevator Music: A Surreal History of Muzak, Easy-Listening and Other Moodsong* (London: Quartet, 1995), p. 56.

38 Brown, *Overtones and Undertones*, p. 35.

39 Roy M. Prendergast, *Film Music: A Neglected Art* (New York: Norton, 1992), p. 222.

40 Eisler and Adorno, *Composing for the Films*, p. 12.

41 Kathryn Kalinak, *Settling the Score: Music and the Classical Hollywood Film* (Madison: University of Wisconsin Press, 1992), pp. xv–xvi.

42 What Max Steiner called '100% underscore'. 'Scoring the Film' in Nancy Naumburg, ed., *We Make the Movies* (New York: Norton, 1937), p. 220.

43 Quoted in Burt, *Art of Film Music*, p. 81.

44 Eisler and Adorno, *Composing for the Films*, p. 85.

45 Aaron Copland, 'Tip to the Moviegoers: Take Off Those Ear-Muffs, *The New York Times*, 6 November 1949, section six, p. 28; quoted in Noel Carroll, *Theorising the Moving Image*

(Cambridge: Cambridge University Press, 1996), p. 139; Jeff Smith, *The Sounds of Commerce: Marketing Popular Film Music* (New York: Columbia University Press, 1998), p. 6; also Prendergast, *Film Music*, pp. 213–22.

46 Brown, *Overtones and Undertones*, p. 32.

47 Chion, *Audio-Vision*, p. 7.

48 For instance, see James Lastra's discussion of 'funning', whereby popular songs with ironic word implications would be played by cinema musicians. *Sound Technology and the American Cinema: Perception, Representation, Modernity* (New York: Columbia University Press, 2000), pp. 112–13.

49 Although in some cases there was no music to accompany films. Jon Burrows has discovered that some films were projected without accompaniment in transitory British cinemas round about 1908, because of strict music licensing laws regarding the premises being used. Research presentation at the University of Wales, Aberystwyth, December 2003.

50 Pauline MacRory notes that 'action music' consists of 'fast beat, repetitive rhythms, and a continuing movement with no emphasis on any of the violent acts'. 'Excusing the Violence of Hollywood Women: Music in *Nikita* and *Point of No Return*', *Screen*, vol. 40, no. 1, 1999, p. 60.

51 Nicholas Cook, 'Music and Meaning in the Commercials', *Popular Music*, vol. 13, no. 1, 1994, p. 36.

52 However, Anahid Kassabian notes a fundamental distinction between 'composed' and 'compiled' film scores, which creates different forms of audience 'identification'. *Hearing Film: Tracking Identifications in Contemporary Hollywood Film Music* (London: Routledge, 2001), pp. 2–5. Indeed, traditional composed scores tend, by and large, to be momentarily matched to action more than songs, although they may well have the same functions.

53 Burt, *Art of Film Music*, p. 6.

54 Royal S. Brown notes that non-diegetic music is film music 'in its pure state'. *Overtones and Undertones*, p. 22.

55 Seated inert in the dark, we are susceptible to the film's whims and big-screen impact, as well as being forced to listen to loud enveloping music.

56 Gorbman, *Unheard Melodies*. p. 62.

57 Theo van Leeuwen, *Speech, Music, Sound* (Basingstoke, Hants: Macmillan, 1999), p. 28.

58 Exactly like Rick Altman's description of 'audio dissolves' that inaugurate song sequences in the classical film musical. *The American Film Musical* (London: BFI, 1989), p. 110.

59 On other occasions, of course, we can detect the art or artisanry of musical moments that simply do not register in the flow of a film.

60 Cohen, 'Film Music', p. 341.

61 In a laboratory test, G. Sirius and E. F. Clarke found that 'accompanying music (of whatever type) increases the rated "pleasingness" of the visual sequences . . .'. 'The Perception of Audiovisual Relationships: A Preliminary Study', *Psychomusicology*, vol. 13, Spring/Fall 1994, p. 130.

Chapter 2

The Demon of Film Music

Perhaps the most memorable scene in David Lynch's *Lost Highway* involves the spectral 'mystery man' (as the film's credits call him) on the telephone. Here, despite standing next to him, this obscure character informs the film's protagonist Fred that he is at Fred's home 'right now'. He tells Fred to call him up on his mobile phone. Fred makes the call and speaks to the very man who appears to be standing opposite him, and then registers his disbelief. This extraordinary sequence might be related to what Michel Chion calls the *acousmêtre*,[1] the absent power behind sound that is a 'form of "phantom" character specific to the art of film'.[2] While the voice appears dislocated and its origin should have been on screen, it is not difficult to argue that it might be seen as the displaced voice of director David Lynch intruding very directly in the film's diegetic world.

Lost Highway is a film that includes significant degrees of sound dislocation from image as well as prominent and significant musical 'interludes'. Overall, it is a film where music and other sounds occupy far more than the 'supporting cast' role to which they are sometimes assigned. Like non-diegetic music in films, the disembodied voice of the mystery man is reminiscent of the disembodied voices recorded by psychic researcher Konstantin Raudive, ghostly voices in the wilderness that appear disconcertingly and irrationally.[3] In fact, non-diegetic music in films is precisely a disembodied voice, coming through from the 'other side', seemingly emanating from nowhere.

This chapter addresses the enchanting power of the film music in *Lost Highway*, whose musical soundtrack arguably dominates and provides some of the logic for a difficult and perplexing film. Lynch sees music as a paramount aspect of cinema.[4] I wish to account for some of the musical soundtrack's underlying complexity, as well as moments where the music rises in power and 'possesses' the film and its audience. While I will discuss this in relation to one film in particular, my hypotheses and assertions can be extended with ease to examples of music in other films.

Lost Highway exhibits confusion about the diegetic status of its music. This is hardly surprising in a film that is ambiguous about its own diegesis/diegeses. At times, the music appears to be non-diegetic, but then is halted when a space is left abruptly, making it seem like music with a diegetic origin. On these occasions, the film music is effectively seeping from its regular (and powerful) position as underscore, intruding into the film world itself as a force. Like non-diegetic music in films, *Lost Highway* occupies a half-world, a nether world.

Demons and Non-Diegetic Music

Claudia Gorbman likens non-diegetic music to the now rare cinematic devices of the non-diegetic insert (for example, metaphorical trains going into tunnels to indicate intimacy between a couple) and non-diegetic colour (the cosmetic tinting of the whole frame).[5] I think we might also characterise non-diegetic film music as being a device related to a ghost or spectre on screen. Like Banquo's ghost at the dinner table in *Macbeth*, it is something irrational and unaccountable in the seemingly rational world of mainstream film.

Underscores exist within films as a spectral presence, a celestial voice of God, seemingly appearing from nowhere, almost as if from heaven itself. Furthermore, film music can rise up in divine power and possess the film and its audience at significant junctures. This 'possession' is like a demonic force that is seemingly inexplicable, irrational and cannot be easily recuperated by the logic of film itself. Non-diegetic music in films is a 'supernatural' aspect by the standards of the overwhelming majority of mimetic film worlds – film as, or understood as, an illusionistic representation of the world. Film music's relationship with film is parasitic, yet it is also symbiotic. It enhances films, yet at times obliterates their regular processes and dominates proceedings.

At its most potent, it can manifest a demon of film music as bursts of pure effect – not simply film music as the polite clarification of screen activity that some scholars have theorised. Adorno and Eisler described music as warding off the 'ghostly effect' of silent-cinema images,[6] but the reverse may well be the case: that film music in sound cinema furnishes a spectral dimension for films. Non-diegetic film music occupies and cuts out a virtual and problematic space. According to Steve Wurtzler, 'The presence of nondiegetic music in Hollywood films involves a pervasive representational practice that problematizes both the cinema's ability to specify a unitary, centered subject position and its ability to posit an originary event that precedes representation.'[7] *Lost Highway* explicitly problematises both of these, through the division of the central character into two (with resulting confusion for audience) and in the depiction of a world that defies any sense of verisimilitude. Wurtzler goes on: 'Not only does a nondiegetic score specify a subject position different from that of the synchronous recording of voices (whether privileging intelligibility or sound perspective), but it also posits no time or space of origin, no event or source.'[8] It certainly posits no time or space within the illusory world on screen, suggesting an 'elsewhere'. However, it does obliquely posit the time of its own recording, which is implicated as an absence.[9]

Film music is a 'second space' – a different space in relation to the space of diegesis, the spaces of consumption, production, etc.[10] Film music is not simply a practice, there to be described in detail; it is a phenomenon, to be explained and explicated, and furthermore it has also colonised elsewhere, as a 'film music aesthetic'. It has an effect that is not (easily) accounted for and not straightforwardly addressed. Film music is not simply the same as music; its context makes it into far more, which is why music in film adds up to more than the sum of its parts.

This chapter is not simply an elucidation or assay of a single film. *Lost Highway* is extreme, but this extremity illuminates more common practice and makes more transparent the practices that are less evident in other mainstream films. Metaphors provide the possibility of understanding difficult and unapparent phenomena. Film music is a potent organ of control, but film studies commonly sees it as little more than marginalia or footnotes to the 'text' of the film. Yet footnotes can rupture the writing surface from a repressed and powerful unconscious, and this is precisely how I think screen music should be characterised. Film music manifests an (not the only) unconscious level of the film, as well as a level of unconscious within the film (the id – harbouring the unpredictable and sensual). *Lost Highway* has the febrile quality of a dream. Reni Celeste, in a *Cineaction* article, declared that 'Entering the Lynchian universe is like entering a body',[11] and according to the film's press kit, '*Lost Highway* is not only about the human psyche, it actually seems to take place inside it.'

More generally, I would argue, the virtual space of film music and the soundscape might be conceived as the virtual space of mental processes, making film music the unconscious space of the film. It may be more like an unconscious level of the film (or a level of unconscious in the film). We can then see it as a repository of reminders, half-memories and outbursts of emotion and the illogical. These 'ghosts' and 'memories' that can haunt a film are often little more than shapes, momentary configurations or half-remembered sounds. Greil Marcus discusses faint aspects of history in a manner that might also apply to films:

> This is history as disappearance. It's as if parts of history, because they don't fit the story a people wants to tell itself, can survive only as haunts and fairly tales, accessible only as specters and spooks . . . History is a kind of legend, and we do understand, or sense, buried stories, those haunts and specters, without quite knowing how or why.[12]

These 'traces' are available in music, and provide references or implications when included in music in films.

Film music might be seen as an 'unconscious' intervention in the film. *Lost Highway*'s sound space drifts in and out of consciousness and seems to include some key intrusions from the subconscious. Thus *Lost Highway* is a dramatisation not only of film music processes, but also of wider cultural processes, all of which, Adorno reminds us, are also social processes. Caryl Flinn declares that film music is not a transcendent or subversive force under the conditions in which it has been constituted theoretically or in terms of production.[13] Thus, I would argue, we need to *reconceive* screen music's place and effect.

As I suggest in this book's opening chapter, film music sees itself as having power: to discipline us, to tell us things,[14] to make us take notice and to make us emote. Film music embodies film's aspiration to control/manipulate audiences. This is manifested clearly by the standardisation of effect aimed at by THX sound and its environmental counterpart, TAP (the Theatre Alignment Project). We regularly fail to deal with film music as a phenomenon. Film music is not simply a materiality; it is an effect, a ritualistic portal. The best example of this process can be found in horror films, where film music customarily works ritualistically to *invoke* film demons. It is a powerful device – although at face value it may not seem so. As I noted in Chapter 1, Claudia Gorbman alludes to film music's similarity to 'Muzak',[15] signalling it as a minor power, as a disciplining device, used precisely to activate behaviour or reaction. It is Pavlovian in the way that film music can be a 'trigger', embodying Adorno's dictum that music 'trains the unconscious for conditioned reflexes'.[16]

Ghosts and Demons
In his 'Evil Demon' or 'Malin Genie' hypothesis, René Descartes postulated that an evil demon might have taken control of all our senses, making all our perceptions false. It is possible that we might thus live in a completely fabricated universe, of false vision and sound, as well as false touch and smell. The reason for Descartes's rhetorical suggestion about the demon was to make the point that we could not accept 'evidence' for anything that comes from outside our own mind, as formulated in his famous 'Cogito' declaration:

> I will suppose, then, not that there is a supremely good God who is the source of all truth, but that there is an evil demon, supremely powerful and cunning, who works as hard as he can to deceive me. I will say that sky, air, earth, colour, shape, sound, and other external things are just dreamed as illusions which the demon uses to ensnare my judgment.[17]

Film music 'haunts' films, both as ghostly references to somewhere else and something else, and as a mysterious demonic manipulative device. Music in films contains ghostly traces of music and sound that are not fully materialised, while the film music demon involves an (unsubtle) rise in music power in an attempt to possess the audience.

The metaphor of the ghost or supernatural being has had some currency in recent critical theory. For example, Jacques Derrida's *Specters of Marx*, where Karl Marx's concerns and ideas have remained persistent and informative, despite only appearing in an ephemeral form rather than being of direct influence.[18] Similarly, Jean Baudrillard's concept of the 'Evil Demon of Images' suggests an unknowable and potentially malign presence in the midst of films,[19] while his 'revenge of the crystal' notion implies that ultimately we cannot pin down aesthetic objects; they elude our attempts at mastery.[20]

As discussed in the introduction, non-diegetic music acts as a 'supernatural' element within the worlds constructed by cinema, and also manifests an emotional passion and irrational force in films – rather than simply being functional or consistently and reassuringly tame. Describing it as a 'demon' poses film music as bursts of pure effect, not simply as a clarification of screen activity, or a 'communicational' discourse reducible to a couple of semiotic turns. At significant junctures, film music rises up powerfully, possessing both the film and its audience.[21] As George Burt notes:

> There are occasions when the score takes on a more noticeable role, if only for a short period of time – even a few seconds. This can occur at the beginnings and endings of scenes or at climactic points where dialogue and action come to a momentary pause.[22]

Music is all-consuming and enveloping in cinemas, particularly with good sound systems. And at particular moments, when it occupies the foreground, film music is able to use its potent charming methods to manipulate the audience to the full.

A formalistic definition of these moments might focus on musical 'upfalls', where the music rises and comes to the fore while diegetic sound is marginalised, as often occurs during exciting or 'significant' moments.[23] This is related to the song sequences in film musicals, and what Rick Altman calls the 'audio dissolve' – the moment where the regime of mainstream film changes, with music moving into the foreground and diegetic sound and causality receding – a reversal of cinema's dominant regime:

> diegetic events, which seemed to be progressing according to an entirely causal scheme, slide imperceptibly, through an audio dissolve, toward the reduction of diegetic sound and the introduction of transcendent, supra-diegetic music. At this point, the events of the diegesis change motivation. Diegetic sound disappears; the only diegetic sounds which remain at normal volume are those which keep time to, i.e. are subordinated to the music. . . . The image now shows movements which depend more on the music than on one another.[24]

I think this can be applied equally to mainstream dramatic films,[25] bearing in mind Altman's description of the audio dissolve as a bridge from the prosaic everyday to the transcendent.[26] While it may not lead to full-blown song sequences as in the film musical, such moments are marked by music's power, even if only for a fraction of a second.

Illustrations of this 'demon' could include the shark theme from *Jaws* (1975), which indicates the off-screen presence of the shark as a powerful musical presence, and *Night of the Demon* (1957 US: *Curse of the Demon*), where a burst of musical sound is an essential aspect of the appearance of the film's demon. Other examples also include the romance genre's swelling strings, in films such as *Now, Voyager* (1942), where both Steiner's soaring main theme and an excerpt from the first movement of Tchaikovsky's *Pathétique* symphony (No. 6 in B minor, Op.7 4) are used to great effect. We could also cite John Williams's swelling explosion of the main theme from *E.T.* (1982) as Eliot and ET fly across the sky on a bicycle (which also marks the music's first full outing in the film itself). Similarly, Bernard Herr-mann's strident use of bass trombones to impart overwhelming blasts of sound in films such as *North by North West* (1959) or the stabbing bird-calling strings during the shower scene in *Psycho* (1960).[27]

As we have seen, the 'demon' is a form of stinger, the blast of music that empha-sises action (and provides shock) in horror films. The score for *Halloween* (1978) is premised upon a succession of stingers, while *The Shining* contains a number of star-tling moments, such as the appearance of the ghosts of the murdered children to the accompaniment of a Bartók piece dominated by very large gongs. Overwhelming 'demon' music is a convention for dream sequences, as, for example, in the 'death visions' in *Flatliners* (1990). It is transcendent, or at least beyond the banality of film's everyday 'reality'.

Susan McClary notes music's 'ejaculatory' moments in opera.[28] In *Lost High-way*, the impotent Fred gives the impression that he is only able to achieve an orgasm with his saxophone.[29] However, the film's more obvious aural orgasm is not the sex scenes, but non-diegetic musical outbursts, both of which are performed by the German group Rammstein, the kinesis of their sound providing climaxes for the film that are almost physical in their impact.

The musical 'demon' marks an atavistic return of the repressed, where films are haunted by the origins of cinema. Film music is the central aspect of the repressed cinematic regime of *melodrama* – a dominant mode in silent cinema – which might be characterised as film's originary state, its heritage.[30] Caryl Flinn notes that melo-drama uses music in a manner that seeks neither to be quiet nor avoid being heard.[31] In addition to this, these powerful demonic outbursts are the bastard child of the dead classical musical film, existing as a ghostly trace in the present. It is not simply a residual, a 'left-over' syntax, but a whole philosophy, and one that is par-ticularly evident in the films of David Lynch.

Lost Highway

David Lynch's *Lost Highway* has a most unusual narrative: Fred, a tenor saxophone player, lives with his wife. Their life is interrupted by a 'mystery man' who, inexpli-cably, has complete access to their home. Fred wakes to find his wife brutally mur-dered and is incarcerated for the crime. In jail, he metamorphoses into another character called Pete, who then goes on to have an affair with a woman who appears to be Fred's (apparently dead) wife. Inevitably, any story description will be totally inadequate, so there is little point in going into further detail. From this basic out-line, however, you might note a similarity with the story of Orpheus, who was allowed to go into the underworld to find his dead wife Eurydice. Orpheus's music was so powerful it could cross boundaries as important as life/death, and music is central to the film's boundary-crossing.

It is little surprise that the music is so important in *Lost Highway*, as it invokes and provides a direct line to the irrational, a notion that Royal S. Brown has explored.[32] This does not go far enough for me. I think that film music regularly constitutes an irrational element in films – and not simply through its non-diegetic status in films, but through its direct engagement with emotion and physicality (through volume and pitch). In *Lost Highway*, music provides a direct line to the irrational that lies at the heart of the film, although critics like Slavoj Zizek try to recuperate the film's 'supernatural' elements as simply plain old 'fantasy'.

In his book on David Lynch, Michel Chion asks that we listen to his films with our eyes,[33] but perhaps we should see more with our ears. We can often *hear the images* – the use of representational musical figures, themes that double characters' on-screen appearances, etc. – but can we ever *see the music*? Perhaps musicals correspond with this description, but *Lost Highway*, at times, *visualises* songs very directly. It is not unlike Jonas Akerlund's pop video for Daft Punk's 'Around the World', where visual elements are made literally to manifest the song's musical (rather than lyrical) components.

Music is central to Lynch's process of creation: 'Sometimes if I listen to music, the ideas really flow. . . . It's like the music changes into something else, and I see scenes unfolding.'[34] Lynch has released albums of his own music,[35] and *Lost Highway* contains many musical referents, along with cameo appearances by musicians. This augurs the importance of music for the film's construction. During the bowling alley shoot, Lynch had Nine Inch Nails's 'Gave Up' 'blasting through speakers',[36] while the film's cinematographer, Peter Deming, noted: 'all the while [during production] David was blaring the piece of music that would accompany the scene in the finished film, which allowed us to take our camera cues directly from the music'.[37] This is a rarity, with music cueing action rather than vice versa, and makes the film's genesis more like that of a musical!

There is a certain atavism when music takes a central position in the film process – not only are production techniques similar to musicals, but other elements can take on a more 'musical' function. The film's 'mystery man' figure (as he is called in the credits) can be seen as a visual manifestation of film music. He is a ghostly (white-faced) figure, existing without explanation and remaining powerful up to an uncertain end. His fatalistic role denies narrative development, appearing as a visible 'plot device' that simply makes events happen. He is a literal manifestation of synaesthesia. Furthermore, the 'mystery man' might be seen as the on-screen apparition of Lynch the film-maker[38] – who is also Lynch the film's sound designer and co-composer of some of the film's music. Lynch has described himself as more of a soundman than a film director,[39] and according to Ken Dancyger, he uses sound effects the way that most film-makers use music.[40] As an academic discipline, film studies has made the mistake of seeing film as based on visuals, or narrative, rather than on the sonic/aural. However, studies of film music can neglect the sound designer's role in manipulating the raw musical product in favour of valorising the music composer.

Focusing on sound design as a creative process requires a fundamentally different way of thinking about film music from the traditional 'musical studies' perspective.[41] Since the advent of Dolby and digital (or even magnetic sound and compression), sound editors have been able to superimpose sounds with well-defined separation, as well as using sound at the periphery of hearing. This is particularly true for *Lost Highway*. Sound effects and music are very difficult to distinguish, and the whole of the soundtrack can at times be extremely quiet (particularly in the first section of the film).

A production focus on sound design can often mean less music in films, in favour of sound effects. Yet classical cinema often had very basic, even poor sound quality, and the improvement of technology and sound effects means more 'sound' in films. 'Sound design' – often conceived in a 'musical' manner – has largely replaced the 'classical film score' as the musical paradigm for contemporary cinema.[42]

Lost Highway does not contain a musical score in the traditional sense; it has music written by three composers, a music album that was played on set during shooting and a number of songs that helped determine the production itself. Music functions not so much as an accompanying score to the film, but more as a central, integrated part of the whole enterprise.

Lynch's regular musical collaborator, Angelo Badalamenti, provided the backbone of the music for the film. He has retained a close relationship with Lynch since 1986 and their first collaboration on *Blue Velvet*, where he was commissioned to write music to replace the film's temp track of Shostakovich's Fifteenth Symphony. The soundtrack CD includes one of Badalamenti's principal compositions, a slow piece called 'Dub Driving'. As with many of the other pieces in the film, the slow surface rate of the song's tempos works to slow down the action on screen, seemingly moving it out of the time of film activity and into a place of musically apprehended time. The composition is built upon a reggae beat that provides tempo for the pedestrian screen action. It remains relentless and undifferentiated for some minutes, such as during the scene of Pete driving and then having sex with Sheila.

Other sections of the film's music were provided by Trent Reznor from industrial rock group Nine Inch Nails, who supplied a couple of pieces, including the music at the film's conclusion before the end titles and more generally what Lynch called 'drone work'.[43] The concluding music is an amazingly kinetic piece that accompanies the final chase scene as Fred apparently undergoes yet another metamorphosis. Exploiting the characteristic Nine Inch Nails sound of electric guitars driven through amplifiers in series, it provides a terrifically overdriven, distorted sound.[44] The atmospheric ambient 'drone work' was a collaboration between Reznor and Peter Christopherson from Coil.[45]

'Additional music' in *Lost Highway* is credited to Barry Adamson, once bass guitar player with Magazine and Nick Cave and The Bad Seeds. His film noir-style themes for Mr Eddy owe a lot to Elmer Bernstein's main theme for Otto Preminger's *The Man with the Golden Arm* (1955).[46] The pieces are theatrically slow, resembling some of his other work: for example, 'The Big Bamboozle', which has been used on a Murphy's stout advertisement on television. While these pieces for Mr Eddy are 'scored' to the film, other music retains its own temporal structure and appears to be 'cut in' to the film, or indeed, the film cut to music.[47] The first composition, 'Something Wicked This Way Comes', had been written before the film's conception, and is used as seemingly diegetic music for the party sequence when Fred speaks to the mystery man. The application of a little pop music literacy will also note samples from the late 1960s hit 'Spooky' by Classic IV, French singer Françoise Hardy's 'O les temps des souvenirs' and the drop-out from Massive Attack's *Blue Lines* (1991).[48] The last piece was, in turn, derived from a sample of Tom Scott's 'Sneakin' in the Back' from 1974, making for a ghostly superimposition, with the music consisting of a sample of a sample. Such organ-led blues rock is most reminiscent of the music used to accompany party scenes in films from the 1960s. Indeed, it seems that Lynch has concretised images that are already implied in the music.

The second existing piece by Adamson is 'Hollywood Sunset', which is based on a languid reggae beat and employs an extremely slow tempo that continues Badalamenti's 'Dub Driving' cue. Again, it slows the action down while ignoring screen dynamics. Its opening uses a five-second sample of an organ run from Emerson, Lake and Palmer's 'Karn Evil 9', a sardonic song about the grotesque/circus sideshow (part of which is now used, bizarrely, as the theme to family entertainment television programme *The Generation Game* on BBC 1).

Adamson's use of quotes and pastiches entailed a focus on readymades, timbres and cultural clichés/meanings that relegates the importance of melody/harmony.[49] His pieces are founded upon musical referentiality – traces of 'elsewheres' that make the music point outwards instead of inwards. Landscapes have ghosts – echoes and signs of past developments – and so do films and their soundtracks. The ghostly musical aspects of films point to an absent genealogy, and songs in *Lost Highway* reference elsewhere. (Indeed, recontextualised music almost always carries connotative baggage of one sort or another.) Moreover, virtually all the songs appear as bursts of demonic sound, blotting out other sonic concerns.

One of the most prominent songs in the film is This Mortal Coil's 'Song to the Siren', which appears more than once, suggesting some level of significance. Lynch had wanted to use this song from the mid-1980s in *Blue Velvet*,[50] but had had to make do with Badalamenti's 'The Mysteries of Love'. This song has acquired something of a cultural status, having appeared in films and on television (including a 1990s perfume advertisement), while it also has a certain cult value via the performers involved (in effect, the Cocteau Twins) and the early death of the song's writer and original performer, Tim Buckley.[51] The song is based on primary chords, with a thin but sonorous reverb-heavy texture of mostly guitar and solo voice. The siren in the film to which the song seemingly refers is doubtless Renee/Alice. This leads us back to Greek mythology, although we should bear in mind Adorno's pronouncements about culture and the siren song, which I will discuss further in the following chapter. Chris Rodley noted the seemingly organic relationship between song and images:

[the editor] puts up another sequence, a single shot lasting three-and-a-half minutes. It's night. A cabin in the desert is burning ferociously. But something isn't quite right. The spare, painfully melancholic strains of This Mortal Coil's version of Tim Buckley's *Song to a* [sic] *Siren* accompanies the conflagration. It could have been composed for the sequence.[52]

While watching this in an editing room, he fails to notice straight away that the shot is in reverse, such is the music's charm over the image.

The film also includes Marilyn Manson's cover of the camp Screamin' Jay Hawkins voodoo song 'I Put a Spell on You',[53] a malevolent composition about manipulation and possession, and his own 'Apple of Sodom'. Manson also makes a brief cameo appearance in one of the porn films within the film, along with his guitar player, Twiggy Ramirez. A prominent position is given to Lou Reed's version of 'That Magic Moment', a cover of an old rock'n'roll song by Doc Pomus, who wrote 'Viva Las Vegas' for Elvis. Are these song appearances simple 'comments on the action'? I don't think so. It is more as if the action emanates from the songs themselves, particularly from their grain of sound and rhythmic aspects.

Pop songs are integral temporal structures based on a number of highly formalised strategies that allow a maximum of audience cognition of the material. In film, they change the relationship of its components by reorganising the film's temporal aspect/schemes, as well as its audio and visual parameters. The pop song, in particular, has a highly characteristic articulation of time that is based, in most cases, on the primacy of an unerring pulse or beat that functions as a central temporal logic in itself. In sequences that foreground music based around heavily regulated musical time, the other elements of the film, to a large degree, have to cede their importance and roles to the music.

In the cinema, regulated musical time most obviously is polarised into its use either in montage sequences, where it unifies a selection of disparate time images into a whole, or in performances by singers that pose a 'real' or chronographic time. The relationship between pop music and time has to be seen as one of direct affect: pop music harnesses and articulates time. It concretises time by converting real or experiential time into a regulated musical time. One of the central attractions, and indeed the primary uses of pop music – dancing – attests to the musical articulation of time, largely through rhythm in its relation to the human body.[54] The beat of pop music is formalised into what is customarily known as the 'backbeat', characterised by the snare drum's provision of an emphatic accent on the second and fourth beats of the bar. This is precisely a musical and temporal spine. As Theo van Leeuwen notes, 'Western music [became] overwhelmingly dominated by the principle of a regular, unvarying machine-like beat, to which all voices and instruments had to submit.'[55] If pop music is premised upon rigour and repetition, in its rhythmic reiteration, its form sustains this to create a most easily cognised succession of musical material. The beat is (virtually always) harnessed into a repetitive structure of four beats to the bar, the ground zero of pop music, which is extrapolated to yield structures of four, eight and sixteen bars,[56] comprising the simple and basic formal principle of the 'song form' that is a key aspect of western popular music. Theodor Adorno viewed the standard format as one of its essential characteristics: 'The whole structure of popular music is standardized . . . The whole is pre-given and pre-accepted, even before the actual experience of the music starts. . .'[57]

Fundamental differences exist between cinematic and regulated musical time. Cinematic time is primarily *flexible*, able to encompass ellipses and reversals (in terms of flashbacks), while also allowing some degree of ambiguity about its temporal relations between shots and sections of the individual film. Speaking generally, it is based on succession and premised upon development and variation in its discourse. Regulated musical time, on the other hand, is founded upon repetition (of the beat), and in terms of process and cognition, veers more towards the static than the developmental of cinematic time. While these are perhaps extreme models, such forms of time in the cinema constitute profoundly different modes of discourse.

As we have seen, music from the first Rammstein album was played on the set of *Lost Highway*.[58] Industrial heavy metal (I have even heard it called 'dance-metal') with deep declamatory singing in German, their music demonstrates the awareness of component elements characteristic of 'deconstructionist' music, and similarly retains a vague inspiration from minimalism (reminiscent of Kraftwerk, Hardfloor or some of Carter Burwell's film music), where traditional 'ornamentation' is elevated to being a central feature of the music.

Lost Highway uses only the introductions to two of their songs. The first piece is called 'Rammstein' and consists of a static Phrygian-derived harmony that develops only slightly further in the main body of the song (which is not heard in the film).[59] This is adumbrated by a synthesizer bass in solid four down beats, across which appears a sequenced synthesized percussion passage based on the sound of a helicopter. This is phase-filtered to supply a sense of spatial movement, and the increase in higher pitched overtones builds the music to the point where the main body of the song starts – a blast of a guitar chord that matches on-screen activity and signals the end of the song edit in the film. The second segment is the introduction to 'Hierate Mich'. This is based on a descending harmonic pattern in keyboards bass register. The timbre is derived from what sounds like a treated sample of a male-voice choir, on top of which is a vocal line that is more interested in the enunciated words than in any form of melody in the pop/rock sense. Both of these blasts of music use spare textures, lacking instrumental elaboration.[60] Significantly, as introductions, both are ramps of intensity that build up towards sonic punches – providing the film with a wind-up of tension and release. The guitar entry becomes the door closing, this synchresis involving music's replacement of diegetic sound.[61]

As compositions played on the set, Rammstein's music had a central place in the film's conception – and provides an example of music as the 'key' to a film. It signifies a certain atavism, like the ghostly return of the repressed. The film this sequence accompanies is not merely the pornography, the existence of which was denied by Alice/Renee. It is an explicit image of Alice/Renee having sex with someone else.

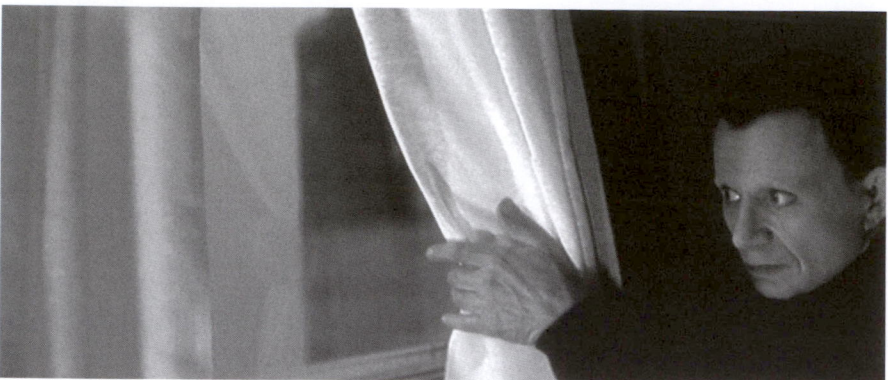

Lost Highway

Could that someone else be Fred?[62] The song 'Hierate Mich' chronicles a man's desire for his dead wife – rather like Orpheus, who pursued his dead wife into the underworld. It *intrudes violently* into the film.

The sequence is most bizarre. Pete is sent upstairs by Alice and, as he ascends the staircase, the Rammstein piece begins. Appearing disorientated, he is framed in a close-up that emphasises his pained facial expression. At the top of the stairs, he encounters the hotel corridor that we have first seen earlier in the film. The space is dramatically lit and the camera moves in a queasy manner. Pete then comes to a door, which he opens apprehensively. Inside, he encounters Alice, in a shot that is heavily processed with saturated colours. She asks him if he is going to ask 'why?' Pete closes the door and goes back downstairs, where he finds an oblivious Alice getting ready to leave. The music has been a crucial part of this sequence. As Pete climbs the staircase, the music builds until it hits the rhythm and guitar riff at the centre of the song just at the point where Pete opens the door. As he walks downstairs, the music is replaced by ambient diegetic sound.

This is the climactic moment of the film – its apogee – and the music manifests an outburst from the id. Here, the spectral presence bursts through twice – crudely, obtrusively – into the consciousness of the film, into its conscious state. Again, this underlines the disjunction between the sound and the image. It is an eruption, not integrated into the flow and seamlessness of the soundtrack.[63] Like the previous example's build-up of pure effect, this sequence demonstrates a demonic moment of raw musical effect in the film, where the non-diegetic music is so powerful that it forces the image to become non-diegetic as well.[64]

Conclusion

Unlike almost all film-makers and writers on film, David Lynch can see film dialogue as less important than music, as is vividly testified to by the club sequence in *Fire Walk with Me* (1992), where dialogue is rendered utterly inaudible by loud music. Chris Rodley also described how Lynch cared less about dialogue during shooting than about having a record played on set during the filming of a scene.[65] Film-makers are regularly inspired by music, as much as if not more than everybody else, and in certain cases, it is fairly clear that the music has been the inspiration, or even dictated, the film action. In the case of *Lost Highway*, Lynch had almost all the songs in place before and during production, a strategy that tends to be a rarity in mainstream film production. At certain moments, the music seems to be the key to what is transpiring, as well as a comment on the screen action. When Pete first sees Alice (in slow motion), we hear Lou Reed's interpretation of 'This Magic Moment'; while when Alice is made to strip for gangster Mr Eddy, who becomes her lover, we hear Marilyn Manson's interpretation of Screamin' Jay Hawkins's 'I Put a Spell on You'. Yet rather than being a facile comment on the action, it is as if the action has emanated from the music. This is underlined by the mystery man's appearance to the tune of 'Something Wicked This Way Comes', an already existing instrumental piece that therefore cannot be construed as a comment on the action. *Lost Highway* has a musical soundtrack that arguably makes more sense than the film itself. In its extremity, it can illuminate more common practice in more quotidian films. It can tell us much about contemporary film music – through induction – and about the relationship of film and music more widely, as well as the place of musical scores and songs in films generally. Although Lynch appeared unhappy about it, the term 'psychogenic fugue' was used in some of *Lost Highway*'s publicity. It is perhaps no surprise that such a singular film can be described in quasi-musical (as well as psychological) terms.

The film soundtrack is a spectral landscape, which, aurally, is haunted by musical ghosts and demonic musical power. This 'demon' is a sign of the residual ancient omnipotence of melodrama, manifested as music, as the possibility of pure sensual effect. The film musical's audio dissolve has emigrated into mainstream cinema. The demonic power of music marks 'key' moments, not only moments of significance for the film's narrative, but those that are 'excessive' to the narrative's significance. It is essential to grasp the fact that music does not just 'underline significance' of these moments, but monumentalises[66] – making it seem more important, which simultaneously makes it physical and emotional. *Lost Highway* illustrates this process well, where the materialisation of Rammstein's music constitutes not only part of the film's ghostly aspects, but also marks a clear manifestation of the power of screen music itself. Indeed, the film might make more sense if it was construed as a visual manifestation of music, a manifestation of a sonic place within film.

Music imported to films ceases to be what it was before. It's place in film adds something to it (as well as taking something away).[67] In *Lost Highway*, songs are fragments, losing their form and integrity. Absolute or 'pure' music is concerned with being a number of different things; non-diegetic music is more concerned with 'pure' effect, at its most auspicious manifesting a white heat of stimulus.

Notes

1 Michel Chion, *Audio-Vision: Sound on Screen*, edited and translated by Claudia Gorbman (New York: Columbia University Press, 1994), pp. 29–31.

2 Ibid., p. 128.

3 Konstantin Raudive discussed 'EVP' (electronic voice phenomenon) and his well-documented recording of disembodied voices in his book, *Breakthrough: An Amazing Experiment in Electronic Communication with the Dead* (New York: Taplinger, 1971).

4 Paul A. Woods, *Weirdsville USA: The Obsessive Universe of David Lynch* (London: Plexus, 2000), p. 184.

5 Claudia Gorbman, *Unheard Melodies: Narrative Film Music* (London: BFI, 1987), p. 33.

6 Hanns Eisler and Theodor Adorno, *Composing for the Films* (London: Athlone, 1994) [originally 1947], p. 75.

7 Steve Wurtzler, '"She Sang Live but the Microphone was Switched Off": The Live, the Recorded and the Subject of Representation' in Rick Altman, ed., *Sound Theory, Sound Practice* (London: Routledge, 1992), p. 100.

8 Ibid.

9 It is worth noting here that non-diegetic status may not be the most significant aspect of film music's standing – aspects such as spatialisation may be more important.

10 Chion discusses the acousmatic space 'off', developed by sound cinema. *Audio-Vision*, pp. 83–4.

11 Reni Celeste, '*Lost Highway*: Unveiling Cinema's Yellow Brick Road', *Cineaction*, no. 43, Summer 1997, p. 32.

12 Greil Marcus, 'History Lesson' in *The Dustbin of History* (London: Picador, 1997) [originally in *Halfpenny Review*, Summer 1992], p. 24.

13 Caryl Flinn, *Strains of Utopia: Gender, Nostalgia and Hollywood Film Music* (Princeton: Princeton University Press, 1992), pp. 6–7.

14 Irwin Bazelon notes that film music regularly tells us what is about to happen. *Knowing the Score: Notes on Film Music* (New York: Van Nostrand Reinhold, 1975), p. 24.

15 Gorbman, *Unheard Melodies*, pp. 56–9.

16 T. W. Adorno, *Introduction to the Sociology of Music* (New York: Seabury, 1976), p. 53.

17 René Descartes, *Meditations on First Philosophy*, translated by Ronald Rubin (Claremont, CA: Arete, 1986), pp. 4–5.

18 'In proposing the title, *Specters of Marx*, I was initially thinking of all the forms of a certain haunting obsession that seems to me to organize the *dominant* influence on discourse today. At a time when a new world disorder is attempting to install its neo-capitalism and neo-liberalism, no disavowal has managed to rid itself of all Marx's ghosts. Hegemony still organizes the repression and thus the confirmation of a haunting. Haunting belongs to the structure of every hegemony.' Jacques Derrida, *Specters of Marx: The State of the Debt, the Work of Mourning and the New International* (London: Routledge, 1994), p. 37.

19 Jean Baudrillard, *The Evil Demon of Images* (Sydney: Power Institute, 1987).

20 Jean Baudrillard, *The Revenge of the Crystal: Selected Writings on the Modern Object and Its Destiny, 1968–1983* (London: Pluto, 1999).

21 A similarity should be noted to what Steven M. Friedson points out as 'such phatasmagories as possessing spirits supported by the Dionysian excess of African music and dance'. 'Dancing

the Disease: Music and Trance in Tumbuka Healing' in Penelope Gouk, ed., *Musical Healing in Cultural Contexts* (Aldershot, Hants: Ashgate, 2000), p. 68.

22 George Burt, *The Art of Film Music* (Boston, MA: Northeastern University Press, 1994), p. 6.

23 Kathryn Kalinak notes that the spectacular in films is emphasised by 'continuous playing and increased volume'. *Settling the Score: Music and the Classical Hollywod Film* (Madison: University of Wisconsin Press, 1992), p. 97.

24 Rick Altman, *The American Film Musical* (London: BFI, 1989), p. 110.

25 K. J. Donnelly, '*Performance* and the Composite Film Score' in K. J. Donnelly, ed., *Film Music: Critical Approaches* (Edinburgh: Edinburgh University Press, 2001), p. 160.

26 Altman, *Sound Theory, Sound Practice*, p. 67.

27 The film's driving scene might also be seen in this light, as Marion Crane (Janet Leigh) drives through the rain with the stolen money.

28 Susan McClary talks of 'the ejaculatory quality of many so-called transcendental moments' in Bizet's *Carmen*. *George Bizet's Carmen* (Cambridge: Cambridge University Press, 1992), p. 67.

29 Michael Henry, 'Le Ruban de Mobius' [interview with David Lynch], *Positif*, no. 432, January 1997, p. 13.

30 Thomas Elsaesser reminds the reader that music is a central aspect of the melodramatic. 'Tales of Sound and Fury: Observations on the Family Melodrama' in Christine Gledhill, ed., *Home Is Where the Heart Is: Studies in Melodrama and the Woman's Film* (London: BFI, 1987), p. 50.

31 Flinn, *Strains of Utopia*, p. 133.

32 Royal S. Brown, *Overtones and Undertones: Reading Film Music* (Berkeley and Los Angeles: University of California Press, 1994), p. 35.

33 Michel Chion, *David Lynch* (London: BFI, 1995), p. 70.

34 Stephen Pizzello, 'Highway to Hell', *American Cinematographer*, vol. 78, no. 3, March 1997, p. 36.

35 Lynch released the record *Lux Vivens* in 1998. The actor who plays Pete, Balthasar Getty, as 'B-Zar', co-produced the hip hop band Mannish's *Audio Sedative* album about a year before *Lost Highway*. The film also includes singer Henry Rollins as a prison guard.

36 Chris Rodley, 'David Lynch: Mr Contradiction', in *Sight and Sound*, vol. 6, issue 7, August 1996, p. 6.

37 Pizzello, 'Highway to Hell', p. 36.

38 Noted by Donald Lyons, 'La La Limbo', *Film Comment*, vol. 33, no. 1, January–February 1997, p. 4.

39 Woods, *Weirdsville USA*, p. 185.

40 Ken Dancyger, *The Technique of Film and Video Editing* (London: Focal Press, 1996), p. 176.

41 Music artist and sound designer Lustmord (Brian Williams) embodies a whole approach to the creation of music as sound environment that has had more effect in films than the 'serious' tradition of electro-acoustic music.

42 However, while film music is a supernatural effect, pieces of music ('music itself') cannot ultimately be approached as a metaphysical unity or plenitude.

43 Chris Rodley, *Lynch on Lynch* (London: Faber and Faber, 1997), p. 241.

44 This piece is in 6/4 time, leaving the concluding action without the expected 4/4 backbeat of rock music but with a bizarre augmented version. The piece is called 'Driver Down' on the soundtrack album, although a bootleg version is called 'Drive Her Down'.

45 Although Nine Inch Nails's 'The Perfect Drug' was the scout single, released before the film for publicity purposes, in the end it was not used in the film itself.

46 Adamson had released a single of Elmer Bernstein's film theme 'The Man with the Golden Arm' in 1988.

47 Called a 'secondary score' in Woods, *Weirdsville USA*, p. 185.

48 The Massive Attack drop-out is removed from the start and conclusion of the piece on the soundtrack album version and thus appears only once.

49 Nicholas Cook notes that this is the dominant form of composition for television advertisements. We might also say it has become a dominant form of composition more generally. 'Music and Meaning in the Commercials', *Popular Music*, vol. 13, no. 1, 1994, p. 36.

50 '*Lost Highway* Soundtrack' (<www.lynchnet.com/lh/lhst.html> accessed 15 October 2003).

51 This Mortal Coil were a conglomerate of a number of musicians from other groups. 'Song to the Siren' is sung by Elizabeth Fraser, singer of the atmospheric group the Cocteau Twins, whose songs had appeared in films such as *Highlander III* (1995) and Bernardo Bertolucci's *Stealing Beauty* (1995), while she sang alone on *Winter Guest* (1996). Fraser's voice – which has very distinctive timbral qualities – also graced Peter Gabriel's *Music for the Millennium Dome* (2000). Interestingly, another singer from This Mortal Coil, Lisa Gerrard, also of Dead Can Dance, provided the music for *Gladiator* (2000), collaborating with Hans Zimmer.

52 Rodley, 'David Lynch', p. 10.

53 Some years earlier, Adamson had played on a version of this song by Nick Cave and The Bad Seeds.

54 Antoine Hennion, 'The Production of Success: An Antimusicology of the Pop Song' in Simon Frith and Andrew Goodwin, eds, *On Record: Rock, Pop and the Written Word* (London: Routledge, 1990), p. 102.

55 Theo van Leeuwen, *Speech, Music, Sound* (Basingstoke, Hants: Macmillan, 1999), p. 38.

56 The four- and eight-bar structure is tabulated by Rick Altman to illustrate the principle differences between score and songs. 'Cinema and Popular Song: The Lost Tradition' in Pamela Robertson Wojcik and Arthur Knight, eds., *Soundtrack Available: Film and Popular Music* (Durham, NC: Duke University Press, 2001), p. 25.

57 Theodor Adorno, 'On Popular Music' in Simon Frith and Andrew Goodwin, eds., *On Record: Rock, Pop and the Written Word* (London: Routledge, 1990), p. 302.

58 Lynch, quoted in Rodley, *Lynch on Lynch*, p. 241.

59 The scale and harmony derived from the Phrygian mode is minor with a characteristic flattened second of the scale, providing the sort of sound prominent in certain traditional music from Spain and parts of the Middle East.

60 This relates to Lynch's use of the beginning of 'Im Abendrot' from Richard Strauss's *Four Last Songs* in *Wild at Heart* (1990), where it appears as romantic orchestral film music, losing any connection with the singing that follows.

61 Chion discusses the crucial notion of synchresis, where music and sound spontaneously weld together. *Audio-Vision*, p. 63.

62 Freudians might see this as a primal scene fantasy.

63 It suggests something of the unity of conscious and unconscious some commentators
    associate with orgasm – and is compounded by the big projection of pornography on screen.

64 This takes us back to Claudia Gorbman's likening of the on-diegetic music to non-diegetic
    film inserts. See *Unheard Melodies*, pp. 5ff.

65 Rodley, 'David Lynch', p. 9.

66 David Huckvale, *Twins of Evil*: An Investigation into the Aesthetics of Film Music', *Popular
    Music*, vol. 9, no. 1, 1990, pp. 1–35.

67 Gorbman points out that film music should not be judged as if it were 'pure' music. *Unheard
    Melodies*, p. 12.

Chapter 3

The Anti-Matter of Film Music: *The Shining*

Film music is commonly thought of as 'background music', but in Stanley Kubrick's adaptation of Stephen King's novel *The Shining*, the music would undoubtedly be better described as 'foreground music'. The overwhelming majority of it was designed solely for consumption in the respectable orchestral concert hall. It is the highest of high art. A cursory perusal of *The Shining* demonstrates that some aspects of the film's non-diegetic music are traditional to the horror film genre. These embrace identifiable musical 'themes' (as in most mainstream films), intermittent bursts of musical sound, the sound of a heartbeat (emphasising the audible thumping of the heart in states of fear), loud gongs (reminiscent of tolling bells), rattly percussion 'noise', orchestral stabs, microtonally shifting undulating notes (giving a sense of the lack of solidity or certainty) and 'satanic' chanting. However, almost all these elements are present, prominent even, in the pre-existing music that has been inserted into, rather than written for, the film. This is 'art music', or modern 'classical' music. Less obviously, *The Shining* contains a significant amount of religious music, inspired by explicit Christian themes and imagery, although the film does not directly engage this theme. The film's story concerns the Torrance family, who are employed to look after a remote and empty hotel for the winter. The son, Danny, is psychic and able to see things by 'shining'. He sees terrible ghostly elements in the hotel. The father, Jack, appears to be affected by these presences, inspiring him to attack and attempt to kill his wife and child. On one level, *The Shining* is a successful horror film, but on another it is an art film, a far more complex piece, which is riddled with ideas, themes and complexities that suggest radically different interpretations.

On a personal note, I first came to Béla Bartók's music through its use in *The Shining*. An excerpt from the *Music for Strings, Percussion and Celesta* (sometimes called 'moosepack' by musicians) was used for key scary moments in the film: when Jack looks into a model maze and apparently sees the reality of his wife and child in the garden maze; when Danny attempts and fails to enter room 237; and finally when Danny asks his father if he would ever hurt his family. These are among the most effective moments of the film, and the marriage of image and music was tight. Now, for audience members who were familiar with the Bartók piece, the film must have presented a radically different experience from those who had never heard it before. My experience has been filtered through *The Shining*. Consequently, when I listen to the piece, I think of the film. Moreover, when I listen to sections of the piece that are not in the film, I still associate them with the film. I imagine them as parts of the film that I have not seen – and, indeed, some cuts of *The Shining* include more material than others,[1] so perhaps there are further missing or incomplete versions in the mind or in the ether. I envisage whole episodes that do not exist, or imagine the music providing the character for the entire film, to the extent that it becomes the unheard soundtrack for the film, the two conjoining somewhere in my mind rather than on a piece of celluloid or videotape.

This opens up a new perspective on the relationship of film and music. It suggests that the music can come to dominate our ideas about films, even when it is not actually present. In the same way, I can remember numerous occasions where I have gone to see a film after hearing a publicity scout single on television or the radio. If it was a pop video, it might even have contained excerpts from the film. Sitting through the film, I found that the song appeared nowhere in the film, yet I was expecting it to, and in the back of my head the song was playing as much as if it had appeared on the soundtrack. Thus music can be a virtual part of the film when it is not an actual part. Many ridicule those CD compilations of 'songs inspired by the film', which represented a growth industry in the 1990s.[2] Yet perhaps these songs were not only inspired by the character of the film, marking an extension to it, but, reciprocally, might also have inspired the film in some way. Returning to Bartók and *The Shining*, I find the character of the *Music for Strings, Percussion and Celesta* wholly in tune with the film. This is particularly the case with the first movement, a fugue for strings, which is not included in the film yet conceivably could have been used as an overture to it. It is almost as if one could conceive of *The Shining* as an emanation from the music, inspired by it, or at least inspired by its flavour or feel. Film-makers are regularly inspired by music, and Stanley Kubrick, judging by the use of music in his films, was inspired more openly than most.

Film Music as Supernatural

Film music has distinct connections with ritual and religious music; indeed, it might even be argued that one branch of film music's genealogy derives obliquely from this quarter. Film music is a ritualised form of music that is purposeful in much the same way as certain forms of religious music. For example, the organ passages played as priests enter the church is a form of 'overture' preparing the congregation for the forthcoming service, in much the same way that the opening title music prepares the audience for the film world and narrative to come. Furthermore, I would argue that just as this music is usually awe-inspiring and provides a bond to the spiritual, the emotional potency of film music offers something of a portal to the transcendent and experience beyond the everyday. While most accounts tend to focus on film music as a derivation of stage music, it would be foolish to dismiss this transcendental aspect in favour of regarding it merely as a sort of prosaic 'functional' music for the screen, like the music for set transitions and intervals in the theatre.

While music is an entity that secures an effect beyond undemanding description and positivist measuring, sound more generally encompasses the strangest phenomena, an aspect I should like to focus on briefly. Strange sonic phenomena pertaining to perception include 'false bass', where the ear can add bass notes to music that do not exist, and 'presence', where a boost to certain mid-range frequencies can give recorded music the impression of being closer.[3] Furthermore, there is the existence of infrasound – ultrasonics and supersonics – sounds that have pitches above and below the human range of hearing, which quite possibly may affect us and our environments without our direct knowledge.[4] This very description suggests that these phenomena might have something in common with film music. One example of supersonics in action is a device that can be inserted into mole hills, and which produces an unpleasant ultrasonic pulse that should drive the mole elsewhere. Despite being beyond our range of hearing, these pulses quite probably affect us as well. Ultrasonic sounds can be 'heard' through the way they change what we can hear directly. Some of it lies on the edge of perception, but other ultrasonics can be heard through their effect on music more generally, such as the gigantic pipes in some cathedral organs that produce frequencies beneath human hearing range but shape our perception of the musical whole. Military research has taken the effect of ultrasonics very seriously, attempting to develop acoustic weapons for covert warfare activities, a subject I will discuss later in this book.

One interesting recent development is Vic Tandy's research into explaining supernatural phenomena through the positioning of standing waves. Tandy appears to have some evidence that the presence of ghosts and other mysterious apparitions coincides with the presence of standing waves emanating from objects such as machines, transformers or radiators.[5] It is worth remembering here that stereo speakers converge to give a 'standing wave' stereo 'image',[6] and that with (non-silent cinema) film music, we are almost always confronted with the product of electronic speakers and their 'image' rather than some pure and originary musical event. We are victim to partials and sympathetic resonance, due to the specificities of the listening conditions of the environment in which we watch and hear film and television. Electronic sound reproduction is hardly a simple process of amplifying and recording 'reality'. Brian Eno discussed the 'third speaker phenomenon' on the sleeve to his 1975 record *Discreet Music*. If an extra speaker is wired (very simply) into the channels for the two stereo speakers and a stereo recording is played, the third speaker provides some extra sounds that do not appear from either of the two original stereo speakers.[7] Such phenomena are difficult to explain and point to the ephemeral and sometimes illogical character of sound. Further still, the celebrated research of parapsychologist Konstantin Raudive into disembodied voices provides another example of electronic recorded sound's extraordinary aspects.[8] He recorded and conversed with ghostly voices 'from the ether' – voices that seem to have no obvious material origin – using both everyday and specialised electronic recording equipment. This bizarre and unexplained phenomenon has something in common with film music, both of which appear as if from nowhere. Such examples, while they may not necessarily be unequivocally pertinent for film music, not only demonstrate the elusive and mysterious aspects of sound but also suggest something of the ghostly and far from straightforward sphere that film music often occupies.

Proto-, Pre- and Post-Soundtracks

Films do not simply have a musical score that is merely a functional part of the film whole. The music, as much as if not more so than other elements, looks outwards and implies other music (other images and ideas, too). These musical connotations could be termed 'proto-soundtracks', 'pre-soundtracks' and 'post-soundtracks', and indeed might be sold as such in relation to the film. The proto-soundtrack might be what was played on set while the film was being shot, and may 'seep' through into the final score as well as being a distant presence in the rest of the film, resembling almost a very quiet remnant within the diegetic location sound. Similarly, the 'pre-soundtrack' might be the temp track, the music added to the film's rough cut, and the inspiration for the composer's final music for the film. The post-soundtrack might be what is appended to the film after its release, as tied-in elements, like the 'songs inspired by the film' albums. These are potential musical extensions of the film. The pre- and proto-soundtracks can sometimes be 'seen', faintly discerned, like a ghost in the film. And of course, the post-soundtrack can add (sometimes quite significantly) to the audience's idea and understanding of a film and its cultural status more generally.

In recent years, theoretical discussions have been veritably haunted by references to spectres of all sorts. In an article entitled 'Ghostly Footsteps', David Pinder discusses an audio walk conducted by artist Janet Cardiff in the East End of London, which aimed to excavate the past as geographical memories.[9] Similarly, there is David Punter and Glennis Byron's *Spectral Readings*[10] and Jeffrey Sconce's *Haunted Media*, the latter of which sees both the paranormal and the electronic media as (inspiring) fantasies of disembodiment.[11] John Fiske also discusses how television texts can work as 'ghost texts', with one layered over another,[12] and, indeed, this palimpsest form might equally be ascribed to films and music as much as any other cultural object.

The 'ghosts' that haunt a film are often little more than shapes, momentary configurations or half-remembered sounds. This ghostly presence of music that may be absent in the final film can be traced to the days of silent film-making when the music played on set was seen as essential in generating a defining atmosphere for the actors. Sometimes this music may be heard in the far distance, picked up by some of the ambient microphones, or it may simply be imagined by the film music analyst. However, in relation to the temp track, we may not need such a vivid imagination. Sometimes the musical references are very obvious. Just listen to the battle scene music in *Gladiator*, which clearly was based on *Mars* from Gustav Holst's *The Planets* suite. The temp track for the final cut, as well as the rough cut, furnishes a very distinct cultural as well as commercial logic. As evidenced by *2001: A Space Odyssey* (1968), this situation marries the already-known (music) with the yet-to-come (film). This has an eerie effect, of a kind of precognition. This logic is now relatively common in mainstream films, which certainly do not blanch from cutting in existing music, particularly if this can be used as an extension of the film as a parallel commodity.

Another form of the pre-soundtrack, the proto-soundtrack, is what one might call the musical ghost of the film, the music that was played on set during the film's production. It is almost as if we can still hear some of this music, which is sometimes the case, as it is part of the final musical soundtrack of the film. If we listen carefully, we might hear snatches of it here or there, where location sound has not been re-recorded, or as a distant echo. On the set of *Performance* (shot in 1968 but released in 1970), Booker T. and the MGs's brand of organ-led rhythm and blues predominated.[13] On the set of *Lost Highway*, David Lynch insisted on playing Rammstein's first album. In the documentary, *The Making of The Shining*, made by Vivian Kubrick, we can hear that Stravinsky's *The Rite of Spring* was played on set during the shooting of the climactic chase in the maze. This is fairly apt, considering that this piece is about human sacrifice to primal forces.

The final cut of *The Shining* evinces strong musical ghosts, through its use of pre-existing pieces with strong historical flavour and specificity. The 'aura' of these pieces haunts the film as a force, albeit an ephemeral one. Quite unsurprisingly, film music composers can live in fear of the tyranny of the temp track. Many have had the music they spent great time and energy writing dismissed because the temp track seems more appropriate to the director/producers.[14] For example, Wendy Carlos's music for *The Shining* was rejected by Kubrick, apart from a couple of sections.[15] Other composers are forced to emulate the temp track and compromise their own musical visions. On *2001: A Space Odyssey*, Stanley Kubrick rejected Alex North's music for the first part of the film in favour of the temp track of concert-hall pieces, which, in effect, he used as the final soundtrack. Listening to the re-recorded album of Alex North's rejected music, it becomes clear that the temp track has acted as a model, inspiring an interesting take on the musical profile of the opening of Richard Strauss's *Also Sprach Zarathustra*.[16] *A Clockwork Orange*, while using Wendy Carlos's arrangements of Purcell, Beethoven and Rossini, bears witness to the use of existing classical pieces as film music. In *Barry Lyndon* (1975), the repeated thematic use of Handel's *Sarabande* (Suite for Keyboard, Vol. 2, No. 4 in D minor) has been described by Claudia Gorbman as 'a fundamentally different aesthetic of film music' from the dominant norms that were established for mainstream cinema under the Hollywood studio system.[17]

The temp track can define the film, which could be fitted to it or built around it as an idea. The screen activity might even be seen to have emanated from it. Therefore, film music has the potential to imply an elsewhere. Not only does non-diegetic music suggest the elsewhere of the music's production, which is literally external to the diegetic screen world, but the music's qualities and the ghostly remnants of other music also can survive as a trace that point somewhere outside of the film. *The Shining*, like many films, has a number of musical reference points, which appear almost like something that can nearly be seen behind a partially transparent film screen.

As a film, *The Shining* is about the power and authority of the 'elsewhere' in cinema, with a nebulous 'evil' sited somewhere around the Overlook Hotel. It denies the 'normal' narrative and diegetic causal and developmental logic and its corresponding authority. Film music is precisely such an 'elsewhere' in films – not quite of its world nor of its logic. It implies an outside, confirming film music's status as an object half in and half out of film. It does this in two ways. First, its non-diegetic status sites it outside the diegetic world on screen (and on the soundtrack), and second, film music, or music in film, can have a life in wider culture outside of the confines of the film itself.

As pieces of art music, with a pre-existing life, the musical pieces in *The Shining* have their own historical implications or oblique reference points. This is a clue as to how film music might be seen as an 'alien' in the system, a volatile element potentially damaging the seeming 'unity' of a film. *The Shining*'s opening music, by Wendy Carlos, is at heart medieval filtered through hi-tech modern.[18] It is founded upon the *Dies Irae*, the medieval mass of the dead, and staple of the musical repertoire of the horror film genre (see later discussion). Some of the considerable amount of music in *The Shining* by Krzysztof Penderecki looks outwards towards a Warsaw Pact central eastern European austerity, Catholicism and 'art for art's sake' forms of highly un-popular music. Representing an almost polar opposite, the film's dance music (which the photograph at the end suggests is from 1921) points to an urbane and sophisticated form of restrained mass culture music. The Bartók piece, perhaps the dominant musical signature of the film, references its time of production, having debuted in Basel, Switzerland, in 1937. Can we hear the Nazi shadow cast over Europe hidden somewhere in its tones? I cannot help thinking that its appearance in the film manifests something of a return of the repressed to match the film's story about evil from the past.[19]

Bartók's *Music for Percussion, Strings and Celesta* opens with a strong and austere movement for strings. As I mentioned earlier, having come to the piece via *The Shining*, I was struck by how this opening movement seemed to be consonant with the film, to the point where it might even be approached as a remnant of a missing film section, the piece being construed as an *extension* of the film; and indeed this might be argued for the unused sections of other musical pieces that appear in the film.[20] Far from mere fanciful imagining on my part, subordinating what some may see as 'great art' to the leviathan of popular culture, this is a pointed admission that some essential parts of the film's character are derived from these musical pieces. Thus, the remaining parts of this music are not really alien to the film, but implicated through ghostly ephemeral connections, adumbrating a larger notion of *The Shining* that spills off the screen and cinema space, and into wider culture most strongly through its use of existing, recontextualised music.

In addition to such associations, the music in the film also furnishes some oblique film connections, providing 'wormholes', in the cosmic (science-fiction) sense of portals between diverse spaces of great distance. These traverse Kubrick's oeuvre, moving from *2001: A Space Odyssey*'s concluding 'lightshow' section, with its use of Ligeti's music, to the use of the composer's music in *The Shining*. Also, from the start of (and again later in) *A Clockwork Orange*, where the theme of the *Dies Irae* forms part of the end of each phrase in Wendy Carlos's arrangement of Purcell's Queen Mary's Funeral Music, to the opening of *The Shining*, where her piece for the title sequence is an explicit variation on the *Dies Irae*, the musical melody for the medieval mass of the dead. These are not simply intertextual references or explicit connections; they do not even really pertain to the terrain of the film's themes (or indeed to Kubrick terrain), but to the terrain of music in film. They are quite possibly not the sort of connection a heavily engaged viewer/listener to *The Shining* might make, let alone a more casual one.

The Sublime

The word 'sublime' means of extremely high spiritual value, inspiring awe. It is an ambiguous and difficult term, having currency in both chemistry and in psychoanalysis, where 'sublimate' means to purify. Philosophers Immanuel Kant and Edmund Burke both connect it to fear. While some have thought the ideas similar, Kant contrasted the sublime with beauty, regarding the former as a profoundly different aesthetic category.[21] According to Kant, a sublime object can seem to be irrational or without purpose, appearing to us as horrible or terrifying. A good example would be the seemingly infinite or an object of overwhelming size. Indeed, he calls the sublime 'an abyss in which the imagination is afraid to lose itself'.[22] The pleasure of the sublime is thus in our response to the object – which oscillates between attraction and repulsion – rather than specifically pleasure in the object itself. According to Burke, the sublime is exaltation to the point of ecstasy, an overwhelming emotion.[23] He wrote: 'I know of nothing sublime which is not some modification of power, [which] . . . rises . . . from terror . . . the common stock of everything that is sublime.'[24] Music has the ability to inspire great awe, while some is capable of arousing terror. Film music can achieve both, while also being a device in films for asserting textual power over the audience.

Yet there is an apparent contradiction between the low status that traditionally has been accorded to film music and the status of sublime high art, as the apogee of western culture. Film music, at its most prosaic, can be functional in a banal manner, as if merely working pleonastically to describe, for example, a door shutting. On the other hand, the sublime of high-art music is a mysterious and highly powerful object, the antithesis, in fact, of such banal functional film music. The music in *The Shining* appears to be both at the same time. It is high-art music, but it is used as functional film music. However, the net effect of this is that art music appears to overpower the film to some degree, while it also takes on a different character by means of its context, within the body of the film. This is *not* postmodernism as it is usually described, as, for example, on Classic FM, where 'classics' are rendered popular through a pop radio format, or on one of many 'Classics at the Movies' CDs, which are like pop song compilations but with excerpts from famous (often overused) orchestral pieces. This is aesthetically quite different.

The art music in *The Shining* seems to dominate the image. While the film is at least partly cut to music, at times it seems that this 'foreground' music is too dominant to occupy a role in the background. This is, of course, reminiscent of certain art music attitudes to film, specifically that of Arnold Schoenberg, who baulked at the idea of having to write his music to fit existing action. He claimed that the only possible way would be for film to follow the demands of the music. Schoenberg wrote a piece of 'film music', *Musik fur eine Lichtspielszene*, which had no film until French avant-garde directors Jean-Marie Straub and Daniele Huillet shot one to accompany his music, entitled *Enleitung zu Arnold Schoenbergs 'Begleitung zu einer Lichtspielszene'* (*Introduction to Arnold Schoenberg's 'Accompaniment to a Cinematic Scene'*) (1972).[25] The primacy of music in this example is reminiscent of Simon Frith's description of the phenomenon of illustrative films, showing images thought to be contained in the music.[26] Music should not always be conceived as merely a secondary aspect to film images, and in the case of very obtrusive 'foreground' music, such an approach is at best folly and at worst a radical underestimation of the power of music.

The Shining exploits the residual or retreating sense of 'difficult' high art as lying 'outside' the normality of popular (mass) culture. Art music in the film functions precisely as Adorno's 'inassimilable' high art that stands outside dominant culture. Music and cultural theorist Theodor Adorno was convinced that some art music was able to refuse collaboration with the strictures and repression offered by mainstream mass culture. Although an inevitable part of this process is that its 'outsider' power is negated through its context, just as its presence in *The Shining* ultimately proves the music's status as an object assimilable to popular culture.

Yet in terms of the sublime, one important stylistic theme runs through *The Shining*: namely, a sense of vertiginous. The film piles on successive heights and shots from high perspectives, looking down and over from a variety of angles, a theme that is emphasised by some of the music. The repeated extract from the Bartók piece includes two passages that could be construed as representations of a vertiginous feeling, a swooning dizzy head. Accompanied by lone string glissandos up and down, the strings create a shimmering sound, some dropping microtonally in pitch while others hold the note. After this 'light-headed', 'vertiginous' moment, a childlike melody is played out, before the music moves towards another similar moment of 'vertigo'. Here, a cacophony builds though a rise in texture density and intensity as the celesta plays fast arpeggios, to create a toneless, shimmering, 'dissolving' sound, a vertigo or dizziness tied explicitly to the sublime of horror in the film. This notion is underlined by one of the Penderecki pieces used, *The Dream of*

Jacob, which represents something of the vertiginous feeling Jacob had upon seeing the great ladder with its foot on the earth and its top in heaven.

The art music in the film becomes the 'unknowable', beyond recognition, specifically on the terms of traditional mainstream film music, and popular culture more generally. In a memorable sequence, Wendy goes to the Colorado Lounge to speak to her husband. Jack is nowhere to be found and Wendy takes a look at what he has been writing while ensconced away during their time in the hotel, only to discover page after page of prose consisting of the same sentence: 'All work and no play makes Jack a dull boy.' This is a moment of vertigo in the face of the sublime, initiated by a shot of Wendy looking down over a box of manuscript paper. Her horror builds (as does the music, an excerpt from Penderecki's *Polymorphia*[27]), in the face of her absolute unrecognition of Jack's literary masterpiece.

Adorno and Horkheimer create an interesting metaphor for a number of issues, including the social reception of high art, based on the episode in *The Odyssey* where, in order to vanquish the sirens, Odysseus must listen to their song.[28] To protect themselves, the crew have stuffed their ears with wax, and Odysseus is lashed to the mast to stop him being pulled in by their irresistible siren song. Similarly, in *The Shining*, Jack is able to see the beauty and logic of his own 'work', while the prosaic Wendy is singularly unable to recognise the 'art' of his writing. This is not surprising, as she spends her time watching cartoons on television with Danny, and from what we are shown knows nothing of more sophisticated culture. Adorno's metaphor simultaneously both defines the highest of high art (transcendent 'sublime' art) and its detractors, the 'cloth-eared' mass audience. The latter, like Odysseus's wax-eared boat crew, are unable to hear the beauty, precluded from an understanding of such art by their need to focus on the banal basics of existence.

The Anti-Matter of High Art

In relation to popular culture, the highest of high art – specifically inaccessible modernist high art – takes on the character of being cultural anti-matter. It is beyond the pale, an alien object to mainstream film.[29] This type of music *should* be the antithesis of popular film and mainstream film music.[30] A precise scientific definition of anti-matter is 'a hypothetical form of matter that is identical to physical matter except that its atoms are composed of antielectrons, antiprotons and antineutrons'.[31] Anti-matter is thus the mirror of matter, anti-particles to those that constitute matter; hence the conjecture that it would annihilate matter if the two came into contact.[32] Like the art music in *The Shining*, anti-matter is by nature totally unlike the everyday, and potentially destructive, which might be one of the reasons why such music has become hidden away and marginalised by contemporary culture.

One particular moment in the film, embodies the intrusion of the absolutely different, and has, consequently, become iconic and metonymic of the film itself: namely, the episode where Jack hacks down the doors to get at Wendy and Danny. At the point where he pushes his head through the hole he has made in the door and shouts, 'Here's Johnny!', the music, which has been a succession of screeches becomes a hail of blasts; the piece is Penderecki's *Utrenja: Ewangelia*. The music adds up to more than simply film music, manifesting what might be called 'non-diegetic sound effects'.[33] It can be interpreted as sounds that express the supernatural world of the film, yet emanate from outside the diegetic world the film has created. Sound effects without diegetic origin are not unheard of in the cinema: for example, the ridiculous noises that accompany comic pratfalls, such as tightened timpani moving upwards in pitch or swanee whistles. Indeed, such things are usually integrated within musical scores, but in the case of the supernatural, such music can take on the quality of being 'off-world sound'.[34]

According to Eisler and Adorno, in *Composing for the Films*, film music is a 'glue' that holds the film together both formally *and* ideologically. Thus, mainstream film music, specifically that produced by the Hollywood studio system, is painted in a negative light in both aesthetic and psychological terms. However, *The Shining* uses music that is some way from this tradition of music for films. It incorporates anti-matter music, potentially undermining the film but then perhaps working for and offering the sort of unity that is traditional to most film music. The question is: does the music in *The Shining* integrate (or even alleviate) the film's aporias, or does the music constitute another aporia of its own within the bounds of the film? Eisler and Adorno recommend that dissonant modernist music should be used as incidental music in films. Writing in 1947, they noted: 'The new musical resources should be used [in films] because objectively they are more appropriate than the haphazard musical padding with which motion pictures are satisfied today, and are superior to it.'[35] They are referring to the unresolved dissonances, formal innovations and technical aspects of modernist concert-hall music. Although the music in the film fits the stylistic bill, Eisler and Adorno certainly were not imagining the wholesale reappropriation of existing art music pieces for horror films. Their suggestion is partly inspired by a desire for music that would not be just a secondary piece of decoration within films, but an aspect with its own logic and integrity; as a result, it would occupy a dialectical relationship with other aspects of the film, the overall film developing through the continuous tension between component parts rather than through a seeming unity that actually degrades music's abilities. This strategy would exploit music's significant powers and capabilities rather than using it merely as 'window-dressing' in the film. As far as I can see and hear, this is precisely the case in *The Shining*.

Music in *The Shining* is one of the stars of the film. Its origin as concert-hall music at least in some measure serves to make it too strong and obtrusive to be simply urbane background music. The fact that the music existed before the film means that large sections of the film are cut to the music, and the action at times seems almost to be staged in accordance with the music's dynamic demands. The music manifests a dimension in its own right, making for a general ambience of unease. Despite a couple of occasions where the original music has been altered minutely in order to fit the images, the fact that substantial sections of pre-existing music regularly appear unaltered proves how dominant these musical pieces are. We should be aware that it is not *necessarily* simply a situation where 'the film is cut to the music'. Little has been made of this as a production strategy in the surrounding discussions involving Kubrick or sound editor Gordon Stainforth.[36] The more likely scenario is that the film was cut only vaguely to the music, fitted roughly together rather than precisely matched. Yet the very force of the music, the way that it dominates the other film elements, means that the action *seems* to follow the music. At times, it is almost as if the images are *emanating* from the music. This is most evident in sequences containing musical excerpts of substantial duration, where the dynamics of the action (dialogue, movement, editing) appear to match the dynamic development of the music (rhythm, tempo, intensity, sound quality).[37]

Featured Pieces

We should note that the raw musical material for *The Shining* does not consist of musical scores but existing recordings. The musical pieces used as excerpts in the film are Béla Bartók's *Music for Strings, Percussion and Celesta* (third movement), Krzysztof Penderecki's *Utrenja, The Dream of Jacob* (also known as *The Awakening of Jacob*), *Polymorphia, De natura sonoris no. 1* and *De natura sonoris no. 2*, and György Ligeti's *Lontano*. The Bartók piece is 'thematic' and thus is credited by name at the end of the film,[38] while Kubrick credits the other more ambient functioning music simply as 'Music by Penderecki and Ligeti'. This tells us a great deal about the director's intention, that while Bartók's piece is featured, the Penderecki and Ligeti pieces are thought of as more of an indistinct sonic backdrop.

In the film, as we have seen, *Music for Strings, Percussion and Celesta* is associated with Danny, appearing when he tries the door handle of Room 237, as he enters the maze with his mother and when he talks to his father on the bed. Ligeti's *Lontano* is the high-pitched whining music that appears as the accompanying sound for 'shining', such as when Danny first sees the two girls when he plays darts and when he hears Halorann 'shine'.

Penderecki's *The Dream of Jacob* first appears during Danny's conversation with Tony and as Wendy and Jack talk on the phone; it reappears when Danny goes into Room 237, when Wendy wakes Jack from a nightmare and finally when Jack sees the woman in Room 237. *De natura sonoris no. 1* appears when Danny sees the two girls in the corridor, and when Wendy goes out to the disabled snowcat. *De natura sonoris no. 2* accompanies Jack as he walks to the Gold Room, and Halorann's journey in the snowcat. Generally speaking, Penderecki's music appears to be used as an ambience in the film, although the excerpt from *De natura sonoris no. 2* includes some memorable rising string stabs, evident as the distraught Jack punches the air on his way to the Gold Room (disorientatingly, his actions are almost but not quite matched to the stabs). The gap or confusion between the music and image homologises the film's disjunction and mixing of 'real' and 'supernatural' worlds on screen.

At times in the film, excerpts from musical pieces are joined together or follow on in quick succession. In the scene where Wendy discovers what Jack has been typing, and he subsequently threatens her, the music starts with *Polymorphia*, then

The Shining

cuts to *Utrenja: Ewangelia* and then back to *Polymorphia* as Wendy drags the unconscious Jack away. The extended sequence where Halorann is travelling in the snowcat, and then Wendy awakes to see reflected in the mirror the word 'murder' written backwards on the door (accompanied by *Utrenja: Ewangelia*), then Jack hacks at the doors with an axe (*Utrenja: Kanon Paschy*) and then Halorann arrives at the Overlook Hotel (back to *Utrenja: Ewangelia*). Jack's pursuit of Danny is accompanied by *Utrenja: Kanon Paschy*, with *Utrenja: Ewangelia* cut in, while *Utrenja: Ewangelia* is used again during the chase in the maze. *De natura sonoris no. 1* is played over images of Jack's frozen body the next morning, while Wendy and Danny's departure in the snowcat is accompanied by *De natura sonoris no. 2*. While the pieces may lack their full musical integrity they nevertheless exploit the music's power.[39]

The film's opening piece of music for the titles is by Wendy Carlos and Rachel Elkind, and accompanies dramatic helicopter shots of mountainous terrain, including breathtaking sweeps over water and in pursuit of Torrance's Volkswagen beetle. This arrangement of the *Dies Irae* mass includes some wailing synthesizer sounds as the title of the film appears on the screen, mixing Carlos's synthesizer with Elkind's mewling vocals. William Rosar has pointed out the iconic musical status of the *Dies Irae* in films and the classical concert hall.[40] Indeed, used repeatedly in horror films, the *Dies Irae* is a Gregorian chant that is known as the 'Mass for the Dead', and translates literally as 'the Day of Wrath'. It appears regularly as a portent of doom, and here are a few examples of some of the films in which it has featured: *It's a Wonderful Life* (1946, music by Dimitri Tiomkin), *Garden of Evil* (1954, music by Bernard Herrmann), *Between Heaven and Hell* (1956, as the basis of the score by Hugo Friedhofer), *The Return of Dracula* (1958, music by Gerald Fried), *The Screaming Skull* (1958, music by Ernest Gold), *The Unforgiven* (1960, music by Dimitri Tiomkin), *The Mephisto Waltz* (1971, music by Jerry Goldsmith), *The Vault of Horror* (1973, music by Douglas Gamley), *The Car* (1977, music by Leonard Rosenman), *Close Encounters of the Third Kind* (1977, music by John Williams), *Poltergeist* (1982, music by Jerry Goldsmith), *The Slumber Party Massacre* (1982, music by Ralph Jones), *Conan the Barbarian* (1982, music by Basil Poledouris) and *The Nightmare before Christmas* (1993, music by Danny Elfman). It has also appeared in the following television dramas: *Doctor Who: The Sea Devils* (1972, music by Malcolm Clarke), *Salem's Lot* (1979, music by Harry Sukman), medieval ecclesiastical television detective drama *Cadfael* (1994–6, music by Colin Towns) and *Buffy the Vampire Slayer* (1997–2003). I am sure that a great deal more might be added to these lists. What this clearly signifies is that the *Dies Irae* is one of the key musical signifiers of doom, evil and death, and is a particularly 'representational' piece in terms of the tradition of gothic and horror films. Probably its most famous rendering, however, is as the basis for the final movement of Hector Berlioz's *Symphonie fantastique*, where it represents a witches' sabbat.[41] As the opening of *The Shining*, this piece of music, in Carlos's electronic arrangement, leaves audiences in no doubt about the character of the ensuing film.

The section from *Music for Percussion, Strings and Celesta* that is used includes a very memorable passage that is the nearest the film comes to traditional film music. This excerpt is repeated three times and so comes to embody something of an aural essence of the film. As I have already discussed, this excerpt includes two vertiginous sounds of 'dissolution'. In the first, the strings play microtonally, creating a shimmering effect as some drop minutely in pitch. This is accompanied by some twangy plucked string glissandi. This leads into a strong melody played in unison on strings and piano that is not 'tuneful' in the accepted sense. It is, however, reminiscent of the sorts of 'mad tunes' and childish tunes that are fairly common in horror films (examples include *Rosemary's Baby* [1968] and *A Nightmare on Elm Street* [1984]). Yet it might also be construed as the sort of mechanical 'indifferent' melody evident in some modernist music, underlined by its highly chromatic rather than the more commonly diatonic character given to prominent melodies. It is four bars long and repeated twice, so in terms of temporal structure is notably traditional.[42] On the second run through, the melody rises in pitch and tension, reaching a climactic point, which is then held, whereupon a passage of three rising piano chords followed by deep timpani rumbles is repeated twice. The piece then goes into the second pitch 'dissolution', which is a dizzy building in intensity dominated by celesta arpeggios accompanied by a cacophony of strings. Out of this mêlée emerges a deep string unison melody. The dynamics of the music appear to be doubled by the visual/narrative dynamics. The film is either cut vaguely to the music, or we make sense of the visuals through the structure of the music. The Bartók piece structures the action in each of its three appearances, with notable synch points in the music matching

(inspiring) edits or significant activity on screen. In its first appearance, the melody proceeds as Wendy and Danny begin walking in the maze, and is followed by a single sforzando piano chord that matches the point where Jack bounces a ball violently on the ground and then looks over the model of the maze. This cuts to what seems to be his point-of-view shot, as he watches his wife and child inside the real maze, the celesta arpeggios building. When Danny reaches the door to Room 237, the melody accompanies a shot-reverse shot between Danny and the door; he tries the handle as the timpani come in, and then sees a flash-frame of the spectral girls accompanied by the sforzando piano chord. He leaves just as the celesta arpeggios begin to build. The third and final appearance is the most sustained, amounting to an excerpt of over four minutes from the *Adagio*, including a significant preceding section that has not been heard in the film previously.[43] Danny enters the family's quarters, then sits and talks with his father on the bed. The first 'dissolution' sound comes as Jack declares that he is unable to sleep. The melody ensues when Danny asks Jack if he likes the hotel, the sforzando piano chord accompanying Danny's question, 'Dad, you'd never hurt Mommy and me, would you?' The timpani rolls fill the time gap before his response, and then as the celesta arpeggios start (accompanied by a precise cut from Danny to Jack), Jack replies that he loves them. While this musical excerpt is used in a manner that clearly exploits its dynamics for shaping the film's dynamics, its character provides something of an essence to the sequence and the film.[44]

The popular music in the film is a more prosaic manifestation of the ghostly presences in the hotel. The seemingly diegetic but spectral music that accompanies the 'ball' in the Gold Room includes *Midnight, the Stars and You* (which is also used for the end titles), along with *It's All Forgotten Now* and *Home*. Although the year from the past that is connected to the present appears to be 1921 (as suggested in the final image of the film), these songs are later. *Home* (by Henry Hall and the Gleneagles Dance Band) dates from the late 1920s, while the other two songs (by Ray Noble and his Orchestra, and featuring the vocals of Al Bowlly) date from 1932. The songs appear as an embodiment of memory – not necessarily our personal memory but more a collective memory of some sort. Indeed, pop songs often serve this function, as exemplified by the BBC's *The Rock'n'Roll Years* (1984), which complemented news footage from the past with songs from the same period;[45] or perhaps slightly differently in the television dramas of Dennis Potter, such as *Pennies from Heaven* (1978, BBC) or *The Singing Detective* (1986, BBC).[46] It may be that when music or song articulates memory, particularly a collective memory as an aesthetic repository, it might possess the power to unearth bad things from the past that we would rather forget, like slavery, starvation or mass murder, more than some individual sexual repression or personal neurosis.

The Horror of Modernism
Howard Shore, discussing his music for David Cronenberg's *The Brood* (1979), declared, 'when I thought "horror movie", I thought "avant garde", because you could go as far as you could go'.[47] Some extreme aspects of sound or vision in art have come to be used in popular arts as indicators of abnormality, of difference from the conventional world of cinema. For example, *Das Kabinett des Dr Caligari* (*The Cabinet of Dr Caligari*) (1920), a German horror film directed by Robert Wiene, famously used Expressionist-inspired set design, constructing a stylised yet very effective nightmare world. The particularly distinctive visual styles of some modern art have been subsumed to cinema much in the same way as some modernist art music, yet, as in this last example, some appears to have been hijacked and redirected,

from being a new way of seeing or hearing to simply being a representation of the world out of kilter, the world of nightmare and disturbed personal psychology.

Horror film music has much in common with twentieth-century 'modernist' classical music, at least horror films seem to think so. It is common for horror films to be adorned with the sort of discordant music that only appears elsewhere in the 'difficult' music of the high-art concert hall: for example, in William Friedkin's *The Exorcist* (1973), which also used pre-existing pieces of respectable art music. How can we understand the connection between the highest of highbrow art music and the most visceral, harrowing and exploitative horror films? On the one hand, it might be argued that the horror genre itself is a popular form of existentialism, and therefore a form of modernism,[48] and that this gives it a certain affinity with modernist classical music. On the other hand, it can be argued that the use of avant-garde classical music as film music creates a use value for the useless, constructing a 'taming' assimilation of the seemingly inassimilable. Twentieth-century art music lost any sense of a large audience or even the level of popularity that some art music had enjoyed in earlier times. In part at least, this was a conscious strategy – to guarantee the music's artistic and 'difficult' status in the face of an onslaught from mass culture and its valorisation of popular music. The more difficult a piece of music was, the less chance that it could become a degraded piece of popular music; instead, it was more likely to be seen as a cultural object that was challenging to the listener rather than being easily consumed in the way that most popular music, and a good deal of earlier art music, had been.[49] So, is the addition of art music to horror films a devaluation of modernist art, where the non-representational is rendered representational? Or is it that such music is destined to become a vibrant and accessible part of popular culture's zones of deepest emotion (such as fear and fright)? Perhaps the answer is a little bit of both. Arguably, modernist art music has now been assimilated by dominant culture (if indeed it was ever outside). Now it signifies 'outside' from within.

Conclusion

Containing a wealth of ambiguities, *The Shining* is particularly open to multiple interpretations. Along with the prevailing 'supernatural' and 'psychological' interpretations, it might be possible to see the whole film as Danny's disturbed fantasy inspired by his parents' clearly turbulent relationship. Another interpretation might be that the film is an allegory of culture, perhaps fuelling the boy's fantasy after the discovery of some art music records in the basement. But more than simply an allegory of culture, *The Shining* is an allegory of high art. Wendy and Danny are associated with, and thus representatives of, popular culture (or mass culture).[50] They cannot understand, indeed will not face up to, Jack's highest of high art (his writing). Thus, he is forced into a position of increased (and increasingly untenable) extremity. An integral element of the sublime is fear, and while Jack at first sees the beauty in Room 237, he then beholds its horrifying aspect. The two are related intimately. Furthermore, the sublime is often linked to the infinite, and as the concluding shots reveal, Jack appears to have been (and indeed will remain) in the hotel for ever.

Bartók, Penderecki and Ligeti's music is not part of the horror of the film. Its relation to the sublime is what makes it seem horrific. The art music that appears in *The Shining* is not a representation of evil – the 1920s dance music appears as a direct representation of the hotel's evil. In Adornian terms, the popular music's embodiment of evil – an appropriation of Hannah Arendt's term 'the banality of evil' could be apposite here – might be in its formulaic pre-digested format and concomitant restriction of thought.[51] The art music could hardly be accused of being formulaic, yet its inaccessibility precludes reflection by audiences unaccustomed to difficult music, and could provoke a reaction of horror – or to the sublime. The high-art music represents/evokes high emotion/abnormality. Indeed, it is the extreme of emotion unavailable to popular cinema, the majority of film music and 'popular culture' more generally.

Notes

1 David A. Cook, 'American Horror: *The Shining*', *Literature/Film Quarterly*, vol. 12, no. 1, 1984, pp. 2–4.

2 Discussed further by Lee Barron, '"Music Inspired by . . .": The Curious Case of the Missing Soundtrack' in Ian Inglis, ed., *Popular Music and Film* (London: Wallflower, 2003), pp. 148–61.

3 Michael Talbot-Smith, *Audio Explained* (London: Focal Press, 1997), pp. 22, 108.

4 See discussion of an experimental concert using infrasound. Mick Hamer, 'Silent Fright', *New Scientist*, 21–28 December 2002, pp. 50–1.

5 Vic Tandy, 'The Ghost in the Machine', *Journal for Psychical Research*, vol. 62, no. 851, April 1998.

6 This invisible 'image' is like a standing wave or ghostly form in itself.

7 This phenomenon has been noted by sound technicians: hi-fi 'matrix decoders can recover ambience and other "difference signal" information in the material and feed it to the rear speakers'. Larry Klein, 'Audio in the Seventies', *Stereo Review*, vol. 28, no. 1, January 1972, p. 80.

8 Konstantin Raudive, *Breakthrough: An Amazing Experiment in Electronic Communication with the Dead* (New York: Taplinger, 1971), pp. 20–7.

9 David Pinder, 'Ghostly Footsteps: Voices, Memories and Walks in the City', *Ecumene*, vol. 8, no. 1, January 2001, p. 1.

10 David Punter and Glennis Byron, eds., *Spectral Readings: Towards a Gothic Geography* (New York: St Martin's Press, 1999).

11 Jeffrey Sconce, *Haunted Media: Electronic Presence from Telegraphy to Television* (Durham, NC: Duke University Press, 2000), p. 200.

12 John Fiske, 'Moments of Television: Neither the Text nor the Reader' in Ellen Seiter, *et al.* eds, *Remote Control: Television, Audiences and Cultural Power* (London: Routledge, 1989), p. 66.

13 According to Anita Pallenberg, quoted in Mick Brown, *Performance, Bloomsbury Movie Guide, No. 6* (London: Bloomsbury, 1999), p. 169.

14 On many more occasions, the temp track is 'copied' by composers. According to Elliot Goldenthal, this is the all-too-easy path taken by most film music composers. Quoted in Richard Davies, *Complete Guide to Film Scoring* (Boston, MA: Berklee Press, 1999), p. 295.

15 This, of course, could be another ghostly aspect: the unheard, imagined missing score.

16 Alex North's *2001: A Space Odyssey*, Jerry Goldsmith and the National Philharmonic Orchestra, 1993, Varese Sarabande VSD-5400.

17 As stated in a paper presented at the Royal Musicological Association's 'Music and Film' conference at the University of Southampton, 20 April 2001.

18 This description could also apply to some of the music that appears in *A Clockwork Orange*, although not Carlos's.

19 *The Shining* may or may not be about the repressed past in the form of the destruction of Native Americans, but the music could well suggest the return of old European horrors. The music's appearance in the film parallels and connects the two events.

20 However, I must concede that the character of the final movement seems to me to be notably out of tune with the film!

21 Immanuel Kant, *Critique of Judgement*, translated by Werner S. Pluhar (Indianapolis, IN: Hackett, 1987 [originally 1790]), p. 101.

22 Ibid., p. 119.

23 Derived from the Greek 'ekstasis', which means standing outside of one's self.

24 Edmund Burke, *A Philosophical Inquiry into the Origins of Our Ideas of the Sublime and Beautiful* (Oxford: Oxford University Press, 1990), p. 59.

25 In 1974, Straub and Huillet also made a film of Schoenberg's *Moses and Aron*.

26 Simon Frith, 'Mood Music: An Enquiry into Narrative Film Music', *Screen*, vol. 25, no. 3, May–June 1984, p. 80.

27 Penderecki's *Polymorphia* has also been pressed into service by *The Exorcist* and *Fearless* (1993).

28 T. W. Adorno and Max Horkheimer, *The Dialectic of Enlightenment* (London: Verso, 1979), p. 34.

29 Although certain zones of mainstream film have allowed dissonant modernist-style music, similar to twentieth-century art music: for example, some of Jerry Fielding's scores, some of the music for the *Alien* series of films and isolated 'artistic' films, such as Joseph Losey's *Figures in a Landscape* (1970), with its uncompromising score by Richard Rodney Bennett.

30 Although the whole 'elitist' v 'mass' dichotomy, which has been important in the past, might easily now be seen as irrelevant by many.

31 Definition derived from *The American Heritage of the English Language* (Boston, MA: Houghton Mifflin, 2000) (<www.dictionary.com> accessed 8 August 2002).

32 However, positrons can be used in medical diagnostics, where tracers are injected before radiography, as their annihilation emits traceable radiation.

33 Indeed, a number of people I have spoken to deny the music in the film's status as music anyway, suggesting that it is 'merely noise'.

34 Perhaps such 'supernatural sound effects' are what non-diegetic film music should be conceived as more generally.

35 Ibid., p. 32.

36 Indeed, editor Gordon Stainforth noted how he synchronised Wendy's movements to cartoon music on television, then as she enters the Colorado Lounge the Penderecki piece is faded up. Kubrick FAQ (<www.visual-memory.co.uk/faq/html/shining/shining.html> accessed 25 October 2002).

37 As images are cut to the music, at times the film appears to display a certain indifference to dialogue.

38 The version of the Bartók piece that appears in the film is performed by the Berlin Philharmonic, conducted by Herbert von Karajan.

39 Penderecki's music has been used in a few other films: *The Exorcist* used *Polymorphia*, the Cello Concerto, music from his opera *The Devils of Loudon* (*Diably z Loudon*), *Kanon* for Orchestra and Tape, and String Quartet No. 1.; *Wild at Heart* used *Kosmogonia*, while *The People under the Stairs* (1991) used his *Threnody for the Victims of Hiroshima*; *Fearless* used *Polymorphia*, and *Twister* (1996) employed *De natura sonoris no. 1*.

40 William H. Rosar, 'The *Dies Irae* in *Citizen Kane*: Musical Hermeneutics Applied to Film Music' in K. J. Donnelly, ed., *Film Music: Critical Approaches* (Edinburgh: Edinburgh University Press, 2001), pp. 110–11.

41 Is this a good example of association breeding reaction, or is it an invocatory piece of music – an ancient mass for the dead that connects us on some primal level with the supernatural?

42 Indeed, the rhythmic contour of the melody is extremely traditional too, almost giving the impression of being the 'wrong notes' to another tune.

43 Indeed, this appearance proceeds from the start of the third movement itself, although it does not run to its full length, and cuts after a cymbal crash.

44 Interestingly, exactly the same section of the Bartók piece that is used in *The Shining* appeared in the *Doctor Who* serial, *The Web of Fear* (1968, BBC), as an accompaniment to a raid on a museum. This is a lost television programme and exists only as a commercial recording of its soundtrack (on BBC Worldwide, ISBN 0–563–55382–0).

45 The notion of songs as hauntings appears on the album *Songs from a Haunted Ballroom* (released in 2001 by V/VM records), by The Caretaker, a record of echoey old songs inspired directly by *The Shining*. This idea was evident earlier in Geoffrey Toye's ballet, *The Haunted Ballroom*, from the 1930s. A waltz taken from it became a familiar piece of light music on BBC radio.

46 Glen Creeber, 'Banality with a Beat: Dennis Potter and the Paradox of Popular Culture', *Media, Culture and Society*, vol. 18, no. 3, 1996, pp. 501–8; for a more general discussion, see Catrin Prys, 'The Singing Detective' in Glen Creeber, ed., *Fifty Key Television Programmes* (London: Arnold, 2004), pp. 183–7.

47 Howard Shore, interviewed in Royal S. Brown, *Overtones and Undertones: Reading Film Music* (Berkeley and Los Angeles: University of California Press, 1994), p. 357.

48 Indeed, Eisler and Adorno note that there is a vague affinity between 'the great sensational film' (like *King Kong* [1934]) and modernist music. Op. cit., p. 36.

49 Ligeti's piece in Kubrick's earlier *2001: A Space Odyssey* was used precisely for its 'otherworldliness' and expression thereof.

50 Indeed, the culture they are associated most prominently with is television cartoons.

51 Theodor Adorno, 'On Popular Music' in Simon Frith and Andrew Goodwin, eds., *On Record: Rock, Pop and the Written Word* (London: Routledge, 1990), p. 302.

Chapter 4

The Accented Voice: Ethnic Signposts of English, Irish and American Film Music

The 'ethnicity' of music and its connection to specific nationality is now widely thought to be culturally accrued rather than innate.[1] However, this is not to deny the national rootedness or implications of certain music. Robert Mackay describes the way that, during the Second World War, the BBC set out to remove German music from the airwaves. The corporation decided on a definition that made no exception for music from Germany:

> a ruling maintained that the political or ideological resonance of a piece of music was detectable in the *sounds of the notes* alone . . . As for the music publishers, who imagined, since they were never told otherwise, that the banning criteria were all to do with copyright, the hidden political filter remained hidden, and they were fobbed off with explanations relating to 'artistic' considerations in the building of music programmes.[2]

The BBC's notion about the 'sounds of the notes alone' is startling and appears unreasonable, at least to more recent ways of thinking about music's intrinsic value and ideas. However, perhaps on another level the BBC got it right. Music is a potent discourse, and its transmission of ethnic information is often one of its most significant powers. The power here does not lie directly in its ability to manipulate on a semi-conscious level, but rather in its ability to establish and guide geographical and social ideas for the audience.

There is a little part of a Hollywood sound stage that is forever England, and a slightly smaller part that is forever Ireland. It is difficult, I would have thought, not to see the power of one nation or ethnic group to represent another as anything other than problematic. This is particularly the case when that representation is tailored to the dominant group's own consumption.[3] At worst, it can be equated to racist jokes – 'Irish jokes' told by the English, 'Belgian jokes' told by the French, etc. – that simply denigrate those who are 'told' in the joke, while elevating those who do the telling.

This chapter is concerned with the way that music can be used to set ethnic and national boundaries in films. This feature is premised upon the use of limited stylistic languages with restricted musical vocabularies that allow music to represent things and ideas. I will delineate this process, the 'tricks' and musical techniques involved, which inevitably relates to the notion of stereotypical ideas and the (largely negative) ways of talking about different peoples. This chapter will deal with 'English', 'Irish' and 'American' film music; in the case of the latter, examining the delineation of Native Americans and white Americans in Westerns. I will deal with the manner in which ethnicity is constructed by film music, focusing on the non-diegetic score, and evaluate how far music sells a distinctive but often restrictive and reactionary view of difference in an unobtrusive manner.

Generally speaking, this will discuss how music can be associated with something else, specifically with types of people and places. This could be seen as a form of 'synaesthesia', where musical sounds immediately invoke more remote ideas related only through convention.[4] This is music as representation, and consequently, music as a primary bearer of ideology. For example, such screen music synaesthesia means that whenever experienced film audiences hear a Spanish guitar, there is a tendency to think of the American West – perhaps even when the film is representing Spain! This amounts to a subtle form of mental control, through the (often insidious) use of ethnic stereotyping.[5] While this may not be the sort of 'control' (at least, not of the order discussed in some other sections of the book) that would worry psychologists or those looking for covert brainwashing, it could well be seen as a socially negative means of controlling ideas, and thus is a form of power worth scrutinising in more detail. It is the power of culture and cultural meanings, rather than a situational power led by the physical and psychological specificities of cinema. Here, for example, films have created 'Indians', whose rich culture is reduced to a fake sonic (and visual) film prop that could easily be unrecognisable to Native Americans. The opposite of this has been to build a sense of tradition for white America through 'Americana' that excludes (or, at the very least, marginalises) Native Americans and much else besides. These are seemingly 'natural' representations, imbued with distinct ideological positionings. Music in film is less obviously 'up front' than other elements, perhaps. It does much of its work in the background of the film and in the background of our minds, yet it is precisely this fact that makes it a more powerful agent for engaging and implanting such ideas.

Music is often seen as the essence of national/ethnic communities, and a paramount signifier of ethnic or cultural difference in films. Ethnic clichés and representative gambits have been imported from musical culture and developed.[6] Edward Said's notion of 'Orientalism' is nowhere better exemplified than in film music. According to Said, the notion of the 'Orient' in western thought is constructed by, and exists precisely for, the West, thus becoming an image of what the West thinks it is not: exotic, barbaric and of less worth. As he puts it, 'The Orient was almost a European invention, and had been since antiquity a place of romance, exotic beings, haunting memories and landscapes, remarkable experiences.'[7] Ideas about the

'Orient' manifest a fully integrated system of thought and understanding. Similarly, film music, particularly in mainstream cinema, regularly counts as one of its main functions the delineation of place and national or ethnic type, initiating and reinforcing divisions. Geoffrey Bennington observes that 'The frontier does not merely close the nation in on itself, but also, immediately, opens it to an outside, to other nations. Frontiers are articulations, boundaries are, constitutively, crossed or transgressed';[8] while Georgina Born and David Hesmondhalgh note: 'in certain circumstances music does function primarily and powerfully to articulate the boundaries defining the collective identities or mutual antagonisms of pre-existing sociocultural groupings, groups defined by shared cultural systems quite distinct from music'.[9] The whole idea of setting an ethnic boundary – expelling that which you disown and reconfiguring the outside to fit your fears – might be seen in a particularly vivid form in much film music. The same goes for much television music, although arguably in a more obvious manner.

The process of how this is achieved is quite clear, following a strong tradition of techniques and a specific repertoire of film music language. This is a form of 'shorthand', taking certain musical aspects and using them as an essence of different musical cultures. According to Thomas Fitzgerald, modern ethnicity works through the wielding and manipulation of symbols.[10] There are some extremely obvious musical examples: the large warpipe version of the bagpipes are regularly employed to denote Scotland; the use of the simple five-note pentatonic melodic scale tends to suggest the rustic, bucolic or folk music; while modes with flattened seconds,[11] such as the Phrygian mode and the 'gypsy' minor scale, are used to provide a clear denotation of the Orient, particularly the Middle East.[12] In film scores both old and new, the 'trick' is to use these shorthands in a manner that foregrounds them as an effect within a musical fabric that is not premised upon such ethnic musical language. Thus, their communicational content very often outweighs their material and sensual aspects.

The use of these clichés is premised upon music as a system of representation, which uses quite circumscribed codes in order to evoke certain distinctive images and ideas. The rigidity of such music-image coding can be illustrated with recourse to the 'problems' noted by some commentators when James Horner used the Irish bagpipe, the uillean pipes, that are played under the arm and sound far more intimate than the larger warpipes, for the Scottish-set *Braveheart* (1995),[13] or when Lisa Gerrard and Hans Zimmer's score for *Gladiator* employed the Armenian-Turkish doudouk to depict the Roman Europe. The very nasal double-reed doudouk is more commonly and less controversially used to denote oriental aspects, as in Peter Gabriel's music for Martin Scorsese's *The Last Temptation of Christ* (1988).

More commonly, the use of music to provide conventional ethnic associations is unremarkable, yet powerful. Mainstream film music embodies something of a 'universal language'. Music in film functions through the invocation of archetypes, working synaesthetically to articulate identity and difference, but particularly in formations where that specific difference is of some cultural value. Hence, depictions of Scotland or Ireland tend to require emphasised musical representation, while in American-made films, the United States usually requires little or no overdetermined representation. Music works as a signpost, like a sonic establishing shot, while it also functions as a boundary marker, setting national and other borders and demarcations.[14]

England on Soundtrack and Screen

In the American Film Institute's documentary *Bernard Herrmann: Music for the Movies*, composer Elmer Bernstein noted Max Steiner's (and more generally the classical film score's) use of 'intellectual musical connections'. He cited the appearance of the tune 'Rule Britannia' in the fabric of a film score to denote unequivocally that a warship on the screen is British.[15] Similarly, in more recent times, in the Hollywood film *Three Men and a Little Lady* (1990), a British location cues the underscore to blare forth 'Rule Britannia'over a helicopter shot of rolling green fields and a Mini Cooper (the iconic British-made car) containing Tom Selleck and Steve Guttenberg. However, we should note that this leaves the audience in little doubt that it is England rather than any other part of 'Britannia'.

In the 1930s and 1940s, Warner Bros. produced a cycle of action films with English subjects and starring Errol Flynn, with music by Erich Wolfgang Korngold.[16] These included *Captain Blood* (1935),[17] *The Adventures of Robin Hood* (1938), *The Private Lives of Elizabeth and Essex* (1939) and *The Sea Hawk* (1940).[18] One of the striking aspects of this outstanding series of musical scores is that they eschew any attemp to evoke the English (and colonial) settings or concerns through music, and deal in an 'international' musical style. While the musical blueprint may be derived from *mittel*-European late-Romantic concert-hall music, the syntax and substance embodies Hollywood film music as the 'one size fits all' film score. Each of Korngold's classic scores is a model example of the 'classical film score', at least in its 'prestige' version.[19]

Another good example of a classical Hollywood film score for a film set in England is *Mrs Miniver* (1942). The film chronicles the impact of the Second World War on a 'middle-class English family', as we are told by a rolling title card at the film's opening. Herbert Stothart's score is in many ways a typical product of the studio system. There is, in fact, little to mark it out as specific to the film in question, and little in the music that paints an English wash on the film. The title sequence is accompanied by lyrical string-led orchestral music that segues into the melody of the hymn 'Oh God, Our Help in Ages Past' while the screen contains rolling narrative-establishing prose. Once the diegesis is properly engaged, and we are shown street scenes, the English nature of this representation is underlined by a variation on the 'Westminster chimes', a common musical signifier of London. *Mrs Miniver* contains rather more reminders for the audience of the film's setting in its diegetic music. The milkman whistles 'British Grenadiers', a group of home-guard soldiers with a prominent Scotsmen sing 'A Hundred Pipers', and at the end of the dance, all present stand to attention for 'God Save the King'. The score refrains from these patent signs of 'Englishness' (or rather Britishness and a moment of Scottishness) until the film's conclusion. Here, in the bombed-out church, the vicar gives a lecture about the war, followed by the church congregation's rendition of 'Onward Christian Soldiers', which, as the camera alights on a hole in the roof and a number of Spitfire fighter planes fly past, is superceded by the score's arrangement of Elgar's *Pomp and Circumstance March No. 1*, better known in the form of its patriotic song adaptation, 'Land of Hope and Glory'.

More recent attempts to represent England (i.e. post the Hollywood studio system) have also tended not to use heavily 'ethnicised' film music. International 'Swinging London' productions, such as Michelangelo Antonioni's *Blow Up* (1966), used 'American' jazz-rock by keyboard player Herbie Hancock, along with a memorable cameo from British group the Yardbirds, playing a blues-inspired song. Similarly, *Alfie* (1966), which starred Michael Caine, had a jazzy underscore by American jazz musician Sonny Rollins. For Sam Peckinpah's *Straw Dogs* (1971), Jerry Fielding wrote a bleak score that was too sophisticated to countenance the inclusion of 'English' musical signposts, and was inclined toward the atmospheric rather than the functional. Indeed, in the 1960s and 1970s, film music developed more towards providing differentiated atmospheres with less emphasis on functional narrative pointers and markers. However, simultaneously, it might be argued that scores diverged into either modernism as a musical 'international style', with concert-hall dissonance replacing the classical film score's 'one-size-fits-all' symphonic scores, or the showcasing of pop music, in which songs became more prominent in non-musical films and scores bore certain stylistic influences from popular music. In British films, this was particularly pronounced in the 1960s, due to the protean character of British pop music at the time.[20]

In terms of representing other countries, a perennial problem arises, in that the version on screen (and from loudspeaker) manifests a touristic version of the location being constructed. This problem is most apparent in British-set US costume pictures.[21] Perhaps the musical *Brigadoon* (1954) is one of the best examples. While constructing a charming world for American audiences, this is built upon a sub-tourist brochure version of Scotland that speaks the language of the most basic stereotypes or ethnic shorthands. Colin McArthur points out the charged aspects of the 'tartan and kailyard' through which Scotland is represented (both by Scots and foreigners).[22] McArthur also suggests that because of its common currency, such a system of representation might better be seen as a 'discursive position' rather than simply stereotype. It is worth noting, however, that some ethnic film music is more prevalent than others (for example, Scottish or Irish more than English), and that all such 'representative music' engages complex debates about national representation more generally.

The manipulation and fabrication of accent can be seen as homologous to the fabrication of musical signifiers of 'Englishness' (and indeed other ethnicities). Many American-made films set in Britain could be seen as constituents of the costume drama genre. As part of the 'Englishness' on display, which runs the gamut of tourist signs, there are also some archetypal accents. One of the best known, indeed the most notorious, was Dick Van Dyke's extraordinary take on the cockney accent as the chimney sweep in *Mary Poppins* (1964). While this causes great mirth among audiences in Britain, it is not an isolated instance. Keanu Reeves made a most notably poor attempt at an English accent in *Bram Stoker's Dracula* (1992).[23] Interestingly, in the same film, American actors Tom Waits and Winona Ryder's efforts were more successful. Sitting through a film apparently (partially) set in England, in which Hollywood actors make half-hearted attempts at speaking 'English', English audiences may feel alienated from what appears to be their own country. Audiences often become particularly aware of how their country is sold and used as a commodity aimed at those abroad and excluding those at home. Film music is a crucial part of this process.

Three Men and a Little Lady certainly has something of the costume picture about it. The film displays English locations like a travelogue and sites English people (rather than British) in a world of aristocracy, unfeasibly large country mansions, polite garden parties, brutal boarding schools and stiff-upper-lip emotional repression – not to mention a dearth of honesty matched with a scheming sense of superiority. The English are not used to being presented in such negative cultural terms.[24] From what I can gather, English (and British) audiences found this film – which clearly was not 'aimed' at their consumption – either wryly amusing or simply horrifying.[25]

In contradistinction to these Hollywood versions of England, the British film industry has produced representations for home consumption as well as some similar ones for export. Perhaps the slippage between 'British' and 'English' is less pronounced in films made in the UK.[26] Generally speaking, Britishness on screen seems to have been embodied by the costume picture, particularly one that represents the ruling classes and their concerns while marginalising the working classes.[27] The fact that costume dramas appear as an incontrovertible space for the discussion of British nation and English ethnicity may well be due to the fact that images of British modernity prove problematic both for British audiences as well as for overseas consumption and sales.

Music occupies a strange position in historical films such as costume dramas. It regularly appears as a guarantor of the film's depicted period: for example, ensuring that images depicting the early 19th century should be accompanied by music that would have been used during that period, or at least music that apparently does not disturb the film's sense of historical period. However, it is surely a rarity when films use music that completely retains historical veracity throughout. More often, film music acts as a frame or conduit, allowing the audience access to what appears to be the past, but through music that, in a reassuring manner, retains a solid foot in the present in terms of style.

There is perhaps something of a tradition that the music in costume dramas, as well as the genre itself, provides an ironic commentary on the action. Music is often in a prime position to do this: to cock a snoot at the film, in a manner that might or might not be registered by the audience, or indeed by the film-makers. However, this appears to be an isolated rarity in a sea of functional scores that furnish place and time for the film as much as any of the *mise en scene* on screen.

Music in British films of the 1940s and 1950s was either of the prestige sort – corresponding to many of the films it accompanied – or, more commonly, of a cheaper and more functional variety. The strategy of procuring respected 'classical' composers to write music for expensive British films is one of the characteristics of British film music from the 1930s to the 1960s.[28] For instance, Sir Arthur Bliss composed the music for *Things to Come* (1936) and William Walton wrote the music for Olivier's *Henry V* (1945). Similarly, prestigious Charles Dickens adaptations like David Lean's *Great Expectations* (1947) had music by respected émigré Walter Goehr, while aristocratic dilettante Lord Berners (born Gerald Tyrrwhitt-Wilson) wrote the music for *Nicholas Nickleby* (1947).[29] Neither of these films play upon Britishness as much as they could, or indeed as much as more recent television adaptations of Dickens's novels that were more explicitly aimed at export.

Working to a different blueprint, the music in some of the less prestigious British films of the time used more functional music that was itself valued rather less.[30] A good example is in the music for costume dramas produced by Gainsborough Studios in the 1930s and 1940s, which eschewed the prestige mode of film music production that guaranteed a quality product by conferring music with a veil of high art that was more overt than many of the other elements. Witness Ralph Vaughan Williams's unprecedented full-screen card (one might even say 'starring') credit at the opening of *Forty-Ninth Parallel* (1941). Instead, the music for Gainsborough and Gaumont-British productions was often written by unsung journeymen, and a fair amount was cobbled together by musical director Louis Levy from odds and ends. These films were less overtly proud of being British – indeed, the studios' output regularly problematised Britishness.[31] Yet when the music was called upon to evoke England or Britain, it sometimes reverted to the more crass styling evident in Hollywood films.

In the 1950s, Britishness was embodied by military marches in war films, where the British routinely vanquished the Nazi forces. Some of the most prominent marches that incarnated Britishness on film were those from *Cockleshell Heroes* (1955), *The Dam Busters* (1954) and *The Bridge on the River Kwai* (1957), although the latter's most memorable piece was the Victorian 'Colonel Bogey' march. By the 1950s, of course, these were historical films, and arguably war films constitute a kind of costume drama, yet Britishness – or, more properly, Englishness – was more tangible (and more problematic) in costume dramas set deeper in the past and showing a concern with the rural ruling classes.[32]

A significant moment in the British costume film, and particularly for its music, is *Tom Jones* (1963). The film was directed by Tony Richardson, with music by John Addison, and was remarkably successful, including in the American market. In fact, Addison's music won the Oscar for best musical score. The music, however, is extremely self-conscious and contains a degree of irony throughout. The film's opening was shot to look like a silent film with no diegetic sound, title cards for dialogue and speeded-up action. Correspondingly, the accompanying music parodies the lone piano accompaniment common in film theatres before the advent of sound cinema, yet instead of a piano, it is played on a baroque keyboard instrument (either the harpsichord or virginal).

Nearly twenty years later, a similar, although reversed, disjunction between musical instrumentation and musical style was evident in *Chariots of Fire* (1981). Greek synthesizer player Vangelis chose to score the film with a mock classical main theme that was played on electronic keyboards and drum machine. In the same year, a very successful television miniseries, *Brideshead Revisited* (1981, Granada), had music that again parodied the classical, although retaining a traditional instrumentation. It was written by Geoffrey Burgon, a conservatoire-trained orchestral composer who had also composed music for the BBC's science-fiction serial *Doctor Who* a couple of years earlier. Since the early 1980s, the vast majority of screen costume dramas had been made for television as prestige productions, many adapting internationally famous novels.[33] As with *Brideshead Revisited*, music in these historical dramas perhaps reflected less their Englishness or Britishness than their interest in the ruling classes. Hence, the music is almost uniformly quasi-classical, as this style of music was associated firmly with the upper classes, although this notion has eroded somewhat following the success of middlebrow commercial classical music radio stations, particularly Classic FM in the mid-1990s. I will return to this discussion in Chapter 6.

The Draughtsman's Contract

A year after *Chariots of Fire* came a less celebrated costume film, Peter Green-away's very singular drama, *The Draughtsman's Contract* (1982). The film's sumptuous but often static visuals were complemented by music by Michael Nyman, which gave a distinct energy to the proceedings. The film played with a sense of historical veracity, and this is nowhere more evident than in its music. Nyman's music works as a 'frame', based on fragments from the music of 17th-century composer Henry Purcell, but subjected to a very modern process.[34] The fragments of actual antique music are used in a repetitive systems format, reminiscent of minimalist music by art composers such as Philip Glass, Steve Reich and John Adams. This makes the music a far cry from traditional film scores, although Philip Glass has since scored a number of films without significant compromise to his distinctive musical style. The film's highly individual music reflected Nyman's interest in experimental music, minimalism and postmodernism,[35] while also making use of his unfinished doctoral thesis on repetitive music of the 16th and 17th centuries. Such a self-conscious attempt to deal with historical veracity, in which the music is a central aspect of the film, constituted an attempt to negotiate or critically discuss the past, rather than simply make it seem normal and natural, as could have been the case with much mainstream film music. The film's sense of Englishness is not only problematised by the visual rendering of the country house in the film, but also by Nyman's musical representation of history and Englishness through a veil of musical modernity. As Nyman notes, he and Greenaway did not 'consider indulging in the pointless activity of musical pastiche usually found in the soundtracks of films located in the "historical past". . .'[36] While *The Draughtsman's Contract* is far from the norm, a more recent film that has similar concerns is another costume picture, *Plunkett and Maclaine* (1999), which also attempted to use music to subvert the costume genre. The music was by Scot Craig Armstrong, and at one notable point in the film, accompanying a party at an English country house, appeared more inspired by current trends in electronic dance music. While this was thirty-six years after John Addison had attempted similar things with *Tom Jones*, it was nevertheless an audacious move.

A series of films that exploits an ambiguous yet internationally marketable version of Englishness is the James Bond films. Although they are British productions, their background and assumptions are less English or even British, but more 'mid-Atlantic'. Arguably, the music has precisely the same (mid-Atlantic) tone as the other elements. Despite the use of some British singers for the title songs, there is nothing to mark this film music space out as particularly English or British.[37] 'British' as distinct from 'English' rarely registers in films and probably never registers in film music. The key, however, is to realise that obvious ethnic pointers in the music (such as the example cited earlier of *Three Men and a Little Lady*) posit an audience outside England.

Ireland Represented

For a country without an established film industry, and prey to representations from strong cultural players on the outside, problems with portrayal are far larger. Ireland has had to endure visions of itself emanating not only from Hollywood, but also from the British film industry.[38] Some examples of British representations of Ireland include *Odd Man Out* (1946), which encompasses much Belfast location shooting, *Black Narcissus* (1947), which contained a short sequence set in Galway, *Captain Boycott* (1947), *Hungry Hill* (1947) and *Jacqueline* (1957), which was shot on location in Belfast. The music for these films was written by English composers William Alwyn (*Odd Man Out, Captain Boycott, Jacqueline*), Brian Easdale (*Black Narcissus*) and John Greenwood (*Hungry Hill*). Alwyn's scores have the most 'Irish' elements and style to them. Generally, films that were either British-made or British co-productions tended to use composers from the more developed British film industry. Examples include Roy Budd for *The Flight of the Doves* (1971), George Fenton for *High Spirits* (1988) and Colin Towns for *Rawhead Rex* (1986). All of these film have scores that to a lesser or greater extent attempt a certain 'Gaelic' sound. This tends to manifest itself in simple lyrical and emotional pentatonic melodies, or in jigs and reels,[39] even on occasion using sounds derived from Irish folk music and traditional instruments such as the uillean pipes, tin whistle and bodhran drum.

According to Noel McLaughlin and Martin McLoone, Irish music was constructed as an ethnic category by the Victorians

> as an expression of the people, a reflection of their innate feelings and sensibilities. Music, therefore, became a feature of 'race', taking on properties for the coloniser that appeared to transcend the passage of time, that remained fixed and unchanging.
>
> In this way, the various musics of Ireland were homogenized and categorized as an 'ethnic' music, a process that was begun by the Protestant Anglo-Irish Ascendancy in the eighteenth and nineteenth century, was adopted in the late nineteenth century by Irish nationalism as a response to negative stereotyping and continues today in Ireland by government bodies like the Folklore Commission.[40]

The British cinematic version of Ireland is confused, most notably with respect to Northern Ireland. The province is culturally as well as politically ambiguous and problematic; it is half inside and half outside Britain in cultural terms. While politically it may be a part of the United Kingdom, culturally it is clear that a significant proportion of the population identify with the Republic of Ireland rather than Britain, and that this culture sees itself as decidedly outside Britain.[41]

Odd Man Out is set in Northern Ireland, yet tries to some degree to avoid direct representation of the sectarian divide and conflict. It attempts to portray a 'universal' narrative, but projects a view of Northern Ireland from Britain, for an implied audience on what some call the 'British mainland'. The film's music demonstrates clearly the processes involved in this attempt at universality, mixing 'neutral' film

Odd Man Out

music language with 'Irish'-style material to fabricate ethnicity and location. It provides a mixture of Hollywood's highly developed action-matching underscoring with the predominantly British mode of autonomous pieces (with their own musical logic) counterpointed with screen activity. As Michel Chion points out, 'music enjoys the status of being a little freer of barriers of time and space than other sound and visual elements'.[42] So we might expect the music to exhibit a process that is not shackled by the film, which does not directly follow the film's ethnic construction. However, in *Odd Man Out*, it follows slavishly the film's other ethnic strategies, and indeed, it might be argued, does important work to define them.

William Alwyn's score engages with stereotypical musical formations to represent 'Irishness', as Robert Moss notes: 'Occasionally the melodies suggest haunting old Irish airs . . .'[43] Music such as this trades upon the 'already known', in this case British discourses about a general Ireland rather than the more specific and historically distinct Ulster or Northern Ireland. This is articulated through musical as well as iconographic and narrative stereotyping and clichés. Seen from this perspective, the music in *Odd Man Out* works as a frame for British audiences, a marker for a particular point of view, allowing easy entry to a world of cliché and formula.

Odd Man Out includes one repeated and overwhelming main musical theme,[44] the Irish-style tune that is also pointedly the funeral tune for Johnny.[45] This represents a musical paucity compared with the thematic wealth of Hollywood film scores of the time. The point of the music is primarily to repeat Johnny's theme, a funeral threnody, and thus to remain static, freezing and fetishising the action of his slow death.

The music creates a fabric through which the film's visual representations are filtered, providing a grounding for the narrative activity as well as fashioning a perspective upon the tale. As such, the music tells of inevitable death: the main theme
is one long funeral march (the finale of the concert-hall suite created from the film's
music is entitled 'Nemesis'). It starts with a rhythmic version of the 'Fate' motto that
inaugurates Beethoven's Fifth Symphony and is marked 'lento funebre' (slow and
funereal). It even goes so far as to include the tolling bell of Belfast's Albert clock,
which marks out the eight hours of the film's action and is a palpable aural icon of
the funereal.[46] Towards the conclusion of the film, this music comes into its own as
an accompaniment for images of Johnny staggering about the streets of Belfast in
the rain and snow.

Alwyn's musical underscore is fully integral to the film, having been conceived and
built up before the shooting started. The poetic quality of the film derives partially
from the fact that it was shot as well as being cut to the music, as Alwyn recalled:

> Long before the shooting in the studios started . . . we worked on the pace of the music . . .
> Most of the scenes were shot to prerecordings and transformed and orchestrated afterwards. I
> worked in the closest collaboration with the editor, so that we knew what we were doing indi-
> vidually with sound effects and music, and the final result is a complete integration of sound
> and visuals – a sound-film in the real meaning of the word, where music had been allowed to
> speak in terms of film and fine art.[47]

The integral status of the music and its frequent appearance in the aural foreground
means that it keys into an immersion in *emotion* and the dreamlike quality of the
film.

A very different, far less sombre but nevertheless fascinating example is the children's film *The Flight of the Doves*. It exemplifies films set in or representing Ireland
that are produced by overseas interests and for overseas audiences. It also typifies
this in narrative terms, marking a flight to Ireland from England, and embracing a
narrative 'discussion' of ethnic difference. One of the main songs in the film, 'You
Don't Have to Be Irish to Be Irish', and sung by the English lead, sums up the
process of cultural cruising at the heart of this type of film.

The film was directed by Ralph Nelson, an American whose previous excursion
had been the revisionist Western, *Soldier Blue* (1970). The main theme music of *The
Flight of the Doves* has something of a 'Western' character to it, and, indeed, the
film's underscore by British composer Roy Budd displays rather less of the 'Irish
pastoral' tradition of film music. A more 'up-to-date' score, it is very much of its
time (the early 1970s), and thus appears dated today. It includes some 'Irishness',
songs, jazzy passages, short dramatic sections and popular (King's Singers-style)
vocal selections.[48] The film music still includes some characteristically Irish aspects,
particularly the appearance of Irish singer Dana (a Eurovision Song Contest
winner) as Sheila, who sings 'The Far Off Place', partly in English and partly in

Irish; while to establish location without any doubt, the film also includes some diegetic Irish-style folk music at the fair.

Interestingly, the film has a semi-submerged sense of postcolonialism to it. The story concerns two children, Finn and Derval Dove, who escape from England to Ireland and the possibility of safety from their evil uncle, Hawk Dove, a master of disguise who wants the children dead for the purposes of inheritance. The film seems unaware of a whole arena of ideas about the relationship between Britain and Ireland into which it is entering. For example, the evil stepfather is named 'Cromwell', clearly after the English leader responsible for what would now be called ethnic cleansing in Ireland. Some of this must have seeped through from Irishman Walter Macken's original novel, but the film seems only partly conscious of the themes and ideas with which it is dealing. Indeed, this process is comparable to the wielding of ethnicised music in the film.

Certain images of Ireland sold well overseas in the 20th century, and were almost always accompanied by a soundtrack of Irish-style music, an easily identified and important international means of differentiation. Hollywood film music stalwart Max Steiner tended to use a basis of seemingly indigenous folk music as a principal means of designating location in his scores. Good examples are his music for John Ford's *The Informer* (1935) and his later Western scores. This technique persisted in classical film scores, resulting in probably the most famous Hollywood take on Ireland, Ford's *The Quiet Man* (1952), with music by Victor Young.[49] More recent Hollywood versions of Ireland have followed a remarkably similar strategy. For example, *The Devil's Own* (1997), the first half of which is set in Northern Ireland, used very Celtic-sounding orchestral music by James Horner. Interestingly, Horner has increasingly used Gaelic musical aspects as important elements of some of his more general film music, employing uillean pipes and other Irish aspects in both *Braveheart* and *Titanic*, to some degree uncoupling Irish signifiers from their expected or anticipated images. The strategies evident in films set in Ireland are designed to furnish a sense of Irishness through their music as much as, if not more so, than the visual aspects of the film. This is simply a more extreme version of the stereotypical 'Irish' representation evident in films like Disney's *Darby O'Gill and the Little People* (1959), which starred Belfast-born Albert Sharpe, and *Finian's Rainbow* (1968), both tales of fantastic adventures peopled with leprechauns and the like.[50]

John Williams wrote an epic orchestral score for *Far and Away* (1992), which included many standard Hollywood action cues mixed with a delicate Celtic-style theme. The film was shot in the United States as well as in Dublin, the Dingle peninsula, Galway and the Bray studios. As an action-adventure film, *Far and Away* perhaps required music that is less than subtle in making its point. A more recent Irish-set film scored by Williams, *Angela's Ashes* (1999), called for a less ethnicised approach. An Irish-American co-production shot wholly in Ireland, the film's emotional content was underscored mostly by solo piano, without a hint of the stereotypical aspects that usually signify Ireland in film music.

Irish-produced films set in Ireland often follow the lead of international productions and are compelled to announce Ireland in the most basic and blatant musical terms. The cosmopolitan status of the film industry in recent years has meant that many Irish films are scored by composers from overseas. Irish films such as Jim Sheridan's *My Left Foot* (1989) and *The Field* (1990) were scored by veteran Hollywood composer Elmer Bernstein. Indeed, American composer Bernstein has established something of a track record for scoring Irish-set films, having also written the music for *Da* (1988), *Into the West* (1992) and *The Rising of the Moon* (2002), a short about Bobby Sands, the IRA man and elected MP who died on hunger strike in the early 1980s.

In contrast, it is fairly rare to find music by Irish composers and musicians in Irish-made films. *The Disappearance of Finbar* (1996, Ireland/UK/Sweden) had music by uillean pipe player Davy Spillane, who had composed music for, and appeared in, Joe Comerford's *Traveller* (1981, Ireland), a film full of traditional Irish music. Irish composer Shaun Davey, who provided music for the television serial *Ballykissangel*, scored *Waking Ned* (aka *Waking Ned Devine*) (1998), which, although purporting to be Ireland, was shot on the Isle of Man and starred a Scot, and *The Abduction Club* (2002, UK/Ireland/France/Germany). *Agnes Browne* (1999) had music by Paddy Moloney from famed Irish folk group the Chieftains, while *The General* (1998) was scored by Richie Buckley, one of the foremost Irish saxophone players, renowned for playing with Van Morrison's band. However, Thaddeus O'Sullivan's remake of *The General*, *Ordinary Decent Criminal* (2000), starred Kevin Spacey and had music by Damon Albarn, the singer in the British pop group Blur. Indeed, it is more common to have music by composers working in the more heavily developed British screen industry, such as Dario Marianelli (*I Went Down* [1997]) and John Keane (also know as John E. Keane) (*Trojan Eddie* [1996]).

Thaddeus O'Sullivan's black-and-white art film *December Bride* (1990) is one of only a few films to focus on Northern Irish (Protestant) Unionists. In musical terms, the film neglected to use the standard aspects of 'Irishness', and had a score by German film music composer Juergen Knieper. While the film's status as an art film, rather than a mainstream film made for wide distribution, meant that it did not have to pander to a sense of expressing Ireland to the outside world in simplistic terms. However, while it avoided archetypal music, it did use music to provide an essence of the Ulster Protestant culture by showing people playing the characteristic gigantic lambeg drums.

Jim Sheridan's *In the Name of the Father* (1993) had a score by South African-born British composer Trevor Jones, but included notable songs for the opening and closing titles that exploited the buoyant state of Irish pop music.[51] They were collaborations between Bono (of U2) and Gavin Friday, along with Maurice Seezer, singer Sinéad O'Connor (on the end titles) and British producer Tim Simenon. The opening song, 'In the Name of the Father', included a repeated digital sample of a piece of traditional Irish music, *An Ras* by Tommy Hayes. While the music had a sheen of modernity to it, the Irish folk music sample made it a self-conscious play with Irish musical signifiers. Gavin Friday and Maurice Seezer went on to compose the music for *The Boxer* (1997), with a score that contains none of the 'Irish' clichés that have often been used to sell Ireland abroad. Another film set in Northern Ireland was *Resurrection Man* (1998), which was scored by another Irish (this time, Northern Irish) pop musician, David Holmes, who came to prominence as a producer of electronic dance music. This music fed upon a tradition set apart from the musical 'Irishness' that has dominated films. Oddly, Holmes's opening music for the film bore distinct similarities to the opening track on his album *this films crap lets slash the seats* (1995), which had been inspired by *In the Name of the Father*, making for circular inspiration but with a foot outside film music.

The vast majority of films from the Irish film industry are co-productions, usually with the United States or the UK. On occasions, this exerts a certain amount of pressure to depict an Ireland that will register for the international market, and explains the often prominent use of 'Irish'-style film music. Some international co-production period pieces exhibit less of a sense of Irishness in the music, such as Stanislas Syrewicz's music for *Nora* (2000, Ireland/UK/Italy/Germany) and Neil Jordan's epic biopic *Michael Collins* (1996, Ireland/UK/US), which had a very strong score by Eliot Goldenthal that contained no obvious ethnic signifiers.

While the Irish often remain 'musicalised' on film, the divide between music as an essential signifier of Ireland and not remains. In *The Commitments* (1991, UK/US/Ireland), a successful Irish-set musical about a pop group, one of the characters claimed: 'The Irish are the blacks of Europe'. The film dealt with a whole musical tradition acquired from American black popular culture, specifically the blues, rhythm'n'blues and soul, but was built upon an international notion of the Irish nation's innate musicality.

On rare occasions, there is some confusion about the musical signifiers of Irishness. English composer Benjamin Britten wrote the music for a documentary short film called *Around the Village Green* (1937, UK). The most prominent piece of music in the film is an Irish reel, which seems quite bizarre in a film that represents a typical village in England. As I have already noted, *Braveheart*, which was shot in Ireland, used Irish-sounding music by James Horner, while his score for *Titanic* also had a notably 'Irish' flavour. A film like *Hear My Song* (1991, UK) presented a Liverpool replete with Irish people and as an adjunct to Ireland, while the music featured international music sung by Irish tenor Josef Locke. Such confusion often envelops Ireland's screen image, although musical representation is less ambiguous but perhaps no less problematic in ethical terms. Jeffrey Richards is content to see depictions of Irish people in British culture as 'a cultural construction of Irishness in which the Irish themselves have collaborated' and so seemingly has nothing to do with British hegemony.[52] Yet this is in stark contrast to scholars such as Richard Ned Lebow who see cultural representations as primary influences on (historical and continued) colonial activities and discrimination.[53]

Hollywood's Ethnic West

Westerns represent an indigenous American film genre, with a significant interest in delineating both white cowboys and the Native Americans, and indeed other ethnicities.[54] In this way, the Western is a uniquely American genre. It invokes and replays ideas of nation and race, among other important issues.[55] Some of the best books about the concept of the American West have concentrated on the massive importance of films for perpetuating and developing American popular history. For example, Jim Kitses's *Horizons West*, Michael Coyne's *The Crowded Prairie* and Richard Slotkin's *Gunfighter Nation* (while the latter is not about films per se, it does include a chapter called 'The Western in American History').[56]

Robert Warshow describes the Western as 'an art form for connoisseurs, where the spectator derives his [*sic*] pleasure from the appreciation of minor variations within the working out of a pre-established order'.[57] Classical Westerns certainly followed a standard formula and indeed might be seen as one of the most obviously 'classical' genres of cinema. Musicals aspects, as much as any other, also followed the limited prescriptions that defined the Western genre, making for the sort of music that is easily identified as belonging to Western films. The music for the vast majority of Westerns has been very traditional, following the blueprint of the classical film score well into recent years. Of course, there have been innovations along the way. Yet the relatively standard aspects of Western scores primarily serve as a testament to the genre's longevity and the limits of its aesthetic boundaries. Classical Westerns have music that follows the patterns of traditional film music, yet with specific 'Western' aspects, of which the most important would be the use of 'Western' folk songs and the music assigned to Indians. It is worth noting that these are also the key ethnic definers that manifest genre through music, setting out an opposition upon which a large number of Westerns rest. While many Westerns include songs, the underscores also contain melodies that sound as if they are, or might be, Western songs (although they are sometimes European folk songs). Westerns often include theme songs, such as those sung by Tex Ritter for many Westerns in the 1950s, and it is worth noting that the tradition of cowboy and Western songs had a strong life outside the cinema. On the other hand, the 'Indian' music in Westerns had no life outside the cinema, as it was not based on real Native American music, but more fitted an idea of what Indian music should sound like for film audiences. Claudia Gorbman notes that 'In the classical pre-World War II western, the film score represented Indians by means of a small inventory of stable and unambiguous musical conventions.'[58] A close relation of the music associated with Native Americans is 'Mexican music', which is also the music of the Other and marks a musical-ethnic border with the white cowboys, cavalry and settlers. Interestingly, this music has seeped more into the main flow of Western film music since the advent of the revisionist Western and European version of the Western. Other notable aspects of Western film music include the copious use of action cues, for horse-riding and gun-fighting sequences, and the employment of expansive 'vista' music – panoramic for shots of landscape – often characterised by the use of the pentatonic scale and related to the simplified melodies evident in many of the folk songs that appear in Westerns.

Western film music tends to use quite distinctive timbres, most of which have some existential connection with the American West. These would include the Spanish guitar, sometimes castanets, harmonica, Mexican 'mariachi' trumpet, banjo, Jew's harp and, in the most clichéd of cases, coconut halves to represent the sound of horses' hooves. In the classical film score, these were only occasional features, ornamentation added to the basic model of the orchestral score. In post-classical Westerns, they became far more common and, indeed, often represent the principal constituents of current Western film music.

The two defining types of what might be characterised as 'featured' music appeared early on in sound Westerns. The first included songs sung by and associated with cowboys and settlers. The second, a type of music that was associated with their perpetual screen enemy, Indians. This basic opposition, or dichotomy, is evident in the vast majority of Western films, with underscores adopting each type of music at different points in the same film. The 'American Indian' tended to be evoked by a combination of drums and chanting,[59] the 'white man' by songs. The most prominent and obvious manifestation of the latter was that now moribund genre, the singing cowboy film.[60] In the 1930s, it was a vibrant sector of the cheaper end of Hollywood film production, with singing cowboys such as Gene Autry, in films like *Tumbling Tumbleweeds* (1935), and Tex Ritter, who made his debut in *The Utah Trail* (1938). In the same year, Roy Rogers starred in his first film, *Come on Rangers* (1938), which also featured singing group the Sons of Pioneers, who went on to grace a number of John Ford films, including *Rio Grande* (1950). In fact, John Ford liked to use folk songs for both the underscore and as featured songs. This was particularly evident in his Westerns, where ballads and ethnic songs form an integral part of the sheen of Americana. Well before the trend for naming films after songs in the 1980s and 1990s, Ford entitled some of his films after folk songs: for example, *She Wore a Yellow Ribbon* (1949) and *My Darling Clementine* (1946). Ford's monumental *Stagecoach* (1939) used 'Bury Me Not on the Lone Prairie', while *The Searchers* (1956) used 'Lorena'.[61] As an essential part of his Western scores, Dimitri Tiomkin judiciously used title songs that might become hits in their own right, much like the tied-in hit songs in films of the last twenty years. A fine example was arguably Tex Ritter's most famous moment, his rendition of 'Do Not Forsake Me' for *High Noon* (1952), although he performed the title songs to a vast array of other Hollywood Westerns in the 1950s.

High Noon starts with a repeated muffled drum pattern that was characteristic of Hollywood music's representation of Indians. This is, in fact, the start of the song and the drums carry on throughout in this manner. Composer Tiomkin, a veteran of Western films, unified the two central defining aspects of Hollywood Western music in the song, although Indians do not play a significant part in the film. Less conventionally, auteur directors such as Fritz Lang entered the Western arena with *Rancho Notorious* (1952) and its bizarre sung Greek chorus, in which each entry builds upon the opening song telling the audience about the hideout 'Chuckaluck'. Equally eccentric was Nicholas Ray's compelling *Johnny Guitar* (1954), which had a score by Victor Young, a very non-Western title song sung by Peggy Lee and a hero, Stirling Hayden, who plays the guitar (very unconvincingly) to accompany the gunfighter 'the Dancing Kid' as he dances.

Max Steiner scored many Westerns at Warner Bros., utilising folk songs from the Civil War to impart the atmosphere of Americana in these films. His Westerns included *Dodge City* (1939), *The Oklahoma Kid* (1939), *Santa Fe Trail* (1940), *Virginia City* (1940) and *They Died with Their Boots On* (1941). His position as one of the founders of the classical film score was underlined by the fact that his Western music broadly followed the same stylistic principles he used for other film genres.

Aaron Copland may be regarded as the grandfather of the Western film score as a characteristic entity. His Western-style ballets, like *Rodeo*, and the score for *The Red Pony* (1949) certainly influenced many composers who later wrote music for Westerns. Copland was one of the first composers to define and establish an orchestral American 'sound'. These stylistic aspects were assimilated into Western scores along with those of Jerome Moross, whose influential score for *The Big Country* (1958) was at turns both epic and intimate. Some might call Dimitri Tiomkin the 'greatest Western composer', due to his prominent involvement in many of the main feature Westerns of the 1950s, as well as the successful title songs he co-wrote with Ned Washington. The most notable films were *Duel in the Sun* (1946), *Red River* (1948), *High Noon*, *Gunfight at the OK Corral* (1957), *Rio Bravo* (1959) and *The Alamo* (1960). His musical output during the 1950s certainly was dominated by the Western genre, while a number of his title songs were massive hit records. The main theme music for *The Alamo* consisted of the sort of extended melody that was rare in Western film music or Western songs, but was more common in eastern European music. However, it was made into a song called 'The Green Leaves of Summer', which was a hit for country singer Marty Robbins.[62]

As we have seen, there is a tendency in classical Westerns to use songs as the foundation of scores, usually structurally in opposition to some 'Indian' music. A good example is John Ford's *She Wore a Yellow Ribbon*, which has a score by Richard Hageman. The titles are accompanied by the ensemble singing (as if by cavalry troopers) of 'She Wore a Yellow Ribbon', which then segues into 'The Girl I Left Behind Me'. In the first shots of the 7th Cavalry riding by, they start to sing 'Yellow Ribbon', whose melody is taken up by the non-diegetic score and leads into the tune of 'The Girl I Left Behind Me'. The first is a cavalry song about a woman who wears a ribbon for the cavalryman she loves, while the second is an Irish song about being apart from a lover.[63] This song had been adopted by the cavalry. This succession might be construed as the more specific song of trade (cavalry) giving way to an older identity (Irish ethnicity, immigration). In opposition to this music of 'civilisation', we then experience the music of the 'savage' Indians. As John Wayne enters the Indian camp,the young braves are preparing for war, accompanied by, as Wayne puts it, 'the medicine drum talking'. At this point, we see the long tubular hollowed-out tree drums, which appear to make 'wooden' sounds, as well as hear the more prevalent (added) sound of deeper drums playing a repetitive but basic mantra rhythm, which, although the cast includes some actual Native Americans, represents the archetypal version of 'Indian' music in film.

Another film notable for its music is Ford's *My Darling Clementine*, which starred Henry Fonda as Wyatt Earp and Victor Mature as Doc Holliday, and dramatised the 1881 gunfight at the OK Corral. The film's music was written by Cyril Mockridge (along with David Buttolph, who was uncredited). The film contains very little non-diegetic music, most notably before and during the shoot-out at the film's conclusion, which is accompanied by silence. However, *My Darling Clementine* contains a number of important songs, the most notable of which furnishes the film's title. When Clementine (Cathy Downs) arrives on the stagecoach, watched by Earp, the score plays 'Oh My Darling Clementine', and later, Earp whistles the tune, without noticing her, then meets and talks to her. As the film finishes, he tells her: 'Ma'am, I sure like that name', and then rides off into the distance as the score plays the song's melody on the organ. The song around which the film was set (i.e. the American Gold Rush of 1849) is about a miner who is unable to save his drowning lover/wife.[64]

While the film may not include much in the way of non-diegetic score, it contains a considerable amount of diegetic music, and Ford biographer Tag Gallagher notes that the film has an 'expressionist, music-drama style'.[65] It includes bar songs, as well as songs associated with the church, thus demarcating social lines and morality. Chihuahua ('Doc's girl', played by Linda Darnell) plays the guitar in the bar as Clementine arrives, and later sings 'The first kiss is always sweeter from under a broad sombrero' to Doc Holliday in the bar (fairly briefly, as his interruption halts the song). As Earp punches Holliday unconscious, the bar pianist begins to play 'Oh, Those Golden Slippers'. Towards the conclusion, the church congregation in their half-built church sings 'Shall We Gather at the River' off screen, as Earp and Clementine (arm in arm) walk towards the church; then the congregation hold a barn dance, and all watch as Earp and Clementine dance a polka. Thus, the film concludes with music and songs of civilisation and celebration, superceding the more 'trivial' values prominent earlier in the film.

John Ford's *Rio Grande*, scored by Victor Young, demonstrated the eclecticism of music in Westerns. The film is about a cavalry commander York (John Wayne) and the trouble he has with his estranged trooper son and wife. It includes many songs, most of which are performed diegetically on screen. The cavalry troop sing the American folk song 'The Eerie Canal', while the Sons of Pioneers sing around the campfire with guitar accompaniment. On occasions, the songs overwhelm the functions of the underscore, as York walks away from the fire and the music, in effect becoming an off-screen, almost non-diegetic accompaniment to screen activity.

Born to Irish immigrant parents, director John Ford certainly emphasised the Irish aspect of his American heritage in this as well as other of his films.[66] *Rio*

Rio Grande

Grande includes Victor McLaglen as an Irish sergeant, who comically talks about the 'well-known Irishman Sir Walter Riley', and despite the seemingly non-Irish status of Wayne's character (despite the actor's ethnic Irish background), the film is overrun with Irish musical signifiers. The appearance of Wayne's wife, Kathleen, repeatedly cues the non-diegetic use of the Irish song 'I'll Take You Home Again, Kathleen' as her theme tune (she was played by Irish actress Maureen O'Hara). Also, as part of the score, the Irish dance tune 'The Irish Washerwoman' appears in the score as Kathleen washes clothes in a tub. More bizarrely, the Sons of Pioneers perform the Irish rebel song 'The Bold Fenian Men' around the campfire, which seems more like a song sequence in a musical. Interestingly, Tag Gallagher notes the relevance of the words of the song to the visiting General Sheridan (J. Carroll Naish), but fails to note the Irish republican nature of the song.[67]

Rio Grande also sets more obvious ethnic boundaries, with its musical representations of Native American Indians and Mexicans, although the Indian ethnic aspect seems of less importance than the Irishness. When the Indians chase the wagon train and troopers, the non-diegetic music is barely audible under all the diegetic noise. The music just hangs there, adding to the noise but offering little; that is, until the melody of 'I'll Take You Home Again, Kathleen' enters. This melody is them alternated with a brief pentatonic 'Indian' riff using parallel fourths, and some whirling arpeggios for tension. The representation of the Mexicans is expressed purely through the underscore, with some Phrygian-type music[68] accompanying the confrontation with the Mexican soldiers on the river. Here, the music reinforces a sense of 'border'. This incident (and indeed the film) takes place along the Rio Grande River between the United States and Mexico, but the appearance of this obvious border on screen is also signalled by the underscore's use of stereotypical Mexican-type music.

While *Rio Grande* includes a number of American folk songs sung by the Sons of Pioneers, its delineation of 'American' is not straightforward, and is filtered through musical ethnic signs that subdivide American with immigrant groupings, in this case Irish.[69] However, the film concludes with a more solid sense of Americana. As the cavalry troopers receive their commendations, the Yorks's son included, the troopers all file past on horseback. The band then, rather unexpectedly, plays the Confederate anthem 'Dixie'!, a particularly fine example of the classical film score's ethnic boundary setting. 'Irishness' in this film works as a white ethnicity in the face of a blanket, undifferentiated whiteness,[70] while also being a sign of an older culture and the construction of the United States through immigration.

Another Ford film, *The Searchers*, was scored by Max Steiner and followed the standard blueprint of Western scores. The non-diegetic music has two particularly notable themes. The first is Ethan's theme, which appears for the title sequence as 'The Song of the Searchers' sung by the Sons of Pioneers, after which the melody appears in the underscore. The second is first heard as Ethan (John Wayne) famously stands framed in the doorway at the film's opening. This is accompanied by an orchestral rendering of 'Lorena', a traditional ballad whose melody Steiner associates with the family in the film, which then runs into 'Bonnie Blue Flag' to accompany the arriving Confederate horseman. The 'Lorena' melody reappears on solo violin when associated with Debbie's locket, and on the spinet when Ethan leaves. One of Steiner's musical cues for the Indian camp had been written earlier for *Jim Thorpe – All American* (aka *Man of Bronze*) (1951) (a film starring Burt Lancaster and about a Native American athlete), and was reused in *The Searchers*.

The 'revisionist Western' was not only a chance for film-makers to revise the images, protagonists and narratives of the American West, but also to revise the soundscape of the Western film. One traditional aspect that became more prominent was the use of Mexican-style music, reflecting the more extensive use of locations around and across the Mexican border. A good example is Jerry Fielding's score for Sam Peckinpah's *The Wild Bunch* (1969), which includes numerous Mexican songs and inflections in the score. *McKenna's Gold* (1969) had music by Quincy Jones, and included a song sung by Flamenco-style singer José Feliciano. A more oblique take on Western film music was the delta blues music written by John Hammond and used sparsely throughout Arthur Penn's *Little Big Man* (1970). While the film is mostly about plains Indians, it refuses their traditional musical representation, although one might argue that the music represents protagonist Jack (Dustin Hoffman) as stuck between two worlds. According to John Saunders, 'Jack's first period with the Cheyenne involves quite conventional Indian material. Yet already Penn is preparing the ground for its later development as an attractive counterculture – the bluesy, Sonny Terry-Brownie McGee-type soundtrack helps too . . .'.[71] This highlights the essence of this breed of revisionist Western, as an embodiment of the potential worlds and discourses evident in the hippie and youth counterculture of the late 1960s.

This cultural phase also partially accounted for an updating of the propensity to use songs in Westerns, leading to the inclusion of Bob Dylan, not only through his commentative folk-style songs, but also through his acting appearance in Sam Peckinpah's *Pat Garrett and Billy the Kid* (1973). This was a form of folk music that was not directly derived from the tradition of folk song related to the Western film. A member of Dylan's band, David Mansfield, went on to write the music for Michael Cimino's *Heaven's Gate* (1980). Picked to take the part of one of the band members in the film, fiddler 'John DeCory', he also played the instrument for the sake of 'realism'. John Williams pulled out of scoring the film, and Mansfield's collection and arrangement of traditional (mostly European) songs on set was accepted as the score by director Cimino when they were mixed onto the film rushes.[72] The tunes include the 'Battle Hymn of the Republic' and 'The Blue Danube', along with more obscure folk melodies, while the music restricts itself to simple development devices, such as changing the metre from 4/4 to 3/4, while retaining the 'authentic' skeletal instrumentation of the band in the film. Mansfield noted that only some of the score was precisely matched; the rest was simply 'layed in'.[73] The 'authenticity' of relating Western film music to settler music was increased by a more authentic representation of Native Americans.

This desire for a new sense of authenticity was evident in films such as *A Man Called Horse* (1970). Much of the dialogue was in the Sioux language, although perhaps rather too much was made of the film's dubious credentials of 'authenticity'. The music was written by Leonard Rosenman, in a dissonant modernist orchestral idiom, which also mixed in some 'real' Native American music by Lloyd One Star. Its sequel, *The Return of a Man Called Horse* (1976), had music by Lawrence Rosenthal, which went further, mixing traditional orchestral music and Native American chanting to a far greater degree.

The desire for more authenticity was accompanied by something of a return to Western tradition. *Silverado* (1985) and *Tombstone* (1993) were scored by Bruce Broughton, while the television miniseries *Lonesome Dove* (1989) was scored by Basil Poledouris. Kevin Costner's *Dances with Wolves* (1990) had a notable score by John Barry, which included the sort of broad and lyrical main theme that could almost have graced Westerns years earlier. The film eschews traditional 'Indian' music to represent Native Americans. Claudia Gorbman notes how the film seems to erase much of the traditional film music associated with Indians, replacing it with more traditional 'white' Western film music.[74] Does this mark a possible de-ethnicisation of Western film music? If so, the cost is that the Indians' culture is simply 'assimilated', 'normalized' – which is exactly what happened by force to Native American culture in the United States.

Another form of updating the Western involved the import of younger actors and a more current sensibility in *Young Guns* (1988). The sequel, *Young Guns II*

(1990), had a score by Alan Silvestri, but also tied-in rock songs, including ten pieces (one of which was the hit single 'Blaze of Glory') by Jon Bon Jovi (who also made a cameo appearance in the film). Jim Jarmusch's *Dead Man* (1995 US/Germany/Japan) had a most untypical Western score of distorted guitar by Canadian-born singer and guitarist Neil Young.[75] This film and its music demonstrate how the Western has become a format that can be dipped into by an auteur art film director like Jarmusch, rather than a living genre that generated a regular run of films based on a generic blueprint, as was the case with classical Hollywood Westerns. Chuck Berg declares that while Westerns 'will undoubtedly continue to be made, the western as a means of transmitting epic and unifying tales of the American experience has passed'.[76]

The demise of the classical Western has allowed the form to focus more on ethnic minorities, pulling the background into the foreground. While African Americans have been more commonly associated with urban American films, a number of 'black Westerns' have emerged in recent years. This film phenomenon has started to open up the historical blind spot, perpetuated by American cinema, regarding the absence of black people in the American West.[77] Bearing some similarities with the representation of Irish people, black Americans have been associated with a musicalised representation, manifesting something of a non-verbal but singing and dancing Other. The tough blaxploitation pictures of the 1970s may (or may not) have expanded the representation of African Americans on screen, yet their representation was still associated with defining music, as testified to by the impressive soundtracks from these sorts of films.

In terms of Westerns, there were only a few antecedents. These included B-pictures starring black actor Herb Jeffries, such as *Harlem on the Prairie* (1937), *Two Gun Man from Harlem* (1938) and *Harlem Rides the Range* (1939), and later, 'white' Westerns, in which black actors occasionally took the lead, such as John Ford's *Sergeant Rutledge* (1960), starring Woody Strode, and Mel Brooks's comedy *Blazing Saddles* (1974), starring Cleavon Little.[78] The two most prominent black Westerns in recent years have been *Glory* (1989) and *Posse* (1993).[79]

Set against the backdrop of the American Civil War, *Glory* was directed by Edward Zwick and depicted black soldiers in the 54th Regiment of Massachusetts Volunteer Infantry, which was made up of black freemen from the North along with some escaped slaves – but was led by white officers. The film is based on an actual incident, an engagement at Charleston in 1863 that resulted in a great loss of life. The music for the film is by James Horner, one of the most prominent of Hollywood composers during the 1990s, using the sort of musical idiom that at least partially looked back to the styles of the classical film score of the 1930s and 1940s.[80] The music in *Glory* includes some material that one might expect in a military film, such as 'last post'-style military trumpet, flute and snare-drum marching music. The sumptuous string music for the attack on Darien bears more than a passing resemblance to Ralph Vaughan Williams's *Fantasia on a Theme of Thomas Tallis*, and although the prominent use of choir has some gospel touches, there is little in musical terms to mark it out from traditional Western films.

Posse was directed by and starred Mario Van Peebles. It concerns a group of mainly black soldiers who, returning from the Spanish-American War, are pursued by a bad white officer and try to establish justice in the face of white racists. The singular cast includes Isaac Hayes (of *Shaft* and *South Park* fame), rappers Tone Loc and Big Daddy Kane, Pam Grier, Melvin Van Peebles (the director's father and blaxploitation veteran), Woody Strode and ex-wrestler Tom 'Tiny' Lister Jr. *Posse's* underscore is by French composer Michel Columbier, and is dominated by energetic and loud action cues; indeed, there is very little that sounds like traditional Western music, with the featured use of the Sounds of Blackness gospel singing. Other cultural reference points in the music include some pop backbeats for a scene when protagonist Jesse jumps into the water. During the fireworks celebration, some diegetic unaccompanied singing sounds much like contemporary 'r and b', and the film finishes with a rap song over the end titles. According to Chuck Berg, 'What might have been an important film winds up being a style-obsessed vanity piece, indeed, a hip-hop western.'[81]

While Steiner's scores were archetypal genre music, based on clichés but structurally and functionally solid, Aaron Copland's music was more personal but with an added 'Western' flavour, and Jerome Moross's music for *The Big Country* (and to a lesser extent Elmer Bernstein's score for *The Magnificent Seven*) became the model for film music in Westerns. The inclusion of songs and song melodies helped define a sense of the West, although in some cases through the songs of immigrants, which led to an ethnic ambiguity. Apart from the appearance of Irish songs such as 'The Girl I Left Behind Me' and 'The Bold Fenian Men' in Ford's Westerns, Raoul Walsh's *They Died with Their Boots On* uses the Irish tune 'Garry Owen' for the cavalry. This was adopted as the unofficial song of the 7th Cavalry, allegedly after Custer had heard a trooper singing it.

John Ford's Westerns in particular, but Westerns more generally, often have a strong mythic dimension, and music is an essential aspect of this. Thus, music in Ford's Westerns tends to illustrate the genre's aspects more vividly than many other films, and its musical processes are illuminated more here than elsewhere. The revisionist Western allowed new ethnicities to be brought to the fore and old ones to be rethought. As a consequence, music changed to reflect this strategy, and, as might have been expected, was a crucial signifier of ethnic difference in these films.

European Westerns

Foreign depictions of the United States on film are not particularly common, although perhaps one could cite the growth in Canadian film portrayals of the USA in recent years. In terms of Westerns, the most characteristic of American film genres, something of a European industry emerged in the 1960s and 1970s, producing films that are generally corralled under the rubric of 'spaghetti Westerns'.[82] While many of these were Italian, some were Spanish and some German, while many more were European co-productions. The majority were shot in Europe, frequently in the desert-like areas of Andalusia or Yugoslavia.[83] The locations often suggested the region around the Mexican border rather than the greener (or snowy) more northerly America, and Sergio Leone's canonical film trilogy, *A Fistful of Dollars* (*Per un pugno di dollari*, 1964), *For a Few Dollars More* (*Per qualche dollaro in piu*, 1965) and *The Good, the Bad and the Ugly* (*Il buono, il brutto, il cattivo*, 1968), firmly established new aspects of the Western film. The more Mexican visual iconography was matched by music that also emphasised a more 'Mexican' aspect, while Leone's trilogy had music by Ennio Morricone that became internationally famous and added some significant new sounds to the Western. *A Fistful of Dollars* has the usual Spanish guitar, but it also uses whistling, twangy electric guitar, high Mexican 'mariachi' trumpet, wordless vocal effects, while his later music included whips, tolling bells, percussive anvils and organs.

Other spaghetti Westerns tended to employ similar soundscapes; indeed, Morricone wrote the music for many of them. The most prominent films were *Django* (1966), directed by Sergio Corbucci and starring Franco Nero, *The Big Gundown* (1966), starring Lee Van Cleef, and *A Bullet for the General* (1966), directed by Damiano Damiani. Film historian Peter Bondanella declared the latter to be an allegory of the United States' intervention in Vietnam.[84] Leone and Morricone went on to a larger-budget Western, shot in the USA, *Once Upon a Time in the West* (*C'era una volta il west*, 1968). Uniquely, a number of different themes were written before production and played on set. The film was then cut to them. Each of the three principal characters had a distinct timbre: high soaring wordless female vocal, banjo and harmonica.

British Westerns are rare. *The Sheriff of Fractured Jaw* (1958) was directed by American director Raoul Walsh, yet was UK-registered and produced. Funded by 20th Century-Fox, it was made by British producer Daniel M. Angel and shot in Britain. This Western spoof starred Kenneth More as an English gentlemen (or perhaps a better description would be a gentle Englishman) adrift in the West, and playing opposite Jayne Mansfield. The film's music score, by British-based Canadian Robert Farnon, is fairly standard, traditional fare, and includes the occasional use of the melody from the verse (rather than the more common chorus) of 'Rule Britannia' as accompaniment to More's activities. It also uses stereotypical 'Indian' music for the film's Native Americans, and has some songs mimed to by Mansfield but voiced by American singer Connie Francis.

A more recent 'British' Western is *Ravenous* (1999), which was produced by a Hollywood studio, yet was a British production and registered as an international co-production between the USA/UK/Czech Republic/Slovakia/Mexico. It was produced by a British producer (David Hayman), written by an American screenwriter (Ted Griffin) and directed by a British director (Antonia Bird). *Ravenous* was shot primarily in the Czech and Slovak Republics (as well as in Poland and Mexico), and starred an Australian (Guy Pearce) and a Scotsman (Robert Carlyle). Two weeks into the production, Macedonian director Milcho Manchevski was replaced by

Bird. In terms of the film's score, it included music written by English musician Damon Albarn and Michael Nyman, an experienced film composer.

Albarn was inexperienced in writing music for films and got Nyman onto the project to co-write the music, although, in fact, much of the music was eventually written by one or the other rather than as a collaboration.[85] Albarn conducted research into Appalachian folk music, listening to recordings at the Smithsonian. Following the musical divide common to Westerns, he separated the film's music into music inspired by white folk music and Native American Indian music. For the latter, he recorded Milton 'Quiltman' Sahmi (with help from his wife) singing traditional songs on a reservation. In the film, this traditional chanting appears as Native American Martha waits for the men to arrive, and a similar one is also used when Boyd wanders around the fort in the snow supporting himself with a stick.[86] Albarn produced the music that accompanies Calhoun's narration (an extended flashback sequence) by making a loop of one bar of an Appalachian-style jig, and then adding a dulcimer melody with flute accompaniment.[87] The chase sequence, where Toffler is pursued by cannibal Calhoun/Ives, is accompanied by a fiddle-led country jig with yodelling. This is a striking musical moment, as a grave situation is accompanied by ironic and happy music, getting the audience involved with the energy of the chase but remaining anempathetic, as Claudia Gorbman puts it, to the plight of the soldier who is about to die.[88]

Ravenous also includes some music that aims to create a vivid sense of place, namely some American brass band music. This includes the pieces 'Hail Columbia' and Steven Foster's 'Way Down Upon the Swanee River'. Nyman is responsible for these pieces, which are played in a shoddy, amateurish manner. On the one hand, this gives a strong sense of the sort of music that might well have been played at that time and in that place. On the other, it engages with Nyman's connections with 'out-of-tune' experimental music ensembles in Britain in the 1970s, such as the Portsmouth Sinfonia and the Scratch Orchestra. Apart from this music, another distinctive Nyman contribution is the music for the end titles, which superceded the film's main theme. This piece appears earlier (and more briefly) over Boyd's dream of killing another soldier in the fort. It has something of string-dominated broad orchestral sound of more traditional Western music, and this is indeed one of the only musical pieces in the film that comprises the traditional orchestral sound palette. The film contains a wealth of 'Western' instrumentation, including a band of dulcimer, violin, guitar and Jew's harp, banjo, percussion, accordion and voices from the London Voices as well as the Native American chanting. Albarn commented that while the dulcimer was clearly not an instrument used notably in the American West, he employed it because of Morricone's use of it in spaghetti Western scores.[89] The film's main theme exploits electronic keyboards as well as more traditional instruments.[90] The film's climactic cue is an additive waltz, including electronic keyboards, electronic drums and synthesizer drones and bass notes. It is based on eight-bar blocks of 3/4 and runs for over nine minutes – covering the entire denouement of the film, in which, following their final confrontation, Boyd and Ives both perish.[91] This, like some of the rest of the music in the film, includes a number of elements that betray Albarn's origins as a pop musician, yet it nevertheless remains highly effective within the context of the film. The score is certainly singular and reflects the notion of film music as a 'featured' aspect of the film. It also seems to set some slightly different ethnic boundaries (of the mind, perhaps, more than physical) than is evident in Hollywood Westerns.

The revisionist Western made some significant changes to the film music model established by the classical Hollywood cinema, yet perhaps the European Western, particularly Sergio Leone's spaghetti Westerns scored by Ennio Morricone, has had a more notable impact on the sounds of the Western film. They had a significant influence on Hollywood films: for instance, Clint Eastwood's *High Plains Drifter* (1972) was to some degree a remake of the spaghetti Western *Django the Bastard* (1969), directed by Sergio Garrone. A recent Hollywood Western, *The Quick and the Dead* (1995), contained a score by Alan Silvestri that emphasises the film's allusions to Leone's Westerns with music that references Morricone. It included instrumentation such as a lonely harmonica, whip cracks and a high 'mariachi' trumpet, all of which is reminiscent directly of spaghetti Western music rather than the more traditional expansive Western-type music.

Indeed, the influence of Morricone's Western innovations in the 1960s cannot be underestimated. Less of an impact was made by the attempt to import pop songs in the 1980s, which was far more successful in other film genres. Apart from these developments, much of the music in Westerns remained traditional. It seems that, despite the occasional innovations in musical style, audiences are not upset at radical developments or departures, despite the genre fostering many preconceptions about what Westerns should be like, and in some cases promoting notions of authenticity.

Conclusion

In *The Red Shoes* (1948), Julian Craster (Marius Goring) plays some of his music for the ballet's ballroom scene at the piano and declares, 'Anyone who understands anything about music will see a ballroom.' While equivalence is untenable, there is a robust tradition of musical aspects representing ideas and images. One of film music's principal functions is to work as a signpost, the musical counterpart to an establishing shot. A limited musical vocabulary furnishes a sense of place and people for films, while also supplying significant boundary markers, which set zones of difference and national or other border lines. In 'ethnicised' film music, we can see the embodiment of 'synaesthesia' through musical association with something else (certain peoples, places). Through this process, music is an obvious bearer of ideology. Whoever might be wielding ethnic musical signifiers is a crucial question, yet whoever decides that they are common currency for international representation should be an equally important concern. The use of 'ethnicised' music usually has implications for the power relationship of the different ethnic bodies involved, but most manifestly for those being represented. Screen music is a powerful device, one that is able to reinforce and impose a sense of stereotype (or arguably archetype) in a manner that barely registers as questionable for naïve film audiences.[92]

Film music tells us important things, adding a semi-hidden level of structure to films. In John Ford's *Rio Grande*, for example, the music hints at certain things – most notably an Irishness that lies just beneath the film's surface of white American-ness. Furthermore, film music has done much to define more general musical representations. For example, internationally available music recordings that are inspired by ancient Egypt, such as Dale Sumner's *Egypt*,[93] apparently owe more to filmic musical representations than to any ethnic or historical veracity, while film scores such as those written by Bernard Herrmann and Alfred Newman for *The Egyptian* (1954), by Franz Reizenstein for Hammer's *The Mummy* (1959), by Tristram Cary for *Blood from the Mummy's Tomb* (1971), by Jerry Goldsmith for *The Mummy* (1999) and by Alan Silvestri for *The Mummy Returns* (2001) have drawn upon film music tradition while instituting and perpetuating popular convictions about 'Ancient Egypt' in musical terms.

Despite exceptions, 'English' films, 'Irish' films and Westerns seem to epitomise standardised film music. The Western *Little Big Man*'s use of delta blues seems somewhat incongruous, although extremely effective, but is perhaps not as incongruous as the use of a blues soundtrack in British-set comedy *Funny Bones* (1995). These exemplify how malleable film music can be, while suggesting that its ethnic boundary setting might sometimes be easily undermined. After all, the use of the conclusion of Rossini's *William Tell Overture* as the theme music for *The Lone Ranger* (1949–57, ABC) on television is proof of the mutability of musical 'imagery', and especially ethnic musical aspects, although the underlying activity – swashbuckling action and adventure – may have been similar.

Notes

1 Although Richard Middleton (also similarly Antoine Hennion) states that there is an accrued (and generally accepted) 'meaning' that can be seen as 'interior' to pieces of music. *Studying Popular Music* (Maidenhead: Open University Press, 1990), p. 10.

2 Robert Mackay, 'Leaving Out the Black Notes: The BBC and "Enemy Music" in the Second World War', *Media History*, vol. 6, no. 1, 2000, p. 79.

3 The dominant 'imagination' school of thought about ethnicity has less to say about situations like this, where people extrinsic to the grouping are doing the imagining.

4 In a discussion of synaesthesia, Kathryn Kalinak declares: 'In a process not unlike the Kuleshov effect, emotion stimulated in the spectator by music is transferred to the image which seems to produce it. Feeling thus resonates between spectator and the image in such a way as to encourage the perception that the emotions depicted on the screen are not only natural, but ours.' '"Disturbing the Guests with This Racket"': Music and *Twin Peaks*' in David Lavery, ed., *Full of Secrets: Critical Approaches to Twin Peaks* (Detroit: Wayne State University Press, 1994), p. 83.

5 David Burnand and Benedict Sarnaker note that film music tends to deal in racial stereotyping. 'The Articulation of National Identity through Film Music', *National Identities*, vol. 1, no. 1, 1999, p. 7.

6 Hanns Eisler and Theodor Adorno are very negative about such film music. *Composing for the Films* (London: Athlone, 1994) [originally 1947], pp. 14–15.

7 Edward Said, *Orientalism* (London: Random House, 1979), p. 1.

8 Geoffrey Bennington, 'Postal Politics and the Institution of the Nation' in Homi K. Bhaba, ed., *Nation and Narration* (London: Routledge, 1990), p. 121.

9 Georgina Born and David Hesmondhalgh, 'Introduction' in Georgina Born and David Hesmondhalgh, eds., *Western Music and Its Others: Difference, Representation and Appropriation in Music* (Berkeley: University of California Press, 2000), p. 32.

10 Thomas K. Fitzgerald, 'Media, Ethnicity and Identity' in Paddy Scannell, Philip Schlesinger and Colin Sparks, eds, *Culture and Power: A Media, Culture and Society Reader* (London: Sage, 1992), p. 116.

11 David Burnand and Benedict Sarnaker note: 'the flattened supertonic appears to arouse a strong sense of "otherness" or "faraway" in Western audiences' imaginations. It is modal, rather than tonal, complex rather than simple, and this indicates more than the primitivism or folkiness of the pentatonic scale. It indicates a lack of Northern European musical influence and, hence, it might be interpreted as meaning "uncivilised" within the discourse of . . . a film.' 'Articulation of National Identity through Film Music', p. 8.

12 Or historical connections to the East, such as Moorish Spain, European Gypsies or Jews.

13 According to Ciaran Carson, the bodhran and the uillean pipes were both ancient instruments that had long been only marginally important in Irish folk music. Both were popularised by folk group The Chieftains in the 1960s and 1970s. Interestingly, the present version of the uillean pipes was standardised in Philadelphia in the late 19th century. Ciaran Carson, *Irish Traditional Music* (Belfast: Appletree, 1999), pp. 13, 17, 37.

14 In television series such as *Jason King* (1971–2, ITC), exotic locations would simply be signified by an establishing shot of a signpost reading 'Monte Carlo' or something similar.

15 *Bernard Herrmann: Music for the Movies*, American Film Institute documentary (1992).

16 Korngold had a unique position within the heyday of the studio system, having a contract at Warner Bros. that allowed him to pick and choose the films for which he would write the music.

17 Although it seems to be firmly about the English, Peter Blood is in fact supposed to be an Irish physician living in England, and Errol Flynn repeatedly informs the audience of the character's Irishness.

18 *The Sea Hawk* extensively uses a simple fanfare theme for Flynn and contains over an hour of music.

19 Kathryn Kalinak, *Settling the Score: Music and the Classical Hollywood Film* (Madison: University of Wisconsin Press, 1992), pp. xv–xvi.

20 K. J. Donnelly, *Pop Music in British Cinema: A Chronicle* (London: BFI, 2001), p. 19.

21 This is not only the case for costume pictures. In *Wayne's World 2* (1993), the protagonists apparently visit London but clearly signal it is phoney. This not only satirises the cost of real

location work, but also points to how locations are metonymised, made into a thumbnail sketch of a few key elements.

22 Colin McArthur, 'Scotland and Cinema: The Iniquity of the Fathers' in Colin McArthur, ed., *Scotch Reels: Scotland in Cinema and Television* (London: BFI, 1982), p. 40.

23 However, despite the 'Englishness' on display in the film, Wojciech Kilar's score never attempts anything approaching a musical representation of England.

24 The Hollywood tradition of English-accented 'baddies' notwithstanding.

25 I would imagine the effect to be similar to the shock English people often experience on finding out that the Irish tell jokes about them.

26 Andrew Higson's book *English Heritage, English Cinema* (Oxford: Oxford University Press, 2003) declines to use the term 'British' at all, or even to pursue any sustained discussion about the difference between 'British' and 'English' cinema.

27 See further discussion in Andrew Higson, *Waving the Flag: Constructing a National Cinema in Britain* (Oxford: Oxford University Press, 1997).

28 This might be seen as a British retort to Hollywood's standardised film music, pursuing a notion of 'quality' in film music that exploited the 'prestige' of using established, respected 'classical' composers.

29 Another aristocrat, the Marquis of Zetland, under his birth name of David Dundas, had a number one hit record in the 1970s and has also collaborated with Rick Wentworth on a number of film scores.

30 K. J. Donnelly, 'Wicked Sounds and Magic Melodies: Music in Gainsborough Melodramas' in Pam Cook, ed., *Gainsborough Pictures* (London: Cassell, 1997), pp. 155–69.

31 Discussed in Cook, ed., *Gainsborough Pictures*.

32 Cf. Higson, *Waving the Flag*.

33 This certainly describes the BBC's position. On the other hand, ITV has screened regular series of Catherine Cookson adaptations that are made with more modest budgets and aimed primarily at home consumption.

34 For example, the opening motif from Purcell's 'Dido's Lament' (from *Dido and Aeneas*) is remade as the bass ground in the Nyman piece, 'Bravura in the Face of Grief'.

35 Nyman wrote the book *Experimental Music: Cage and Beyond* (Cambridge: Cambridge University Press, 1974), which documented the British post-avant-garde music scene in the 1960s and 1970s.

36 Michael Nyman, sleeve notes to *The Draughtsman's Contract* CD (Virgin CASCD1158, released 1989).

37 Bond is a problematic figure in ethnic terms, having been played by a Scot (Sean Connery), an Australian (George Lazenby) and an Irishman (Pierce Brosnan), despite the appeal to Englishness evident in the films. (Even Timothy Dalton was born in Wales.) Film songs have also included two Welsh singers (Shirley Bassey and Tom Jones).

38 Lance Pettit, *Screening Ireland: Film and Television Representation* (Manchester: Manchester University Press, 2000), p. 264.

39 Reels are usually fast and in 4/4 time, while jigs are more often in 6/8.

40 Noel McLaughlin and Martin McLoone, 'Hybridity and National Musics: The Case of Irish Rock Music', *Popular Music*, vol. 19, no. 2, 2000, p. 181.

41 I use the term 'Britain' without including Northern Ireland, following the official description
    as stated on British passports: 'The United Kingdom of Great Britain and Northern Ireland'.

42 Michel Chion, *Audio-Vision: Sound on Screen*, edited and translated by Claudia Gorbman
    (New York: Columbia University Press, 1990), p. 81.

43 Robert F. Moss, *The Films of Carol Reed* (New York: Columbia University Press, 1987),
    p. 142.

44 The main theme is reminiscent of other vaguely 'Celtic'-style music such as Hayden Wood's
    Mannin Veen (Dear Isle of Man), which has the same slow, grand and austere Celtic sound at
    the start.

45 Apart from this, only one other character consistently has music associated with them:
    Kathleen, who has a romantic string lullaby attached to her screen appearances (although
    Shell is also accompanied by a semi-comic clarinet tune on a couple of occasions). Kathleen's
    theme is precisely coded to indicate 'emotionality', using gentle but chromatic strings. Apart
    from these musical themes, there is only a repeated 'Delerium' theme that cues Johnny's state
    of mind and hallucinations.

46 Indeed, tolling bells seem to be the aural icon par excellence for films set in Northern Ireland,
    as evidenced by examples such as *The Boxer* and *Resurrection Man* (1998).

47 William Alwyn's journal, quoted in the sleeve notes to *The Film Music of William Alwyn* CD
    (Chandos CHAN9243, released 2000), and corroborated by Moss, *Films of Carol Reed*, p. 143.

48 In the CD's sleeve notes by Geoff Leonard and Alexander Walker, they note 'Budd's
    predominantly gentile [*sic*] background score' (!) (Cinephile CIN CD010, released 1999).

49 Martin McLoone notes that the film is seen to embody the notion of 'paddywhackery', a
    stereotypical and mythic form of representing Ireland. *Irish Film: The Emergence of a
    Contemporary Cinema* (London: BFI, 2000), p. 35.

50 The proliferation of Irish folk music and 'Celtic' new age CDs testifies to the persistence and
    international popularity of 'musicalised' Gaelic culture. *The New Oxford Companion to Music*
    states: 'That the Irish are a naturally musical race is evident from the beauty of their folk
    music, which is abundant and vital.' Percy Scholes in Dennis Arnold, ed., *The New Oxford
    Companion to Music* (Oxford: Oxford University Press, 1983), pp. 947–8.

51 Indeed, these were more than songs just stuck on the titles. The melody of the closing song,
    'You Made Me the Thief of My Heart', appeared at key moments in the film's non-diegetic
    music.

52 Jeffrey Richards, *Films and British National Identity: From Dickens to Dad's Army* (Manchester:
    Manchester University Press, 1997), p. 229.

53 Richard Ned Lebow, *White Britain and Black Ireland: The Influence of Stereotypes on Colonial
    Policy* (Philadelphia: Institute for the Study of Human Issues, 1976), p. 45.

54 Running from Irish actor Richard Harris's portrayal of an English aristocrat in *A Man Called
    Horse* and 'English Bob' in *Unforgiven* (1992) to the Chinese characters played by Jackie
    Chan and David Carradine in *Shanghai Noon* (2000) and the television series *Kung Fu*
    (1972–5, ABC) respectively.

55 They also have other unique interests, including landscape, ideas of the law, individualism in
    relation to the collective, etc.

56 Jim Kitses, *Horizons West* (Bloomington: Indiana University Press, 1969); Richard Slotkin, *Gunfighter Nation: The Myth of the Frontier in Twentieth Century America* (London: HarperCollins, 1992); Michael Coyne, *The Crowded Prairie: American National Identity in the Hollywood Western* (London: I. B. Tauris, 1997).

57 Robert Warshow, *The Immediate Experience* (New York: Anchor, 1964), p. 66.

58 Claudia Gorbman, 'Scoring the Indian: Music in the Liberal Western' in Georgina Born and David Hesmondhalgh, eds., *Western Music and Its Others: Difference, Representation and Appropriation in Music* (Berkeley: University of California Press, 2000), p. 235.

59 Ibid.

60 Peter Stanfield, *Horse Opera: The Strange History of the 1930s Singing Cowboy* (Chicago: University of Illinois Press, 2002).

61 Ford also used the 'Red River Valley' in *The Grapes of Wrath* (1940), scored by Alfred Newman.

62 Tiomkin included in the film a solo trumpet version of a piece he had already used prominently in his score for Howard Hawks's *Rio Bravo*.

63 There was a successful Broadway Western play called *The Girl I Left Behind Me* in the 1890s.

64 Although, in an interesting final verse, he drops his tone of loss and takes the dead woman's sister as a surrogate.

65 Tag Gallagher, *John Ford: The Man and His Films* (Berkeley: University of California Press, 1988), p. 225.

66 Something perhaps not borne out by history, as most Irish (rather than Scots-Irish) immigrants preferred to remain on the eastern seaboard.

67 Gallagher, *John Ford*, p. 260.

68 Using a scale and harmony that emphasises a flattened second, as discussed earlier in relation to 'oriental' and 'Spanish' generic music.

69 Gallagher notes that Ford may have been 'warming up O'Hara, Wayne and McLaglen for the Irish movie' (*The Quiet Man*), *John Ford*, p. 257.

70 Richard Dyer suggests that 'Whites must be seen to be white, yet whiteness as race resides in invisible properties and whiteness as power is maintained by being unseen.' *White* (London: Routledge, 1997), p. 45.

71 John Saunders, *The Western Genre: From Lordsburg to Big Whiskey* (London: Wallflower, 2001), p. 96.

72 David Mansfield interviewed by Bruce Lawton, sleeve notes to *Michael Cimino's Heaven's Gate*, Original MGM Motion Picture Soundtrack, 1999 (Rykodisc RCD 10749).

73 Ibid.

74 Gorbman, 'Scoring the Indian', p. 248.

75 It also included cameo appearances by Iggy Pop and Gibby Haynes, singer in the Butthole Surfers, and two of the characters in the film are named after American pop musicians.

76 Chuck Berg, 'Fade Out in the West: The Western's Last Stand' in Wheeler Winston Dixon, ed., *Film Genre 2000: New Critical Essays* (Albany, NY: SUNY Press, 2000), p. 224.

77 Cf. Quintard Taylor, *In Search of the Racial Frontier: African American in the American West, 1528–1990* (New York: Norton, 1998); Monroe Lee Billington and Roger D. Hardaway, eds., *African Americans on the Western Frontier* (Boulder: University of Colorado Press, 1998).

78 We could add *Take a Hard Ride* (1975), a fairly obscure blaxploitation spaghetti Western, which was partially made by US film-makers and included music by Jerry Goldsmith. It had two black leading actors, Jim Brown and Fred Williamson.

79 Also notable is *Wild Wild West* (1999), with black leading man Will Smith as Jim West.

80 K. J. Donnelly, 'The Hidden Heritage of Film Music: History and Scholarship' in K. J. Donnelly, ed., *Film Music: Critical Approaches* (Edinburgh: Edinburgh University Press, 2001), p. 13.

81 Berg, 'Fade Out in the West', p. 223.

82 The first included the Winnetou series inaugurated by *The Treasure of Silver Lake* (*Der Schatz im Silbersee*) (1962), with music by Martin Boettcher, and starring ex-Tarzan Lex Barker.

83 Indeed, north-west of Almeria in Spain, one can visit a theme park based on these films, called 'Western Leone'.

84 Peter Bondanella, *Italian Cinema: From Neorealism to the Present* (New York: Continuum, 1996), p. 268.

85 Albarn notes this on the *Ravenous* DVD commentary, including the fact that some of the music had to be turned down to allow the dialogue to be heard. (20th Century-Fox DVD FS1-SGB 00323DVD).

86 On the *Ravenous* soundtrack CD, the track is called 'Weendigo Myth'.

87 The two instruments play around between the major and minor key: dulcimer in minor, flute moving to major. Then monotone strings enter and build in density (sounding very characteristic of Nyman's work).

88 For discussions of anempathetic music, see Claudia Gorbman, *Unheard Melodies: Narrative Film Music* (London: BFI, 1987) ('Anempathy: Hangover Square' chapter), and Chion, *Audio-Vision*, p. 123.

89 Noted by Albarn on the *Ravenous* DVD commentary.

90 The main theme has a sense of irony about it that is slightly reminiscent of Nyman's music for *The Draughtsman's Contract* and *Drowning by Numbers* (1988).

91 It is called 'Saveoursoulissa' on the soundtrack CD.

92 It should be borne in mind that those being represented are often *not* those being addressed by the film.

93 On Global Journey Records, 2001.

Chapter 5

Demonic Possession: Horror Film Music

Music is often a featured aspect – indeed a vital participant – in horror films. It can be a scary entity in itself, or at least an ambiguous one, which can confuse and undermine the audience's feelings of security. A good example is the ghost story *Haunted* (1995). At one point in the film, protagonist David Ash (Aidan Quinn) looks intently, as if he hears music, and we, the audience, hear a solo piano being played in a neighbouring room. He goes into the room and examines the piano, which has no player; the music has stopped. How do we know that this music is not non-diegetic music? Ultimately, we do not. We assume that Ash is responding to the music from the other side of the closed door. It turns out that the music is, in a way, non-diegetic, as it comes from outside the 'normal' world on screen; it is music produced by a ghostly presence, clearly emanating from another dimension or logic. While it might not be what many would understand as 'horror film music', its status underlines the central power of film music more generally and shows how it can be a fundamental and unsettling element in horror films.

Horror film music is particularly apparent in its techniques and functions, and therefore also in its effect. As we have seen, film genres function as mental frameworks, which guide the way we watch and experience the images on screen, and film music can be seen not only as a part of that, but also as almost a microcosm of the process. I focus here on the music in horror films as a very particular musical language with very specific effects, positing it as symptomatic of the way that film music works more generally, but perhaps as an extreme and special case.

This chapter will deal with the crucial distinction between the way that music works through conscious and semi-conscious linguistic codes or conventions, and the possibility that it can have a 'direct access' to the listener, producing physiological effects that bypass learned structures, and arguably inserting frames of mind and attitude much like a direct injection. This will include a discussion of film music 'beyond representation' and of music as 'effect'. The first part of this chapter examines how the music in horror films functions first as a language, and second as an element that works beyond plain representation, and thus is a crucial device in producing the horrifying effects of this film genre. This is followed by a detailed historical review of the music in horror films, attending to important films and noteworthy developments.

The music for horror films is often as distinctive and easily identifiable as the films themselves.[1] Horror film scores certainly share similar characteristics, as Hammer musical director Philip Martell noted:

> there is a pattern. As long as it's horror you have to make frightening sounds, and they do come in a pattern. . . . The general practice is to make a great noise on your titles and give everybody the impression that this is a terrifying and very important film. But it is true that on horrors as a rule you need a lot of brass. If the Werewolf sinks his fangs into someone's throat then you've got to make a lot of noise to terrify the audience. . . . All the murders will be covered with music, and the chases. There's a long sequence in the sewers which wants a lot of music. . . . I would rather the prologue had the natural effects of the forest, the sounds of the birds or whatever. And hold back everything until the title *Legend of the Werewolf* comes up and then hit people with all you've got and lift them out of their seats if you can.[2]

The horror film genre is a fairly distinct entity, having evolved its own core iconography, stars, set of narratives and types of character. Moreover, it has developed its own auteur directors, tradition of special effects, specialist production companies, fan magazines and means of publicity, even sometimes distribution. Consequently, there is little need for me to delineate and delimit what I mean by the horror genre in this chapter. The music in horror films is often very distinct from the music used in other film genres. However, on rare occasions, generic horror films employ music that is not of generic 'horror film music' character, while, on even rarer occasions, films that are not from the horror genre appear to use music that derives from generic horror film music.

The transcendent and the mystical are common aspects of the supernatural horror film, and thus there is a correspondingly strong religious (as well as ritualistic) strain in horror film music. Hammer's *Dracula* series, for example, is premised upon the theological readymades and pre-existing moral framework that defines much in the way of supernatural horror. For instance, in *Taste the Blood of Dracula* (1970), the film opens with an anti-Christian ritual and concludes with salvation through Christianity. Both of these key sequences in the film's theoretical framework are accompanied by pseudo-Christian church music (as well as being set in a church), positioning music at the very centre of the film's ideological construction and the ritualistic aspects of cinema more generally.[3] *Taste the Blood of Dracula* is far from atypical in the horror genre.[4] According to Paul Wells: 'The [horror] genre has been addressed in the light of its moral and theological perspectives, its sociological and cultural dimensions, its politics of representation, and its configuration as a set of texts particularly conducive to psychoanalytic approaches.'[5] My approach to film music does not embrace psychoanalysis, which, as Wells rightly notes, has had something of a stranglehold on analyses of horror films. In many ways, horror films are more straightforward than many other films, in that their aims are often quite palpable and their format can be stylised to an extreme, making for some of the most formulaic films of popular cinema. They are also more interesting, to the extent that they seem to have a more direct access to some of the most primal and unconscious aspects of human existence. Horror films often evince very *apparent* technique, both in film (as a genre) and film music. Good examples are the three *Scream* films (1996, 1997 and 2000), which include a central parodic level, like so many recent horror films, and which work through the assumption of a 'horror film literate' audience. The music is very much a central part of the apparent (not 'invisible' but clearly readable) process in horror films. Its activities are transparent – on one level, audiences can hear what it is doing without having to concentrate too much on the music's activities.[6]

Functions and Effects

Horror film music is often very clear and identifiable to audiences, even when removed from its context. As I have noted, it epitomises the mental frameworks that are constructed by films and their music. Like other film music, it works with recourse to both conscious and semi-conscious linguistic codes; however, in its sheer material aspect in horror films, sometimes it works more obviously through a kind of 'direct access' to the audience. Perhaps related to this in some way is horror film music's importing of style (and attendant existentialist angst) from modernist classical music, which I have discussed in Chapter 3. By linguistic codes, I mean transitive communication, where 'this sound means precisely that idea'. For example, 'La Marseillaise' denotes the French nation and associated patriotism, often accompanying war images or a story set within the context of a war.[7] Max Steiner's scores regularly have recourse to such devices, as evident in films like *Casablanca* (1942).

Horror film music's narrative employment is perhaps more obvious, yet it clearly has an additional psychological use, based on fundamental notions of presence/absence, perceived origin and physical volume. So, non-diegetic music appears to have a closer relationship to the horror genre than any other area of cinema. Its 'supernatural' status seems particularly fitting here, often working precisely as another dramatic player in the drama. Functioning as a specific 'device' in this way emphasises film music's existence, and points some way towards the 'essence' of non-diegetic music, and its potential and possibilities. Horror film underscores tend to have a very specific sound, defined usually by a number of stylistic aspects. A common feature is the use of melodic lines of deeply pitched strings, which are often slow and tend not to be particularly memorable or tuneful. Related to this is the principle of the drone, where tension is built through anticipation. Another defining aspect of music in the horror film is the use of unresolved dissonance. In tonal art music (and other musical forms), dissonance seems to suggest a resolution to musical consonance. Should the dissonance in film music suggest the possibility of resolution, then this can upset the audience by allowing them no audio repose. Royal S. Brown argues this case in relation to Bernard Herrmann's music for

Psycho;[8] yet this is far from straightforward, as much dissonant music does not suggest the possibility of tonal resolution, and, indeed, some of it is not based strongly in the tonal system (with its harmonic rules and logics of standard chord progression) anyway.

There are a number of different musical timbres (instrumental sounds) that are associated strongly with music in the horror film. Perhaps an all too obvious one is the organ, as traditionally played in *The Phantom of the Opera* and *The Abominable Dr Phibes* (1971), both of which display a hint of the funereal. The organ also adds a gothic edge to the score for *Batman* (1989),[9] and provides an overwhelming ghostly ambience to *Carnival of Souls* (1962). Another characteristic sound was noted by Eisler and Adorno in 1947: 'The tremolo on the bridge of the violin, which thirty years ago was intended even in serious music to produce a feeling of uncanny suspense and to express an unreal atmosphere, today has become common currency.'[10] A tremolo involves the rapid alternation between two pitches, and over fifty years after Adorno and Eisler's pronouncement, this device is still the staple of much horror film music.[11] Indeed, the opening of one of the canonical horror films, *The Bride of Frankenstein* (1935), entails a succession of tremolos in the strings. The first action in *House of Dracula* (1945), after the opening titles, involves a bat outside a window accompanied by an insistent and sustained tremolo. A similar technique, although limited to stringed instruments, is playing *sul ponticello* ('on the bridge'), where the instruments (violin, viola, cello and double bass) are played near the bridge to give a reedy, nasal sound that eradicates the warmer tones of the instrument. This is a staple of horror film music, and is particularly evident in Bernard Herrmann's score for *Cape Fear* (1962 and 1991), providing a 'watery' and mysterious ambience to the tense narrative.[12] Many of these musical techniques can be found in art music, particularly the more avant-garde works of the early 20th century. The kind of harmonic language evident in Stravinsky's *The Rite of Spring*, *Petrushka* and *The Firebird* (such as the use of the ethereal whole-tone scale) became part of the musical language of horror films in the 1930s. However, while many of the musical aspects I have described were derived from art music, they were also simultaneously part of a repertoire of musical characteristics used to describe gothic or supernatural situations that existed within more popular forms of music, such as, for example, the music accompanying theatre productions.

In horror scores, memorable melodies and song forms (as temporal structures) are less common than in other cinematic genres. The currency of horror film music comprises a relatively small selection of musical devices. On an overt level, they are linguistic and functional; the audience understands them instantly.[13] This includes the 'stinger' or 'sting', which manifests a physical shock in a musical blast, and the tension ostinato, a loop of music that provides tension through cumulative effect, along with its first cousin, the drone. Despite appearances, the latter two are not closely related to minimalism in art music, with its gradual-systemic development. They are more additive, exploiting the phenomenon of repetition's cumulative effect, like mantra, religious ritual music or even repetitive dance music. A good example of these musical strategies is evident in the opening of Hitchcock's *Vertigo* (1958), which, although not a horror film, displays a number of horror aspects. It starts with a repetitive ostinato, accompanied by deep stinging blasts. It does not involve a 'tune' as such. The title sequence is followed shortly after by one of the most effective stingers in film music: Herrmann's brass-led blasts that accompany Scotty's (James Stewart) disorientating vertigo-vision as he dangles from the roof.[14]

Music in horror films is regularly used as an effect or device. Perhaps the most obvious example would be an attack by Dracula in the majority of the films in which the character appears. An essential element is almost always the sonic aspect of the attack. This is a sequence of which you might well have seen many different versions – there have certainly been plenty of film versions of this dramatic moment. Count Dracula closes in slowly and resolutely on his victim, and then pounces and bites. In most cases, we can predict the music that will accompany this scene. We might imagine a homology with the tension and build-up of drama, leading to a release at the point of attack, embodied by an aggressive burst of musical sound. However, in Werner Herzog's *Nosferatu the Vampyre* (1979), the characteristic sequence in which Jonathan Harker (Bruno Ganz) is attacked is played out with no music. This immediately tells us that the film is no ordinary genre piece (and perhaps that this is not the supernatural as we know it).

On the other hand, music in horror films regularly appears as an invocatory object. It is magical and central to rituals, making demons appear as well as being part of their materiality. Indeed, it often briefly precedes them. A prime example of this is the Hammer film *The Devil Rides Out* (1968) (US: *The Devil's Bride*). James Bernard's scores, a characteristic of many Hammer horror films, illustrate film music techniques in a very straightforward manner. Two sequences, in particular, demonstrate the two central musical techniques of horror music used to signify the invo-

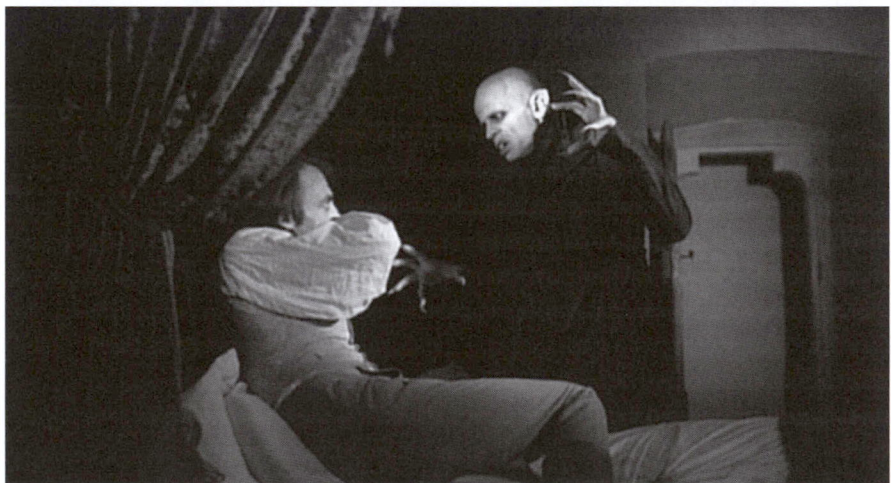

Nosferatu the Vampyre

cation, and indeed substance, of demons. In the first scene, Richleau (Christopher Lee) and Rex save their friend Simon and a woman from a meeting of devil worshippers led by Mocata (the urbane Charles Gray, clearly based on the historical figure Aleister Crowley). The climax of the satanic ritual is the appearance of the devil, which Richleau calls 'the Goat of Mendez'. Its appearance is doubled by immense stinger blasts, which not only emphasise its horror, but partially manifest the horror itself. In the second incident, Rex and Richleau are confronted by a black djinn, which tries to control them through eye contact. This is accompanied by a grotesque ostinato, functioning as anticipation but also as part of the demon's appearance. Indeed, I would argue that the music is a central component of the materiality of the djinn and the devil. In a similar case, in the *Night of the Demon* (1957), the appearance of a gigantic demon is anticipated by the noisy, rattling music, which manifests the apparition as a central component, much like the music for the shark in *Jaws* – which does not merely signify its presence, it *is* its presence.

Functions

Functioning as a sound effect, film music has incorporated various sounds, onomatopoeically one might say, into its language. The most obvious point at which sound effects became musicalised was in silent comedies, where instruments such as swanee whistles and bass drums sometimes stood in for diegetic sounds. This mimicking tradition remained to some degree once synchronised sound arrived, manifesting most obviously in short cartoons like *Looney Tunes* and *Merry Melodies* – both of which took titles alluding to music. While musical sounds are able to represent objects and ideas, they also have a materiality of their own. The stinger, central to the horror film score, has a physical aspect to it, giving it something of a primary effect, more of which I will discuss later. It is worth noting, though, that music has retained one of its important features from pre-synchronised sound cinema: that of mimicking sound effects. This onomatopoeia often takes very stylised forms and can be little more than a hint or an echo of the sounds of objects on screen (or, indeed, off screen).

Film scores do not have 'form' in the sense that symphonies, sonatas or even pop songs have distinctive and individual formal structures. However, they clearly have form as part of the film in which they reside, and arguably, they have a certain form in themselves. They tend to exhibit a coherence of musical character, including themes and range of timbres. This level of consistency aids the film score's status as 'another dimension' in films, one that lies outside the diegetic world as constructed on screen and by sound and dialogue effects, yet it remains very much a part of the audience's experience of that same world. Furthermore, non-diegetic music tends to delineate the form of films more sharply, through underlining important narrative aspects and clarifying the structure.

In horror films, in particular, music can manifest a distinctive and enveloping 'sound architecture' or ambience. This function might be called 'theatrical', as music works like part of the scenery, although its enveloping quality means that it can be more than simply 'backdrop'. Horror films are created as whole environments that the audience enters, equating a mental state with a sonic construct. Indeed, more than any other film genre, they construct a whole sound system, a musicscape, as well as embodying a distinct sound effects iconography of horror.[15] In fact, this is distinct in much the same way as the image repertoire of horror films. When rock star Marilyn Manson was asked to provide the music for *Resident Evil* (2002), he assumed that he would also be providing diegetic sounds and atmospheres,[16] underlining how the horror film is often seen as a coherent atmospheric package that embraces both music and sound effects. In many cases, horror film music follows less the traditional leitmotif symphonic structure of the classical film score than creates a sound architecture combining a concern for ambience with intermittent shock effects.

Beyond Representation

If film music is invocatory, this underlines its nature as something more than the simply representational. Most semiotic approaches would consider music simply to be a selection of signs that are decoded by the listener, translated into words, ideas and narrative. This seems a risibly banal conceptualisation of something that is far more emotional, seductive and mysterious than simple 'communication', as if it were words written on a page. If film music's relationship with the audience involves more than simply 'reading' audio signs, then it might be reconceived as one of partial *subjection* by the materiality of the music.[17] It is possible to make – perhaps purely a temporary, contingent and heuristic – distinction between film music that works primarily through conscious and semi-conscious linguistic codes (and can thus simply be decoded by the analyst using semiotics), and film music that is premised upon having a more material effect, as sound volume and the action of soundwaves upon the listeners. This opens up the possibility of seeing music as having a direct effect, a 'direct access' to the listener, where physiological effects bypass culture's learned structures. Thus, film music might insert frames of mind and attitude in the listener much like an injection from a hypodermic needle. Indeed, there is an obvious direct effect, in that hearing is more immediate than vision. Lacking the physical distance between the viewer and film on screen, hearing seems to take place 'inside' our heads. Headphones, for example, can make sounds appear to exist spatially in the vicinity of our heads, perhaps even inside our brains. Robynn Stilwell notes that

> Sound . . . forces a surrender of control; we cannot turn away. Closing our eyes only serves to intensify our experience of the sound because of lack of interference from visual input; putting our hands over our ears rarely shuts out the sound completely.[18]

The edge of film theory has noted how the dominant notion of film as representation has swamped other concerns about film. Barbara Kennedy, for example, suggests that we should 'consider film as something "outside" the purely representational'.[19]

Inspired by Gilles Deleuze, she argues that we should approach film as 'experiential: a material capture of the processual, rather than being merely representational'.[20]

Concern with representation not only converts the concept of film into a linguistic endeavour, but also limits the concerns of film study to aspects of the social, where sociological aspects can simply be 'read off' from the film by the analyst. Thus, 'representation' can be a restrictive concept for understanding film more fully. Kennedy points out that

> The visual [sic] experience of the cinematic needs to be thought of as an 'experience' as a material capture, as synaesthetic experience on sensation, not merely as representation. Thus an aesthetics of some sort needs to come back into the equation . . .[21]

I find it hard to disagree. While analysis cannot discount the communicational aspects of film, it has found it all to easy to ignore its sensations and emotions – aspects that are far more difficult to write about. I do not intend to investigate them here, but merely to note that there is an experiential level that we can perceive *before* cognition of cinema's representational elements.[22]

Sounds, particularly music, stimulate the arousal of the autonomic nervous system, which is measurable via heart rate, EEG (electro-encephalogram) readings of brain waves and respiration. Music is related to bodily and life rhythms, through the essence of volume, beat and pulse perhaps more than timbre, pitch and harmony. The most primitive (and most primal) musical moments in cinema are stingers, which engage with the audience on the most basic levels. As absolutely fundamental blasts of sound, stingers can tell us much about how film music works. A 'culturalist' argument would suggest that we have to learn how to react to stingers, that we have to interpret their coding before we can make the appropriate response.[23] On the contrary, stingers underline that there is a primary level that precedes learned responses, precedes complex mental cognition and responses. This can be demonstrated quite easily, through the introduction of a loud horror film soundtrack to a young child or a sensitive animal like a cat. Their response – in my experience, one of shock and surprise – to the semi-physical blast of sound is precisely a *reaction*, devoid of any significant cognitive level of mental activity. Or perhaps at least having a precognitive level of activity that is not erased by cognition.[24] At the same time, film music works through the repeated association of certain musical techniques and styles with particular emotions. It is thus able simultaneously to be an emotional primary effect and a learned trigger for representative ideas.

Historical Vista

Horror film music developed into a very distinctive set of stylistic options under the auspices of the classical cinema. These have developed further since its dissolution and remain powerful aspects of genre in more recent mainstream cinema. Music in horror films was often conscious of, and exploited, direct antecedents in art music. Edison's version of *Frankenstein* (1910) used extracts from Carl Maria von Weber's opera *Der Freis-*

chütz, which the composer finished in 1821, and which represents one of the first German Romantic operas. Although primarily concerned with a shooting contest, it includes demons and much in the way of supernatural involvement in the story's shootings.

One of the notable silent horror films was the German Expressionist work *Nosferatu – eine Symphonie des Grauens* (1922), directed by F. W. Murnau and starring Max Schreck. At its premiere in Berlin in 1922, the programme opened with the overture to Heinrich Marschner's opera *The Vampire* (written in 1828).[25] Hans Erdmann's score, which was performed by a live orchestra, is lost but was reconstructed in 1994 by Gillian Anderson and James Kessler from some orchestral suites that Erdmann had adapted from his music for the film, as well as the Erdmann-Becce *Allgemeines Handbuch der Film*,[26] one of the principal sources of silent film library music at the time.

The specific strain of art music called 'programme music' helped to set the model of horror film music. Such 'programme music' aimed to provide an impression of a location or some other visually based idea. Indeed, some of these programmatic pieces of music were readily reused for scary or eerie situations in silent films. Moreover, the origins of horror film music can be traced to a certain strain of Romantic orchestral music from the latter part of the 19th century. One particularly influential piece is Hector Berlioz's *Symphonie fantastique*, premiered in 1830, especially the final movement. This concluding section is premised upon the representation of a vision of a witches' sabbat and is founded on the medieval hymn, the *Dies Irae*. William Rosar notes the influential position of this ancient religious chant, as the basis for Rachmaninov's tone poem *Isle of the Dead* (1909), as well as making trace appearances in Bernard Herrmann's score for *Citizen Kane* (1941) and in Leigh Harline's music for Val Lewton's horror film *Isle of the Dead* (1945).[27] I discussed this motif earlier in the book (see Chapter 3), but it is worth noting again the durability of this religious musical icon as a sign of evil, portent and death. As Rosar's discussion of Rachmaninov's *Isle of the Dead* suggests, the area of art music that tended towards gothic impressionism fed quite directly into horror films. Claude Debussy's impressionistic and atmospheric music had less of an effect than might have been expected, with only isolated examples of its usage, including John Carpenter's electronic adaptation of *La Cathédrale engloutie* in *Escape from New York* (1981). While Richard Wagner's music had a notable influence on film music more generally, the darker sound of some of his works, such as *Götterdämmerung*, had some influence on horror film music. Bernard Herrmann's music often shows a Wagnerian influence, and the disturbing love theme from *Vertigo* definitely displays some aspects of the Prelude and *Liebestod* from Wagner's *Tristan and Isolde*. Werner Herzog used a section from *Das Rheingold* in his atmospheric reading of Murnau's original *Nosferatu the Vampyre*. Modest Mussorgsky's *Night on a Bare Mountain* (aka *St John's Night on a Bare Mountain*, or *Night on a Bald Mountain*), which was meant to depict a witches' sabbat, was used in an advertisement for Maxell videotapes in the 1980s, as well as appearing in numerous horror films. Another Mussorgsky piece, *The Gnome* (in Maurice Ravel's orchestral arrangement) from *Pictures at an Exhibition*, was used in the Amicus film

Asylum (1972) for a tense sequence involving the ascent of a staircase. Indeed, there are a number of 'scary' pieces in classical music, all of which have been used in films: Bach's *Toccata and Fugue in D minor*; Dukas's *The Sorcerer's Apprentice*; Grieg's *Hall of the Mountain King* (from *Peer Gynt*); Liszt's *Bagatelle sans tonalité* for piano (known as the *Mephisto Waltz* No. 4); Saint Saens's *Danse macabre*. While this is not an exhaustive list, it is enough to note the existence of a tradition, and how, by and large, this tradition emigrated across into music for horror films, notably in the early years of cinema. It should also be noted that this is a very different tradition from the sort of dissonant classical music that entered horror films inspired by twentieth-century modernist/avant-garde concert-hall music, which I discussed in Chapter 3.

Early 'pastiche' scores, which mixed fragments of existing music, survived from silent cinema and flourished in the bargain-basement horror films of the early 1930s. The more upmarket horror films followed the same industrial imperatives and aesthetic processes of other, more expensively made Hollywood films in increasingly having specific scores written and recorded specifically for each film. The development of the 'classical film score'[28] solidified in the early to mid-1930s with Max Steiner's score for *King Kong* (1933) and Erich Wolfgang Korngold's Oscar-winning score for *Anthony Adverse* (1936). In fact, *King Kong* used the principal techniques that would define later horror scores.[29]

Classical Hollywood horror is most readily associated with the output of Universal Studios in the 1930s and 1940s. Although the series degenerated somewhat, rejecting its earlier virility in favour of monsters cavorting with comedians Abbott and Costello, the music remained interesting and of good quality throughout. The horror genre developed apace during the 1930s, initiated as a sound film genre by Universal's productions of *Frankenstein* and *Dracula* (1931). Both films use an absolute minimum of music. This was partly due to cost-cutting and the desire not to drown the dialogue, which tended to be the fashion with most mainstream films at that time.[30] This was partly due to the difficulties of sound mixing, and the marginalisation of music in mainstream dramatic films in favour of dialogue and ambient atmospheres. Consequently, both *Frankenstein* and *Dracula* are very quiet films, and by more recent standards the sound is badly defined and muffled. *Dracula* has only a couple of blasts of non-diegetic music, using an excerpt from Tchaikovsky's *Swan Lake* (the famous 'Dying Swan' segment from scene two) across the film's titles. This piece only appears as if to provide a little romantic angst to the static and wordy film, which betrays its origins in a stage version of Bram Stoker's novel. This Tchaikovsky excerpt was used a number of times in the early 1930s in Universal horror films, a series of which appeared in the wake of the massive success of the first two films. Excerpts from respected 'classical music' (especially nineteenth-century orchestral music) was often simply cut in to films at this time. Such 'legitimate' music added a sense of upmarket sophistication and class to films that were made cheaply, a process that is still very much alive in more recent cinema.

According to Kevin Brownlow's television documentary *Universal Horror* (1998), Dracula was more eerie and proved all the more shocking for audiences precisely because of its sustained silences, as they were used to hearing plenty of live music with silent film projections.[31] Films such as *The Invisible Man* (1933) had only a single piece of music,[32] which appeared for the opening and closing credits, yet the piece's versatility meant that it could be reused in other productions, such as the *Flash Gordon* serial later in the decade.[33] The fact that Universal produced predominantly B-movies created a tradition of budget music, which meant reusing music in the same way as sets, actors, characters and bits of narrative, etc. were used again. Sets are a good example, as the mid-European town set used in all the Universal *Frankenstein* films was built for *All Quiet on the Western Front* (1930), and is still partially in existence on the Universal backlot today. *The Mummy* (1933) reused the sets, props and cast from *Dracula*, and even had a comparable storyline.[34] Similarly, it used little music.

Universal's *The Black Cat* (1934) contained a large amount of music, but almost all of it was existing pieces from the classical repertoire. The sequel to *Frankenstein*, *Bride of Frankenstein*, included music that later reappeared in the *Flash Gordon* serial, notably the use of some crypt music in the clay men section. The film was a more expensive production than previous Universal horror films and had a complete and extensive orchestral underscore written for it by Franz Waxman, who employed the whole-tone scale that became associated with the supernatural in films. The score was an essential element of the sumptuous and unique package that was the film, including director James Whale's insistence on a British-dominated cast. Like the rest of the film, the musical score is replete with ironies. For example, when the bride (Elsa Lanchester) is infused with life, Pretorius (Ernest Thesiger) announces, 'The Bride of Frankenstein', inspiring peals of wedding bells in Waxman's underscore.

Although the quality and imagination of the Universal horror series waned as it proceeded, the music tended to still be interesting. For example, *Son of Frankenstein* (1939), a late entry in the cycle directed by journeyman Rowland V. Lee, had a highly effective score by Frank Skinner. The central theme was so effective that Universal reused the recording for the main title of *House of Dracula*. *Son of Frankenstein* was also the model for Mel Brooks's highly reverent comedy *Young Frankenstein* (1974), and although John Scott's score does not reference Skinner's, it follows broadly the pattern of a classical film score for a horror film of the time.

During the 1940s, the mantle of Universal's horror cinema was increasingly taken up by the work of producer Val Lewton at RKO.[35] The Universal cycle descended into farcical productions that wore out the initial impact of the canonical monsters. Lewton's films were cheaply made but very serious, premised upon a desire to build atmosphere rather than simply lurch between moments of shock. Consequently, music played an important part in the creation of the eery atmospheric 'scenery'. In general terms, however, the music in Lewton's cycle of horror films broadly followed the Hollywood norm of the time. Superficially at least, it was similar to the music in the Universal horror films, although, like the films themselves, it was more subtle and measured. Roy Webb, an associate and friend of Max

Steiner, dominated this cycle of horror films, providing the music for *Cat People* (1942), *The Seventh Victim* (1943), *I Walked with a Zombie* (1943), *Curse of the Cat People* (1944), *The Body Snatcher* (1945) and *Bedlam* (1946).[36] Despite, or perhaps due to, their success, RKO kept Lewton making B-pictures, as horror films lost their status as main attractions in the cinema. Composer Roy Webb's subtlety, not often seen as a virtue in classical Hollywood film scores, is evident in his horror film scores for Lewton at RKO. His score for *Cat People* was based almost wholly on a French nursery rhyme, making the music an emanation from the film's central character (played by Simone Simon).[37]

Horror films began to drift out of fashion in Hollywood, spurred on by the progressively risible status of the Universal cycle of films. However, in Britain, where the horror genre had not been an important part of film production,[38] the genre became very successful through the productions of Hammer Films. This small production company had been rocketed to international success by two films that matched Universal's inaugural successes nearly twenty years earlier: *The Curse of Frankenstein* (1957) and *Dracula* (1958). They initiated a run of films that developed those characters (including *Taste the Blood of Dracula* and *Frankenstein Must Be Destroyed* [1969]), as well as embracing mainstays of earlier Hollywood horror films, in *The Curse of the Mummy's Tomb* (1964) and *Plague of Zombies* (1966). In terms of music, Hammer horror films were dominated by composer James Bernard, and later perhaps by Harry Robinson. Music played as important a part in their films as in earlier horror films, exploiting its potential for instant effect, as well as its ability to distract attention from the cheap decor or creaky plotlines of films that in most cases were made with modest budgets. Bernard had worked as an assistant to Benjamin Britten, although his horror film music betrays no influence from the outstanding British composer. In many ways, Bernard's music seems more closely related to the kind of process music that became prominent in the 1960s, some time after his music had graced a number of Hammer films.

While Hammer horror films evinced a number of different styles belonging to the different composers who were chosen for their productions, Bernard's style not only came to be identified with Hammer's output, but was almost instantly recognisable as his music. He scored more than twenty-five films for the studio. In contrast to the composers who wrote the music for Hollywood horror films in the previous decades, Bernard was a specialist, scoring only horror films, rather than turning his hand to whatever type of film came his way, as was the dominant Hollywood mode of practice.

Bernard's music is almost unerringly austere. While it is not atonal, it certainly works through a system that is not premised upon tonal harmonic movement. Dissonance is a central part of the music, exploiting the association of non-consonant music with being 'out of kilter'. He based the title music for all his scores on a vocalisation of the words of the film's title, making the melody an unsung title song. Bernard's short motif for Dracula, which appeared in all the subsequent *Dracula* films he scored, converts the word 'Dracula' into dactyl syllables (where the first of the three is emphasised). Similarly, the title music of films such as *Taste the Blood of Dracula* derives directly from the words of the title, yielding a melodic theme, to which words could easily have been added to make a song for the film. Bernard's underscores have a very particular style and logic all of their own. Fully integrated as a film language, they consist of a relatively small number of devices: ostinati, pitch raises (and, to a lesser degree, falls) in sequence and stingers. These are readily identifiable aspects of the film for filmgoers who are not familiar with musical technique. They are based on repetition (the ostinato), tension of rising pitch (transposition by sequence – simply moving the whole repeated unit of music up a semitone in pitch) and shocking blasts of sound. Indeed, these might be seen as the primary effects of horror film music.

   Plague of Zombies was directed by John Gilling and had music by James Bernard. In the film, Dr Forbes and his daughter go to Cornwall to investigate a succession of mysterious deaths. Aided by Alice, they discover that villain Squire Hamilton is killing people in order to revive them as zombies to work in his tin mine. The music is premised upon supernatural resonance allied with horror blasts and ostinati.[39] The most memorable sequence involves the dead rising from graves in a mist-filled cemetery, to the strains of an ostinato dominated by reverberating vibraphone. Indeed, the film's mysterious aspects use ringing tuned percussion and deep wood-wind, while the zombies' appearances are accompanied by deep and descending severe crashing chords. As I have suggested, Bernard's scores tended towards dis-tinctive sound and habitual practice. Randall Larson notes the small number of themes in his scores, as well as his 'characteristic manner of pairing snare drum beats with horn or piano chords ...'.[40] Bernard regularly worked to one beat to one second (or two beats per second), which made it easier to cut music to fit action. If required to, he could simply lose a beat and start the new bar early.[41]

   Bernard's horror film music was surely the most understandable of film music, being as transparent in its musical processes as it was in its function within the film. The limited roster of techniques, and the predictability of the musical devices led to a comprehensive and instantaneous effect on audiences, as well as manifesting one of the most coherent film music philosophies. Other British horror films of the time demonstrated a different approach to film music. *Night of the Demon* had music by William Alwyn, which was altogether more traditional, while on the other hand, Gerard Schurmann's score for *Horrors of the Black Museum* (1959) used a more mod-ernist palette with dissonance at its heart. Around this time, another Hammer horror film, *Curse of the Werewolf* (1961), became the first British film score to use Schoenberg's twelve-tone serial composition technique,[42] the use of which habitu-ally led to harmonic dissonance and a lack of tonal 'movement'.

   At roughly the same time, Bernard Herrmann wrote the music for Hitchcock's *Psycho*, which is without doubt one of the most easily identifiable pieces of music of the 20th century. Although Herrmann integrated elements that he had used in other scores for Hitchcock films,[43] his music for *Psycho* is distinct in many ways. Using a sonic palette limited only to strings, Herrmann's music lacks any of the empathetic or romantic music that often comprises an important part of horror film scores. Later in the decade, Krzysztoph Komeda, Roman Polanski's regular musical collaborator, provided a haunting score for his *Rosemary's Baby*, where the innocent childish music accentuated the film's horror, a style that was used again later for the childlike main theme composed by Lalo Schifrin for *The Amityville Horror* (1979). Another successful satanic horror film, *The Exorcist*, predominantly used pre-existing musical pieces, including part of Mike Oldfield's recently released *Tubular Bells*, while yet another satanic horror, *The Omen* (1976), had an outstanding score by Jerry Goldsmith. The film opens with *Ave Satani*, a chilling Latin choral chant that establishes satanism as an organised religion through its black mass incantations. Goldsmith's impressive music mixes strident string and choral outbursts as blasts of scary sound, as well as using eerie whispering voices, a staple of horror film music ever since. However, the success of *The Omen* – awarded a film music Oscar – merely underlined how the horror film had become an occasional manifestation rather than the genre it had been under the Hollywood studio system.

Hammer dominated the horror film genre throughout the 1960s, and although the impact of their films declined in the 1970s, production was still fairly consistent up to the middle of the decade. Films such as *Dracula A.D. 1972* (1972) had begun to use pop music as a new option for film music. In the early 1970s, Hammer attempted to modernise its internationally successful horror films by, first, using contemporary settings, second, including copious amounts of female nudity and, third, using pop songs. *Dracula A.D. 1972* not only includes two pop songs, but re-stages in contemporary Chelsea the Dracula stories that had made the studio famous. This new 'swinging seventies' environment included a party where an American pop group, Stoneground, appear and perform. One of Hammer's 'lesbian vampire trilogy', *Lust for a Vampire* (1970), exploited the attractions of soft porn and, to the evident shock of some of the people involved, inserted a pop song as non-diegetic music during post-production:

> Producers [Harry] Fine and [Michael] Style took the editing of the movie out of the busy [director Jimmy] Sangster's hands. Upon viewing the finished picture in a cinema in Hammersmith, Sangster and [star Ralph] Bates were astonished to find that a bizarre pop song, Strange Love – sung by 'Tracy', had been dubbed over one key scene. 'I have never been so embarrassed in my life [as] when that song came on!' recalls Sangster.[44]

This demonstrated the possibility of adding pop songs as an afterthought, as well as indicating the pressure to use pop music as a signifier of 'modernity', explicitly levelled at a young audience. However, these were not tied-in songs, in the sense that they were not made available on disc. In the Hammer films, pop songs were only a momentary attraction, an attempt to furnish the films with a pop culture credibility. These films are evidence that the film industry was not purely interested in pop songs as products placed within and sold by films.

Both the increasing commercial viability and aesthetic options offered by pop and rock music had a significant impact on music in horror films. While I do not intend to discuss pop music and horror films here, it is worth noting that during the 1970s and 1980s, Italian horror films often used distinctive music by rock groups. For example, Dario Argento's films, such as *Profondo rosso* [*Deep Red*] (1975), had music written and performed for the film by the group Goblin, also known as The Goblins. Rather than simply supply a succession of pop songs for the film,[45] Goblin built up a fabric of rhythmic underscore for the film using an instrumentation derived from rock music. The main theme is reminiscent of Mike Oldfield's best-selling *Tubular Bells*, which, as we have seen, was used in *The Exorcist* a couple of years earlier. The music that John Carpenter wrote for his own films was also clearly influenced by *Tubular Bells*, as well as minimalist art music by composers like Steve Reich and Philip Glass. Carpenter's startling unadorned synthesizer music for *Halloween* and *The Fog* was both highly distinctive and an effective part of the films' arsenal of effects. Carpenter's debt to minimalist 'process music', where the listener can hear the music's processes, was most evident. Some time later, a pioneer of this form of music, Philip Glass, turned his hand to horror film music, with *Candyman* (1992). Glass stuck to the use of electronic keyboards, the instrument he had concentrated on in the 1970s, when his music was still seen as part of the new 'minimalist' style of art music.

Carpenter developed a stripped-down, bare bones version of film music. *Halloween* had two principal themes and was based upon regular pitch drops in sequence (where the same musical material is simply moved down in pitch). In a very straightforward manner, the film's music establishes a tense atmosphere through drones and ostinati, then stingers. This tense build-up and climax is a structure that is repeated throughout the film (and, indeed, in many other horror films). The sections of the film with other functions (e.g. dialogue scenes between the girls) are almost wholly bereft of any musical accompaniment. The repetitious character of almost all the music underlines the narrative logic of the film: we know what is going to happen (people will be killed), we just do not know when. Thus, the music does not really build towards climax, but remains a simple and disconcerting reiteration that gives less in the way of clues as to 'when' than the audience would probably like. The on-screen attack and its tied stinger usually appear 'out of the blue', and as something of a relief to the tension built by the relentless musical ostinati. Near the start of the film, Laurie (Jamie Lee Curtis) goes up to the Myers' house to post in a note. Viewed from within the home, Laurie approaches the door and a stinger emphasises the appearance of the shape entering screen left on the near side of the door. This musical stinger is thus the equivalent of a shocking sound effect, which could not be there in accordance with the laws of diegetic sound effects.

The release of *The Exorcist* was a cause célèbre, involving calls for the film to be banned amid stories of disturbed audience members and claims about the film's satanic power.[46] Music provides a different dimension in the film, utilising a selection of twentieth-century classical music alongside the recently released *Tubular Bells*. Lalo Schifrin's score for the film was rejected and replaced with excerpts from existing pieces, such as music by Penderecki and Ligeti. In this way, *The Exorcist* was similar to Stanley Kubrick's *2001: A Space Odyssey* and *A Clockwork Orange*, both of which used the pre-existent music that had 'temped' the film. Kubrick later used the same procedure with *The Shining*, as I discussed in Chapter 3. There are distinct advantages in the reuse of existing but obscure music in films. First, film-makers know the final result, rather than having to wait for post-production to see the composer's product. Second, there is little in the way of mass audience associations with pieces that only attract a small audience. Unlike famous orchestral pieces, such as Rossini's *William Tell Overture* (the concluding *Hymn* part), they carry with them no solid meanings or associations,[47] However, the sounds of dissonance most certainly seem to carry distinct connotations.

While *The Shining* may have used twentieth-century orchestral music to express extreme and supernatural states, the end of Ridley Scott's science-fiction horror film *Alien* used an excerpt from Howard Hanson's 'Romantic' Symphony to give a sense of closure and a return to normality. In the main body of the film, Jerry Goldsmith's dissonant music has accompanied the film's otherworldy representations. Music in the *Alien* films is partially inspired by modernist art music, and as 'music for monsters' could be seen unproblematically as horror film music. Some of these elements of modernist art music were incorporated into more traditional scores. For example, a sophisticated take on the traditional horror film score is Christopher Young's music for *Hellraiser* (1987) and *Hellraiser 2: Hellbound* (1988). This is very haunting music, and the choral music of the second film resembles a requiem, which connects it with the genre's traditional concerns evident in films like *The Omen* and the more general notion of Evil as a religion (and perhaps even the horror film as a ritualistic invocation).

The 1980s saw a fairly widespread return in Hollywood to the use of large orchestral forces and films with extensive film scores that bore a resemblance to the scores of the classical studio era.[48] John Williams's work has been central in this process, particularly his scores for the *Star Wars* films. Williams's score for *Dracula* (1979) evinced a highly romantic conceptualisation of the film and subject matter. As I have noted elsewhere, Danny Elfman's scores for the *Batman* films in the 1990s demonstrated a return to some of the aspects of the underscores in classical cinema. Elfman's music takes a number of gothic horror staples and uses them in an ironic manner, making the music a key element in the films' sense of parody and irony.[49] His music for *Darkman* (1990) includes some overblown action cues but a highly chromatic main title theme with non-functional parallel harmony that avoids establishing a solid traditional sense of tonality.[50]

The early to mid-1990s saw the release of two films with strikingly similar desires to connect themselves with the literary origins of both *Dracula* and *Frankenstein*, both having extended titles that could equally have included the names of their bankable directors: Francis Ford Coppola's *Bram Stoker's Dracula* and Kenneth Branagh's *Mary Shelley's Frankenstein* (1994). *Bram Stoker's Dracula* had music by Wojciech Kilar, who has only done occasional work outside his native Poland. The

Interview with the Vampire

score is far from a traditional horror film score. He was an inspired choice to score the film, writing some achingly romantic music and notably superimposing different musical compositions, such as a Charles Ives concert piece.[51] Scot Patrick Doyle's score for *Mary Shelley's Frankenstein* also demonstrated a resurgent romanticism. While the music is very much in Doyle's usual style, the sheer weight of orchestral forces and the plain volume of the music in relation to other sound on the soundtrack are remarkable.

Another horror film with striking and very individual music was *Interview with the Vampire* (1994). An unusual horror film based on Anne Rice's best-selling book, it was directed by Neil Jordan, an auteur director rather than a horror film specialist. Similarly, composer Eliot Goldenthal attempted in the film to produce a very individual underscore, while retaining many conventions of generic horror film music. A good proportion of the music came from material already composed but not used, as Goldenthal was given three and a half weeks to compose eighty minutes of music for the film, replacing George Fenton's discarded music.[52] The characteristic attributes of Goldenthal's film music – breakneck-speed French horn trills, blaring trumpets, howling woodwinds and avant-garde-style writing for strings – all fit the horror film format well.

Interview with the Vampire makes use of religious music, a staple of the horror genre. The music that Goldenthal uses to open the film, *Libera Me*, has its Latin text changed from 'Save me from everlasting death' to 'Save me from everlasting life', as a reflection of the vampire Louis's weariness of eternal life. As might be expected in a horror film, there are some tense action sequences, some of which Goldenthal scores in a most individual manner. For example, the piece of music called 'Claudia's *Allegro Agitato*'on the soundtrack CD uses a string quartet in front of the orchestra to provide the sound's energy by playing in a scratchy manner and with the repeated use of the snap pizzicato. Such a sound is rare in concert-hall music, although this is clearly an instance of art music technique being brought to the traditions of film scoring.[53] Goldenthal uses this sound again for the sequence where Louis is imprisoned in a coffin and then rescued by Armand. One of the film's most striking moments in musical terms occurs when a dramatic monologue by Lestat is accompanied by a harpsichord as non-diegetic music, providing a parody of operatic recitative. The music is interspersed with his words, making it appear almost like the response to his voice, certainly a complement to the for-malised performance of the monologue by Tom Cruise as Lestat.

Goldenthal's score does not use leitmotifs in the traditional sense. Instead, the film's music is partly built around the notion of historical progression in terms of musical style. The music starts with the use of a viola da gamba, a stringed instru-ment from the early Renaissance, and with a boys' choir singing music derived from the Latin liturgical. It then moves forward in time to the harpsichord accompani-ment for Lestat described above, then to the little girl Claudia with the piano, and to Louis with a full, modern symphony orchestra. The film ends with a more modern musical aspect, employing Guns'n'Roses's version of the Rolling Stones's 'Sympathy for the Devil', as the film moves from the past to conclude in a modern-day setting.

Conclusion

We should always remain aware of the status of sounds in films. They are not two-dimensional like film images, and despite their lack of full aural dimension can be perceived as bearing strong similarities to actual sounds outside of the cinema, notably in the case of loud noises and screams, which also produce a physical impact, particularly at high volume. This imbues sounds in the cinema with a par-ticular virility, which is exploited unequivocally by horror films. Music in horror films often attempts a direct engagement with the physical: for example, through the use of the very high (like the stabbing strings in the shower scene in *Psycho*) or the low (deep stingers or drones). These are not merely extremes of pitch, but are also tied to the intrinsic sounds of the human body: the high buzz of the nervous system and the deep throb of the bloodstream and heart.[54] Music's sensual input provides a physical stimulus that is more than simply quantifiable 'meaning' (which, of course, may be added retrospectively). It is beyond doubt that fear is one of the strongest human emotions as composer John Frizell, interviewed in 2002, noted:

> It's very difficult to write something that involves scaring people, especially to avoid the clichés you find in a score like [*Ghost Ship*]. Fear is a very two-dimensional, rudimentary feeling – I

don't even want to call it an emotion. It's a very primal, simple thing. You're afraid or you're not afraid. This creates the challenge of writing a good, scary score. If you're dealing with drama, you might have the complexity of someone who is elated but slightly anxious and maybe envious, but hopeful. Writing a cue that has those things in it is a lot easier than simply scoring fear. Fear is not a terribly complex feeling. I think a snail goes through some type of fear, but a snail probably doesn't experience envy, and so it's something very primal, deep down in our brain stem that evolved very early and doesn't have the complexities of higher emotional functions. And that's what makes a scary score hard.[55]

Horror film music illustrates the modes of film music more generally. However, in many cases, music in horror films appears to have followed less the leitmotif structure of the classical film score than to displace these concerns through an overriding concentration on a combination of shock effects and ambience or sonic architecture. Horror film music functions as a central 'effect' in horror films, and thus as a principal player rather than simply 'window-dressing' accompaniment for scary visuals. In Lamberto Bava's *La casa con la scala nel buio* (*A Blade in the Dark*, 1983), a composer is writing and recording a score for a horror film. The music he is recording is used in the film as non-diegetic music, confusing the status of the film's diegetic world while providing a central unitary spine to the narrative. Rather than merely providing an accompaniment to screen horror, film music is also able to *embody* horror, providing a demonic presence in itself. In *Night of the Demon*, for example, a significant part of the demon's physical presence is the music. The appearance of the demon is prefigured by the music; that is, it is not merely an accompaniment to the visuals of the demon but starts *before* each appearance. This proves the centrality of music as a physical apparition within films. More than simply anticipation, musical sound functions as an essential part of the physicality of the demon in the film.

Notes

1 This is the case not only with orchestral film scores for horror films, but equally with the certain specific genres of pop/rock that seem to accompany the films. This chapter will not deal with the latter to any notable degree.

2 Philip Martell, quoted in Edward Buscombe, *The Making of Legend of the Werewolf* (London: BFI, 1976), p. 101.

3 It should be noted that outside the film frame, similar invocatory music can be used for ritual and religious purposes.

4 Voodoo might also be seen as a religious ritual.

5 Paul Wells, *The Horror Genre: From Beelzebub to Blair Witch* (London: Wallflower, 2000), p. 7.

6 Film analysis and criticism has not really dealt with the horror film as a succession of physical jolts. However, popular writing about the horror film, especially in horror fanzines, has approached it as merely a succession of special effects set pieces. Lurching from shock to shock is lurching from stinger to stinger in musical terms.

7 We know that this would have been the soundtrack for the picture of a black soldier saluting the French flag, made famous by Roland Barthes's analysis in 'Myth Today' in *Mythologies*, translated by Annette Lavers (New York: Hill and Wang, 1972), pp. 109–59.

8 Royal S. Brown's discussion of *Psycho* relies on a notion of tonality that is, I would argue, not particularly evident in the music's processes. *Overtones and Undertones: Reading Film Music* (Berkeley and Los Angeles: University of California Press, 1994), pp. 3–7.

9 K. J. Donnelly, 'The Classical Film Score Forever?: Music in the *Batman* Films' in Steve Neale and Murray Smith, eds., *Contemporary Hollywood Cinema* (London: Routledge, 1997), p. 148.

10 Hanns Eisler and Theodor Adorno, *Composing for the Films* (London: Athlone, 1994), p. 17.

11 Kathryn Kalinak notes the equivalence between tremolo strings and suspense. 'The Language of Music: A Brief Analysis of *Vertigo*' in Kay Dickinson, ed., *Movie Music: The Film Reader* (London: Routledge, 2003), p. 21.

12 Another occasional effect is to play strings col legno – with the wood of the bow – as used most prominently in Stravinsky's *The Rite of Spring*.

13 Unless, of course, the audience is absolutely unfamiliar with horror films. Although it should be emphasised that these devices are more than simply a semiotic effect anyway (see later discussion).

14 Hitchcock and Herrmann's *North by North-West* (1959) has some startling stingers in the Mount Rushmore sequence. In fact, Herrmann was something of a 'king of the stingers', regularly using clamorous deep (trombone-dominated) brass blasts.

15 Non-film genres of music such as satanic 'black metal' tend to use iconography and some musical aspects derived from horror films and their music. A good illustration is the Cradle of Filth album, *Cruelty and the Beast* (1998), which featured Ingrid Pitt (of Hammer horror fame) as narrator.

16 Stated on the *Resident Evil* DVD (Pathé P9048DVD) featurette extra, interview with Manson and Marco Beltrami.

17 Bordwell's four levels of cognition leave out primary engagement, which has the net effect of attempting to render engagements with all films, such as abstract films like Norman McLaren's, into purely linguistic rather than sensory experiences. David Bordwell, *Making Meaning: Inference and Rhetoric in the Interpretation of Cinema* (Cambridge, MA: Harvard University Press, 1991), pp. 8–9.

18 Robynn Stilwell, 'Sound and Empathy: Subjectivity, Gender and the Cinematic Soundscape' in K. J. Donnelly, ed., *Film Music: Critical Approaches* (Edinburgh: Edinburgh University Press, 2001), p. 171.

19 Barbara Kennedy, *Deleuze and Cinema: The Aesthetics of Sensation* (Edinburgh: Edinburgh University Press, 2000), p. 3.

20 Ibid., p. 16.

21 Ibid., p. 28.

22 This effect might well lie outside cultural codings, situating this section as a reply to the dominant theory of 'culturalism'.

23 This approach would be consonant with a cognitivist viewpoint, too.

24 This counters the 'culturalist' view, which sees everything as learned. A common retort is that music (and other culture) is precisely the way it is because it is a reflection, an emanation from

human emotion and consciousness. There is some (although not conclusive) evidence for this, such as the similarity of the music used to denote happiness or mourning across radically different cultures.

25 Gillian Anderson, 'Reconstructing the Music', sleeve notes to the CD, *Nosferatu – Eine Symphonie des Grauens*.

26 Ibid.

27 William Rosar, 'The *Dies Irae* in Citizen Kane: Musical Hermeneutics Applied to Film Music' in K. J. Donnelly, ed., *Film Music: Critical Approaches* (Edinburgh: Edinburgh University Press, 2001), pp. 103–16.

28 Kathryn Kalinak, *Settling the Score: Music and the Classical Hollywood Film* (Madison: University of Wisconsin Press, 1992), pp. xv–xvi.

29 *Dracula's Daughter* (1936) contained romantic string music.

30 William H. Rosar, 'Music for the Monsters: Universal Pictures' Horror Film Scores of the Thirties', *The Quarterly Journal of the Library of Congress*, no. 40, Fall 1983, pp. 390–421.

31 This would correspond with Adorno and Eisler's formulation of the 'ghostly effect' of images without sound. See discussion in Chapter 1.

32 Composed by Heinz Roemheld, although he was not credited on screen.

33 For cheaper productions, this process of music reuse was common practice. *Flash Gordon* (1936) also reused music from *Destination Unknown* (1932), which in turn had been derived from concert pieces by Wagner and Liszt.

34 David J. Skal, *The Monster Show: A Cultural History of Horror* (London: Plexus, 1993), p. 168.

35 Lewton was inspired initially by the Universal horror films. Skal, *The Monster Show*, p. 218.

36 See chapter on Steiner in Christopher Palmer, *The Composer in Hollywood* (London: Marion Boyars, 1990).

37 His score for *Bedlam* was based on 'English' music, while *The Body Snatcher* had a Scottish-style military theme.

38 David Pirie, *A Heritage of Horror: The English Gothic Cinema, 1946–72* (London: Reynolds and Hearn, 1973); Peter Hutchings, *Hammer and Beyond: The British Horror Film* (Manchester: Manchester University Press, 1993).

39 The film's music is dominated by strings, horn and snare drum.

40 Randall D. Larson, *Music from the House of Hammer* (Metuchen, NJ: Scarecrow, 1996), p. 45.

41 As detailed in a talk given by James Bernard at the Royal College of Music in London in 2000.

42 This was a radical departure for musical composition, eschewing the dominant tonal system, based on key centres, and embracing set rows of notes as musical foundations, leading in most cases to discordant music. Leonard Rosenman had already used serial techniques in his score for *The Cobweb* (1955).

43 Royal S. Brown discusses what he calls 'the Hitchcock chord'. *Overtones and Undertones*, p. 160.

44 *Hammer Horror Collectors' Special*, no. 1, 1994, p. 52.

45 The earliest examples of pop groups writing music for films simply involved them supplying a number of songs. K. J. Donnelly, *Pop Music in British Cinema: A Chronicle* (London: BFI, 2001), p. 20.

46 Mark Kermode, *The Exorcist*, rev. 2nd edn (London: BFI, 2003).

47 A version of this Rossini piece in *A Clockwork Orange* is used precisely for its comic effect.

48 Donnelly, 'The Classical Film Score Forever?', p. 151.

49 Ibid., pp. 151–4.

50 *Darkman*'s title music involves rising and falling semitones in contrary motion towards each other, and non-functional parallel harmonies.

51 Some of Ives's work makes 'variations' upon existing musical pieces through their superimposition, to create different planes of listening where one of a number of musical strains might be focused upon by the listener.

52 Mikael Carlsson, 'Interview with the Composer' <www.musicfromthemovies.com/pages/goldenthal_interview.html> (accessed 10 October 2000). Previously published in *Moviescore*, no. 2, 1995, and *Music from the Movies*, no. 10, 1995–6.

53 Furthermore, this particular sound is enabled by placing the microphone very near to the string quartet.

54 Theo van Leeuwen also notes the physiological basis of musical tempo or beat. *Speech, Music, Sound* (Basingstoke, Hants: Macmillan, 1999), p. 39.

55 John Frizell, in Randall D. Larson, 'Fear and Laughter' [interview with Frizell], *Soundtrack*, vol. 21, no. 83, 2002, p. 42.

Chapter 6

Music on Television 1: Music for Television Drama

It is all too easy to take television for granted. For many, it is just a box that sits in the corner of the room that we switch on and off as we please. But, of course, it is so much more than that. It has become one of the most defining characteristics of our age and the central object in many people's lives. In this chapter, I am not concerned with musical turns or acts on television, but rather with television's use of incidental music, a subject that has inspired very little in the way of analysis or serious discussion. In fact, it is only over the last few years that writings specifically about television have started to cohere into a distinct 'television studies',[1] although television theory remains in its infancy. It has never managed to scale the lofty heights of endeavour that film theory attempted in the 1970s, remaining an altogether more humble body of thought. The most prominent academic texts that have looked at television programmes – such as John Ellis's *Visible Fictions* and John Fiske's *Television Culture* – always fail to deal with the music.[2] This is no surprise. The situation is strikingly similar to the way that studies of film have been in the past. Perhaps the nature of television has dictated that its techniques, including its musical techniques, usually have to be seen as 'transparent' as the medium itself, the 'window on the world' or transmitter of events. In fact, two dominant metaphors for television are the window and the mirror. While the latter is concerned with showing us to ourselves in the broad sense, in which we are aware of a small degree of parallax or difference, the window is premised upon our looking at a world outside. Both of these assume that television has the ability to show audiences 'real life', through the direct relationship of transmitted images and the medium's intimacy,[3] which is at least partially derived from what some commentators see as television's principal defining characteristics: its apparent 'liveness' and immediacy[4]. This sense of 'transparency' meant that 'serious' documentaries, in Britain at least, tended to eschew the aestheticising use of musical accompaniment. In recent years, this tendency has receded. While news programmes do not use musical accompaniment to bulletins, increasingly music has been added to documentary material in special reports. It is possible loosely to divide television into two 'opposing' currents: the 'journalistic' and the 'dramatic'. Such a division cannot really be exclusive, but these two tendencies have defined significant differences in broadcasting, the most obvious one being between news and current affairs programmes on the one hand, and plays and drama on the other. In this chapter, I will look at the latter.

A single chapter in a book cannot deal adequately with all the wealth of incidental music in television, so I will concentrate on broad aspects of music in television drama, and primarily British television. This will involve looking at three 'forms' of television music: underscores (based on the modes of film music), reiterated blocks of music (a form more indigenous to television drama) and the use of library or stock music. These are not exclusive strategies but rather formats of television music that can be discussed separately for the purposes of understanding both mode of production and the effect of the final product.

In comparison with film music, television music deals less with the transcendental and move with the everyday, yet it is still a prevailing agent of control. While there are important similarities and differences between film music and television music, music in television programmes recurrently adds authority and provides an almost tangible sense of quality, through exploiting the cultural value associated with certain types of music. Television is dominated less by developmental drama, as in films, but more by momentary dramatic instants.[5] Television is fragmented[6] within a continuous 'flow'.[7] This tessellated form obviates the need for lengthy sections of music designed to build continuity and reaction through successive progression. Instead, what is required is that certain moments are emphasised, noted as significant, monumentalised and aestheticised. Generally speaking, the vast majority of music for television drama aims less at emotional effect than in film music. This is because television is a radically different context from the cinema. While cinemas are spaces geared towards an uninterrupted experience of sound and image (and where some theorists argue that the audience 'regresses' to an infantile psychic state), television is consumed in an everyday mode, where the attention it receives is often only intermittent.[8]

According to John Ellis, sound retains attention more than image, and while audiences' attention to the image often lapses, they pay more sustained attention to television sound.[9] We listen to television sometimes more than we watch it. It is a talkative medium, and tends to have sound cues that we can follow when our attention is drawn elsewhere. News and documentaries can lose our visual concentration while retaining our aural attention, and we can glance away from the television only to be brought back by sounds that appear to signal action, excitement or interest. Indeed, Rick Altman notes that we often listen to rather than watch television, as we undertake some other activity.[10] It is therefore profoundly different from the context of a film exhibited in a cinema,[11] and although at times it may appear similar, television music usually lacks the traditional procedures of film music.[12] While television may be able to use incidental music in a cognate manner with films, it was never dominated by the convention of scoring music to fit the action, as has been the case with feature films. While some television dramas have been scored in a manner identical to films, television's lower production values, married to its technical differences, have dictated that television music should not be simply film music for a small screen. (It also should not be analysed as if it were simply film music.)

Until very recently, technological limitations have defined television music. The nature of television itself has set severe limitations upon music and its reproduction. The medium has been dominated by sets with very small speakers that are inadequate for good musical sound. Small speakers have a narrow frequency spectrum, creating a middle-based sound that lacks subtlety and the wide dynamics characteristic of feature film sound production (if sometimes not its reproduction). This may be changing slowly, due to the proliferation of 'home-cinema' set-ups with multiple speakers including woofers, meaning that television has begun to catch up with the sort of sonic experience for which many of the films it shows were actually designed. Despite this, and broadcasts in Nicam (Near Instantaneous Companded Audio Modulation) stereo, the overwhelming majority of television programmes still reflect the lack of aural ambition that has perennially plagued television. Music that was transmitted through the sort of miniscule speaker available in the past would have to negotiate the relatively limited dynamic and frequency range. It was music that could not deal with subtleties, and which had to be heard clearly and unambiguously under circumstances that did not favour musical reproduction, both in technological terms and in terms of the domestic space of television's viewing and listening.

Television music has also suffered from another severe constraint, that of cost limitations, particularly when compared with its more illustrious and opulent cousin of film music. Typically, the music budget for television programmes represents a very small proportion of the overall budget. In many cases, this has meant that programme makers have been forced to use stock music, derived from music libraries and bought by the minute. In other cases, very basic musical set-ups would have to be employed. The pilot episode of *Star Trek* (1966–9, Paramount/NBC/Desilu), entitled 'The Cage', used an ensemble that varied between ten and twenty musicians.[13] Even quite expensive productions, such as the miniseries *Dune* (2000), were forced to cut corners when it came to the music. Composer Graeme Revell noted that as they could only afford a certain amount of music for the six-hour miniseries,they had to repeat musical cues by cutting them into the drama again.[14] During the years when television was predominantly a live medium, some programmes would employ musicians to play along live, in some cases single musicians on an organ reminiscent of silent cinema pianists.[15] This aesthetic is still partially evident in some television dramas, such as the soap opera *Sunset Beach* (1997–9, Spelling/NBC), where each programme included an individualised musical accompaniment on electronic keyboards. The simple textures clearly denoted that the music comprised a minimum of overdubs and, indeed, could almost have been played as a live accompaniment to the drama.[16]

Function and Control

While music in television programmes follows similar processes to film music, by and large it is far less sensitive or subtle. As I have already noted, television drama often uses incidental music in a manner highly reminiscent of films. This is crucial for the discussion here. Television dramas include TV movies, single dramas, mini-series, series (a certain number of episodes) and serials (that can run indefinitely). Television programmes other than drama tend to use similar screen music techniques to television drama. Indeed, music used for adverts can be the same as, or similar to, show theme tunes. So, what is the function of television music? How different is television music from film music, particularly in terms of effect and function? Is it really manipulative in any notable way? The everyday domestic familiarity of the television set might mask music's important and powerful role, much as some commentators believe that television has become the all-powerful mind manipulator of our time,[17] 1984's Big Brother screen that is our constant companion (and we its). In some important ways, television music – like film music – aims and works to control us. It aspires to control our behaviour and responses to television – and we should not forget that most television is premised upon influencing our responses to commerce, hence the centrality of advertising, with its all-pervading logic for the formatting of television more generally. Yet television music is not the same thing as film music, although it may have superficially similar ambitions as a controlling device. It has some very clear 'disciplinary' functions, one of which Philip Tagg calls the reveille function.[18] This refers to its role of alerting the listener to the beginning of a programme, or to notable events within a programme, like the reveille played by army buglers to rouse sleeping soldiers in the morning.

We can identify a number of distinct functions for music on television. As we have seen, the reveille function summons the audience to the television set. Of importance here (but not always) is the sense of recognition, that certain music can attract the listener (and potential viewer) by providing an ident-branding of a particular programme. An important structural function is that of aiding continuity, providing portals or thresholds that mark the end, the beginning and advertising breaks, as well as marking off sections within a programme. This is a form of punctuation, which not only marks temporal format (start and finish, etc.), but also indicates significant activity within the programme, as well as movement between spatial and temporal zones. Music can also be an attraction in itself, such as songs performed on music programmes or as isolated activities in dramas, or even title sequences or songs (a number of which have become hit records). Another key function of television music is to signal emotion (or assent to emotional reactions in the audience, authorising their response). It has a heightening function for certain charged episodes, such as action sequences. In this instance, sequences with music seem more effective than those in which music is absent. Along these lines, music on television serves to aestheticise and monumentalise the images and events played out on screen (and in dialogue).

In any examination of television music, there are a number of analytical questions we should ask. Is this music particular to the programme, or not? Was the music written to fit the action, or composed before the action was recorded and simply cut in to the programme? Is the music a small repertoire of distinct musical pieces or an organic continuity, fitted to what happens on screen? In other words, does the music have its own 'integrity'?

It should be noted that simply 'cutting in' music to action is very easy and endemic on television; similarly, editing footage to fit the music is also a common practice. The precise matching of music, written specifically for the finished visual product, is less common in television, in contrast to the vast majority of feature films produced in Europe and the United States, where it is the dominant process. If, for example, we address the incidental music in the quiz show *Who Wants to Be a Millionaire* (1998– , Celador), it is clear that the music goes through the same procedures for each contestant. The action fits the music in the same way that some sports matches use a variety of basic musical accompaniments to complement activities on-field (such as anticipatory tension, and 'Charge!'). In *Who Wants to Be a Millionaire*, different music accompanies different moments in the programme's progression. For example, the early (easier) questions are accompanied by more relaxed music than the later (harder) questions, which have a tension ostinato that you might easily find in a scary drama or film. These are interrupted, quite crudely, by the so-called 'Lifelines' – 'phone a friend', 'ask the audience' or 'fifty-fifty' – which engage a different musical passage that simply cuts in, across the seemingly progressing tension music that dominates the show. Regular viewers interiorise this tension music's development, and will notice the edit to 'Lifeline' music all the more.

According to Jeremy Butler, there are four functions of sound on television,[19] which, broadly speaking, music also follows:

1. capturing viewer attention
2. manipulating viewer understanding of the image
3. maintaining televisual flow
4. maintaining continuity within individual scenes

The first two are concerned with affecting the television audience, while the latter two reflect more formal functions. Music can also be an attraction in itself, as well as performing the more traditional 'theatrical' functions such as maintaining continuity between different scenes, holding together montage sequences and the more 'filmic' function of accompanying visual spectacles.

We can identify different types of television music that cohere around the specificities of television genres. Television drama tends to have its own form of music, which usually bears similarities to the film score. The music for game shows is usually based on reused blocks of music, while documentaries and seemingly 'factual' programmes, like the news, tend to employ a different musical format again.[20] Until recently, British documentaries often rejected the use of music, for fear that it might aestheticise the programme's representations and detract from the illusion of direct access to the real world through the television screen. However, in more recent times, documentaries have begun to embrace the use of music, which begs the question as to whether they really are that different from television drama, particularly when reconstruction has become a central stylistic element of much documentary audiovisual language. So, while we can identify a number of distinct generic formats of television music, there are still a number of distinct functions that work across television as a whole. This is not to say that there is an individual television music aesthetic. Clearly it is derived chiefly from elsewhere, largely from film and radio.

The rest of this chapter concentrates on three types of television music: underscores, cut-in blocks of music and stock music. These are not mutually exclusive categories. For example, a specifically composed underscore might also be reused in blocks as background music in television drama, or a coherent 'score' might be created from stock library music.

Underscores

Many television dramas have musical underscores that closely resemble the scores that are written for films. Indeed, television drama can often resemble film, and there is an intermediate zone between television and cinema that is occupied by films that fail to get a cinematic distribution, television movies and expensive prestige dramas. Certain areas of expensive contemporary television drama exhibit a musical aesthetic that appears to have been derived unproblematically from film. These are characterised by a lot of specially written music, although in some cases this may include less under the dialogue. Arguably, perhaps, this aesthetic derives more from radio drama.

Some television dramas have *no* non-diegetic music at all. In Britain, as noted above, there has been something of a tradition that 'serious' television should be very sparing in its use of music, particularly as an aestheticising device. British documentaries and the social realist tradition led to soap operas such as *Coronation Street* (1960– , Granada), *EastEnders* (1986– , BBC) and *Brookside* (1982–2003, Channel Four/Mersey Television), all of which used no incidental music – except in very exceptional circumstances.[21] In fact, so ingrained is this tradition – which is also partly derived from economy or parsimony – that a British soap opera that uses incidental music is the rarest of exceptions. The only one I can think of in recent years is *Night and Day* (2001–03, Granada), which stylistically aims to be as different from soap norms as possible, and music clearly plays an important role in this. In contrast with this, American soaps tend to use large amounts of musical underscore. This may well be due to their more direct origins in melodrama and the lack of a strong social realist tradition in American television drama. For example, *Sunset Beach* had a musical underscore that accompanied a significant proportion of the show's screen time. In the pilot episode, for example, there are some extended musical cues that accompany action sequences, such as the chase after the theft of a handbag. As is the case in many pilots, more money is spent on these than the following episodes, and the musical score for the pilot is rather more sumptuous than in later episodes. The pilot has a multi-instrumental score, including some very prominent wailing electric guitar. The scores for the ensuing series used more basic textures, apparently based mostly on electric keyboards that could easily be wielded, resembling a silent cinema pianist improvising along with the developing screen action. The important difference is that the unfolding accompaniment is to the dialogue scenes that comprise almost the entire programme. In fact, this is no different from the sort of musical accompaniment that was common in much live television drama, where a musician or few would provide live off-screen music as a drama was being played out in front of the cameras. Equally, they could be 'cut in' – or 'needle-dropped', as it was sometimes known – using already recorded music. However, usually television underscores were produced by smaller ensembles, solo instruments and composers recording their own music on electronic keyboards: good examples are *Doctor Who* (1963–89, BBC) and the *X-Files* (1993–2002, Fox). This tends to produce more spare textures than film music, the result of both cost restrictions and a reflection of television's more intimate character.

However, the close relation between individual composer/performer and the music can allow a certain scope. A most unique score was composed and performed by Malcolm Clarke of the BBC Radiophonic Workshop for the *Doctor Who* story 'The Sea Devils' (1972). Clarke's music is startling in its range of obtrusive electronic timbres and relative melodic paucity. In fact, this programme manifests an interesting period when mainstream television (momentarily) embraced avant-garde music. This electronic music was a featured aspect of the programme rather than simply an anonymous musical backdrop. The shocking new sounds, conjured from the BBC's brand new prototype EMS synthesizer, mixed music and sound effects, presenting uncomfortable sounds to a substantial early Saturday evening audience in a way not duplicated in Britain before or since.[22] In fact, the score was a last-minute replacement, when another Radiophonic Workshop member, John Baker, was unable to write the commissioned score.[23] *Doctor Who: The Television Companion*, a very authoritative source on the serial, notes that Clarke

> came up with a score that can best be described as experimental. It is in effect a collection of atonal sounds that punctuate action, in some parts melodic but in others simply background noise (for example a low bubbling for the sequences set in the submarine). Opinions differ as to the merits of this approach, but one thing that is certain is that no-one who watched *The Sea Devils* can possibly fail to miss what is arguably its most striking aspect.[24]

The malignant 'sea devils' of the story's title are accompanied by a theme derived from the *Dies Irae*, potentially one of the few recognisable melodic aspects of Clarke's score that makes any external reference. The complexity of this sort of television underscore allows for musical references and the opportunity for the music to signify on different levels: one for the viewer, who is only a casual listener to the score, and one for the more attentively listening viewer. Mark Snow's scores for the *X-Files* often make oblique references that are doubtless only picked up by a fraction of the audience. In the episode 'Roadrunners' (season 8, aired in 2000 on Fox in the USA, 2001 on Sky in Europe and March 2002 on the BBC), for example, when Scully first begins to see evidence of the parasite inside a man's back, Snow's music, which largely has retained a spare texture based on single sonorous notes, plays the opening melody of Jerry Goldsmith's score for the film *Alien*. Is this witty reference telling us about the creature Scully is about to see? There is no indication in the rest of the programme that it might be extraterrestrial in origin (yet it does live inside people, as in the Hollywood film). Composer Patrick Gowers declared that his incidental music for the *Sherlock Holmes* series starring Jeremy Brett (1984–8, 1990–4, Granada) is premised upon cryptic clues.[25] For example, the story 'The Priory School' involves the disappearance of a ten-year-old lord from a private school. At the start, he is seen singing *Libera Me* from the Requiem Mass, foreshadowing his own kidnapping.

Since the 1980s, the development of a notable zone of 'quality' drama production in British television has increasingly used music as a guarantor of the high production values that are required in the international market. Prestige dramas, such as BBC costume dramas, use large numbers of musicians, significant amounts of music and expensive 'name' composers, who come together to produce highly evident 'prestige' music that is now more often a star than a bit-part player. In the vast majority of cases, these programmes use film-like underscores, and indeed follow a process of production that is more like film production than the cheaper, studio-based traditions of British television drama. *The Adventures of Sherlock Holmes* was an early example of this, each episode of which contained a score for chamber ensemble by Patrick Gowers. More recent serial costume dramas such as *Vanity Fayre* (1998, BBC/WGBH Boston) and *Great Expectations* (1999, BBC/WGBH Boston) included scores that in their sumptuousness and sheer volume of music could have been film scores. They included the release of the music on CD as a matter of course. Peter Salem's music for *Great Expectations* was striking, including a very quiet, delicate start to the drama, accompanied by images of marshes, and was seemingly radically different from the sort of dialogue-based, studio-shot BBC drama of over a decade earlier (which sometimes resembled nothing more than videotaped stage plays). Similarly, the music is wholly unlike the 'unsubtle' music that had been dominant in television. In fact, the intricacies of the music might well be lost on small television speakers, and although some experienced it on home-cinema systems, the availability of the music on CD provided an opportunity to hear the music 'complete' with full audio fidelity.

The large-scale BBC production for the turn of the millennium was an adaptation of Mervyn Peake's novel *Gormenghast* (2000), with music by two respected composers, Richard Rodney Bennett and John Tavener. While Bennett provided the incidental music, Tavener – who had an art music reputation but had come to a degree of popular prominence when a piece of his music was played at Princess Diana's funeral in 1997 – wrote the ritual music. This was fitting, and Tavener's music had a 'featured' quality within the drama, which positioned it as a sellable object, confirmed by the advertisement for the soundtrack CD broadcast as an appendix to each episode. While, on the one hand, this might be seen as a commodity cluster, on the other, it could be interpreted as a version of Richard Wagner's notion of the *Gesamtkunstwerk*, where a number of artistic aspects of the programme become an integrated complex. Emblematic of the way that large-scale grandiose orchestral music has become a featured and thus bankable aspect of recent British costume dramas are Adrian Johnston's sumptuous symphonic scores for the historical dramas *Shackleton* (2001, Granada) and Stephen Poliakoff's *The Lost Prince* (2002, BBC). Both were prestige productions, and needed to have 'prestige' music. The latter, a four-part serial about a son of King George V, was accompanied by a DVD and soundtrack CD, which were available for purchase the morning after the broadcast of the first episode. Both musical scores were distributed on the associated record label of the BBC and Channel Four Records (for Granada), while music for *The Lost Prince* was also published by the BBC. The style of music, while on the one hand vaguely reminiscent of some of Edward Elgar's music, arguably bears more resemblance to Geoffrey Burgon's incidental music for *Brideshead Revisited*.[26]

Another area of British television where marketable underscores appear prominently in television programmes is natural history. Like costume drama, these have become something of a flagship of BBC 'quality' production that have enjoyed great success in the international market, and consequently have used expensive-sounding musical scores. Nature programmes have increasingly commissioned specially written underscores that are characterised by 'symphonic' sounds, following the logic that big images and ideas (spectacles) need big-sounding music. One of the first to use music prominently was *The Trials of Life* (1990, BBC), which had music written by seasoned film composer George Fenton, including *The March of the Lobsters* to accompany a trail of lobsters crossing the sea bed.[27] However, apart from Fenton, the composers for natural history television programmes are not well known in the world of film music. *Alien Empire* (1996, BBC/Thirteen/WNET) was scored by Martin Kiszko, while faux-documentary *Walking with Dinosaurs* (1999, BBC) was scored by Ben Bartlett.[28] However, the undersea natural history epic miniseries *Blue Planet* (2001, BBC) had a score by George Fenton. His music used a notably traditional orchestral palette and style that worked as an effective counterpoint to some of the images (particularly the virtual 'science-fiction' images from the deep ocean). This might be seen as 'anchoring' the extraordinary images in familiar audiovisual style, while also having a respectable value as upmarket orchestral music, and a marketable status beyond the programme itself.

Musical Blocks

The use of repeated blocks of music is a cheaper option than commissioning an underscore to fit the dynamics across the whole programme. It is in effect a version or variant of having specific underscores written for individual programmes. This format was particularly suited to the series form, where the same characters (and often similar situations) would appear each week. Indeed, its economical and comprehensive format is probably most suited to long-form television drama. Block music scores can either be a selection of specially written pieces or they can be assembled from pre-existing library music, which will be discussed in the final section of this chapter. The use of a small repertoire of musical cues was evident in *Star Trek*, which initially commissioned scores for each episode, but then in later episodes reused that music to match the similar situations on screen. This is a very common process, where a couple of scores are written and then made into a library of musical cues. The effect of this is to provide musical cohesion for the programme through the regular repetition of the same pieces of music. The serial *Twin Peaks* (1990–1, Spelling/Lynch-Frost) used a relatively small number of musical pieces, written by Angelo Badalamenti. The repetition of these pieces provided some of *Twin Peaks'* distinctive character, as well as establishing leitmotifs for certain ideas within the serial.

Mission: Impossible (1966–73, Desilu/Paramount) had an initial score by Lalo Schifrin, which then was reused in blocks in later episodes. For example, 'The Plot' cue was used for action sequences in each episode, providing the tension music that accompanied the team as they fought against time and detection in order to complete a mission. The repeated music in each successive episode underlined the repetitive structure of the series format, where similar action would appear at roughly the same time in each episode, with exactly the same musical accompaniment.[29]

Gerry Anderson, usually in collaboration with his wife Sylvia Anderson, has been the most successful marionette animator in British television history. He produced a remarkable body of work. His programmes started with *Torchy the Battery Boy*, and went on to *Supercar, Fireball XL5, Stingray, Thunderbirds, Joe 90, Captain Scarlet, UFO* (live action), *The Secret Service, Space 1999* (live action), *Terrahawks* and *Space Precinct*. His marionette animation was very much based on a house style, and one crucial element in this was music, usually provided by Barry Gray.

Creative use of music was a feature of the programmes. *Fireball XL5* had a pop song on the titles (which was released as a single in October 1962), and singer Cliff Richard appeared as a puppet in a dream sequence in one of the *Thunderbirds* feature films, along with his backing group The Shadows (*Thunderbirds are Go!* [1966]). Barry Gray had been musical director for Vera Lynn's stage shows in the 1950s.[30] These children's action-adventure shows afforded him the possibility for experimentation. For example, the *Fireball XL5* theme used an ondes Martenot,[31] an electronic instrument that was a rarity in television music at the time and added a real 'space age' edge to the show. Gray's music differed radically from the sort of cartoon music produced by people such as Carl Stalling in Hollywood, which espoused mickeymousing, radical eclecticism and rapid-fire stylistic changes. Instead, Gray's music was more like the sort of music found in film drama, although it differed in its repetitive block usage. This meant the series had a consistency derived from the use of known pieces of music and styles, all of which were parodied. Pieces tended to focus on instrumental timbre, with an exaggeration of sound and style, which allowed for differentiation of sound and function.

The mode of production for these puppet dramas meant that the music was reused regularly across successive programmes. Indeed, Gray's music for *Supercar* (1960–1, AP Films/ATV/ITC) was also used in later Anderson series.[32] Ralph Titterton, curator of the Barry Gray tapes, sums up the musical mode of production: 'Though Barry wrote specific themes for certain episodes, . . . he also used the same material over and over from episode to episode, or (physically) cut musical phrases together to get the sequence he was looking for.'[33] *Captain Scarlet* uses a small number of musical passages, which were then repeated across each episode. This procedure supplies an essential musical character for the series, making it an absolutely integral part of the programme design. Gerry Anderson usually commissioned a main theme for the title sequence, after which the rest of each show's music would be a selection of variations on that theme.[34]

The music triggers emotional stock states as well as anchoring the situation on screen. Particular pieces signify tension or repose. Reused episode after episode, they thus insinuate themselves directly into the viewer's mind. As the audience for *Captain Scarlet* was largely children (at least, that is the way the programme was conceived), the music sets up a simple system of working, supplying recognisable pieces that match the repeated (well, *very* similar) situations that occur with each successive episode. So a small number of stock emotional reactions are elicited to fit a relatively small stock number of narrative scenarios.

In dramas that used puppets, the music to some degree compensates for the limited range of facial expressions, adding a further sense of emotion that was lacking in such 'wooden' drama. Along similar lines, the music also compensated for the lack of body movement, through establishing greater dynamism and sense of activity where, visually, there was very little. Visual activity and drama tended to be most evident in the programme's model shots, which often involved planes, cars and explosions, and were also regularly accompanied by the same musical pieces in successive episodes.

Gerry Anderson's productions are particularly useful for illustrating television strategies more generally and musical strategies more specifically. The fact that Anderson's succession of shows form a distinct progression, while retaining a core of key aspects, allows certain conclusions about television and television music to be extrapolated across other areas of television. However, in the 1970s, Anderson introduced human protagonists in his dramas, yet with little significant change in production strategy or programme character. In *Space 1999* (1975–7, ITC/Group3/ RAI), Anderson used human actors and accompanied the first series with impressive music that ranged from the electric guitar and disco beat of the title theme to

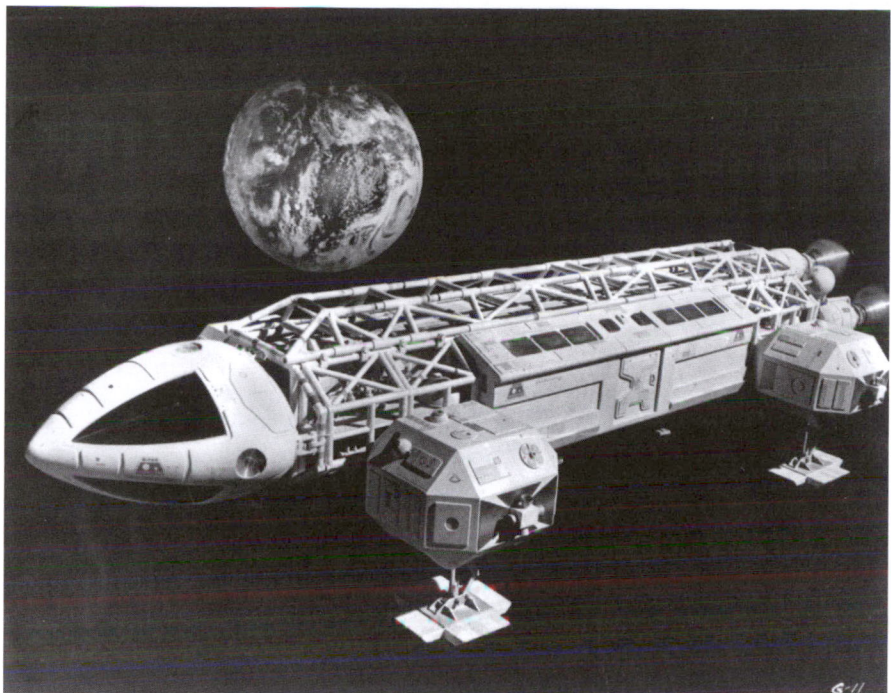

Space: 1999

the electronic space music of the end titles.[35] Gray provided a selection of often very short cues, some of just a few seconds' duration. Originally, Anderson had commissioned music for the series from Vic Elmes, who supplied some pop-inspired music, including the energetic disco-style part of the main titles.[36] Barry Gray was brought in to supply a more symphonic style of music. While on the surface the music for each episode seemed coherent, as if commissioned for the episode, it was either written by Gray to fit specific action or tracked, and picked not by Gray but by the programme's music editor Alan Willis. The early episodes 'Breakaway', 'Matter of Life and Death', 'Black Sun' and 'Another Time Another Place' were the only ones to be scored fully by Gray. Episodes such as 'War Games' and 'Death's Other Dominion' were constructed primarily from tracked cues: 'Barry Gray had only scored four of the five episodes of *Space: 1999* (Year One) with the remaining music culled from Gray's own back catalog and the Chappell, EMI and Delyse Envoy libraries.'[37] 'Dragon's Domain' used Albinoni's *Adagio*, a well-known popular classical piece that had also been used for the space-flight sequences in *Rollerball* (1975).[38] For its opening series, *Space 1999*'s music provided both a distinctive character for the programme and effective dynamics within each episode, although some of the cues were repeated regularly and some had been derived from elsewhere. However, under the tutelage of ex-*Star Trek* producer Fred Freiberger, the programme was reconfigured for the American market, and significant changes were instituted for the second series. On the musical side, Gray was not engaged for the second series, and the programme's music was provided by Derek Wadsworth, with some additional music written by Canadian-born composer Robert Farnon, who had been writing library and light music for decades.[39]

The repetition of musical blocks has a very particular effect in television programmes. The same musical cues appear for different action. However, what this demonstrates vividly is just how similar and repetitive screen action and narrative situations can be. We might theorise certain television programmes, drama in particular, as a stereotypical blueprint of narrative with the same stock situations each week. Consequently, the same car chase, gunfight or whatever can easily accommodate the same piece of stock music. In the vast majority of cases, audiences will fail to notice that the same piece of music appears over and over again. The use of repeated blocks might simply be seen as manifesting a cheaper version of the symphonic score's repeated themes. Indeed, the art of cheap television music is to make a small amount of music go a long way. Ralph Titterton notes that

> in the early years, Gray almost never fully scored a single episode [in this case, of *Supercar*] beyond the first. Instead, he would record bits and pieces for several episodes at once, tracking in whatever he could to get the most out of his meagre budgets (often he'd record overlays at home, performing most instruments himself).[40]

Gray's scores for Gerry Anderson's productions underline how formulaic action-based shows aimed at a child-youth audience could be. Yet within these constraints, the programmes managed a degree of subtlety and great invention. The same should be said of Barry Gray's music, which provided an essential character and more depth to the programmes. While television music largely has been the poorer and more cheaply made relation of film music, in television drama, the production values of film music have provided an optimum model, even if rarely met. The gradual change from live television to recorded programmes that began in the late 1950s instituted the model of the film score as what could and should be the sort of musical accompaniment to television drama. As was the case with television's cousin, radio drama, a common strategy was to commission music to accompany a few episodes of a series or serial and then use this music to 'track' the following episodes. In certain television programmes, such a small repertoire of musical pieces provided the essential character of the programme. In *Twin Peaks*, as already noted, Angelo Badalamenti wrote a small number of pieces. These were either repeated by being cut in to accompany the action, or were later rearranged slightly while retaining their essential character.[41]

Jeff Bond, in his book *The Music of Star Trek: Profiles in Style*, notes that in the late 1960s, the Musician's Union (in the USA) allowed repeats of music, as in *Star Trek*, but by the 1980s, when *Star Trek: The Next Generation*, *Voyager* and *Deep Space Nine* were made, the union's rules had changed, decreeing that with a few exceptions each programme must have music that has been written especially for it.[42] One of the *Star Trek* composers in the 1960s, Fred Steiner, pointed out that this union ruling

Star Trek

had the greatest influence on TV film scoring methods in that era. It allowed the producer to *reuse* any or all music recorded during a production season in other episodes filmed in that same season, as many times as he saw fit, without further payment to the musicians. However, he was not permitted to use tracks recorded during a previous season, or tracks from other series. Nor could he employ music from outside services, such as commercial recorded music libraries.[43]

The original series of *Star Trek* used five composers: Steiner, Alexander Courage (who also wrote the title theme), Sol Kaplan, Jerry Fielding and Gerald Fried. A number of the first episodes were scored and then subsequent episodes assembled musical accompaniment from the existing cues. Bond points to the perennial use of a cue called 'Ship in Orbit' (by Alexander Courage), a sedate version of the *Enterprise* fanfare over ascending chords, which first appeared in the episode 'Catspaw' from season 2. This was one of the most prominent musical pieces of the series, regularly appearing after advert breaks and over shots of the *Enterprise* in space. He also notes Fred Steiner's 'Ruk Attacks' and Courage's 'Vena's Dance' from the pilot episode 'The Cage',[44] while Sol Kaplan's suspense music from 'The Doomsday Machine' episode was reused for anticipation in tense situations on the bridge of the *Enterprise*. Bond's book provides a list of the library cues written for and used in the series from 1968 to 1969; there are fifty-one of them.[45] As already noted, the use of repeated music in this manner provided something of an essential character for a television series. Years later, on hearing a CD of incidental music from *Star Trek*, I was devastated to realise how familiar I was with music that I had heard as a child (admittedly from constantly repeated re-runs). This music had made an indelible impression on my musical memory. Viewings of the series itself produced at least as strong a memory of the incidental music as of the stories. This is a profoundly different form of screen incidental music from that in mainstream cinema, where a specially written score usually contributes to the impression of the uniqueness of the experience of that single film.

In the case of *Star Trek*, recorded musical cues that were not specifically linked to one piece of action were thus better suited as cues that could be reused, to be cut in by the music editor as blocks of music. As I have noted, the aesthetic assumption, derived partially from economic expediency, is that the stock music is perfectly suited to the stock situations that appear in such a series. Virtually every successive episode will have similar tense situations, perhaps fights, perhaps mystery. Thus, the music comes to represent the idea behind the action more than it supports the action itself. The logic is that whole series of programmes are based upon *stylisation*. In historical terms, this emanates from the increased dominance of the *series* in television production and scheduling in the 1960s – a format that is now overwhelmingly dominant. It is a structure that supplies its own formal and aesthetic logic. For a start, each programme begins with a problem, leading to danger, suspense, and a final showdown and story closure – the same every week!

Stock Music

The process of simply 'cutting in' stock or library music rather than writing music for the particular screen situation had existed since the early days of cinema. Silent films regularly created 'scores' from cobbled together excerpts of existing music, and ever since, the very low-budget sector of film production had rarely been able to afford composers to write music.[46] More recently, copyright laws have demanded that producers secure a 'synchronisation licence' (allowing the existing music to be synchronised with an image track) from the music's copyright holder, be it the composer, the publisher, record company or an agent of some sort. Library tracks, or 'bands' as they are sometimes called, can be assembled into a coherent 'score' for a programme or simply used in repeated blocks.

Like cheaply made films, television regularly had recourse to using library music, also known as stock music, which is then cut in to the programme, or 'tracked' as it is known in the industry. Pre-existing library music, like stock footage, is supplied by the metre, or in music's case by the minute. It would then be 'tracked' (or 'needle-dropped') into the sequence where it was required. Stock music has proved profitable for certain music companies who have sold 'music by the minute'. One such British company is DeWolfe, who have large rosters of 'canned' music, some of which is officially 'unauthored', while large music publisher Chappell also has a lucrative trade in stock music. While such companies paid composers to write music to fit 'stock' situations in television, these pieces were almost never credited.[47] Cheap films and television, and almost all industrial screen culture (such as training films), will use library music. They tend to use it very occasionally, often repeating the same piece of music they have paid for.[48] Stock music is not written to fit a particular piece of television, but has been composed beforehand (and possibly used many times already), before it is simply edited into the final programme. It is unlike the overwhelming majority of context-specific feature film music, and is usually written blind, without the benefit of images. The use of stock music has been commonplace in cheaply made films both during the classical Hollywood era and since. It was also common in radio drama, and then in turn became a principal means of providing music for television. The strategy of using stock music emanated from budgetary restrictions as much as, if not more so, reasons of aesthetic control. Stock music is the aural equivalent of stock visual footage. Some television programmes consist of musical cues that have been written especially for the programme but are then reused in a stock manner, sometimes as a supplement to newly written music (as in many of the earlier episodes of *Star Trek*) or as a small repertoire of musical cues that are used systematically (as in *Thunderbirds* [1964–6, AP] or *Twin Peaks*, as already noted).

Apart from very cheaply made films and television programmes, almost all training films/videos and other bargain basement audiovisual culture will be furnished with stock music. One clear benefit is that no specialised musical knowledge is required to endow the images with music, although it may be an advantage. In certain cases, stock music written by different composers can be assembled into what resembles a coherent musical 'score'. Examples of this include British dramas *The Avengers* (1961–9, ABC Weekend/ABPC)[49] and *Randall and Hopkirk (Deceased)* (1969–71, ITC), *Dallas* (1978–91, Lorimar) and *Perry Mason* (1957–66, CBS/TCF), the latter of which used music from the CBS music library, including many cues written by Bernard Herrmann. During the Hollywood strike in the 1980s, British-written stock music was imported for use in American shows such as *Dallas*. In the 1980s and 1990s, Australian soap opera *Neighbours* (1985– , Grundy) used only occasional blasts of stock incidental music that was supplied by 'Mushroom Records' until Sony recently took over. The same company still supplies stock music for *Home and Away* (1988– , Red Heat/Network 7/Southern Star).

The CBS TV music library was founded in 1956, based upon retaining a number of pieces of music that could be reused in subsequent television programmes. CBS reused music from its own dramatic productions (both radio and television) from as far back as the 1930s (which had to be recorded, as the original music had been played live). This large body of music provided a significant musical resource for reuse in CBS programmes. Some of this music was written by prominent film composers such as Herrmann, Dimitri Tiomkin and Lyn Murray, all of whom at one time worked with Alfred Hitchcock. Herrmann composed *Outer Space Suite* and *Western Suite* in 1957, as part of CBS's pool of generic cues, which were composed and recorded without any particular programme in mind. Television shows that used this library music included the Westerns *Fort Laramie*, *Gunsmoke* and *Rawhide*, the science-fiction series *The Twilight Zone* and the detective series *Perry Mason*. The majority of the music in *The Fugitive* (1963–7, ABC) was derived from the CBS music library, while other programmes that took advantage of the library included *Wild Wild West* (1965, CBS) and *Hawaii Five-O* (1968, CBS).[50]

In his book *The Music of Star Trek*, Jeff Bond describes both the process and effect of tracking episodes with stock music, although the music was written especially for the series:

> One of the reasons the music of the original *Star Trek* is so deeply embedded in our memories (whether we realise it consciously or not) is the matter of simple repetition. . . . the musical cues themselves were repeated endlessly, not just in ensuing episodes, but often several times within the *same* episode.[51]

So the same cues are regularly used for different action, meaning that stock music fits stock situations, and was the logical choice for standardised genre drama, particularly in the series format that now dominates television.[52] There is, therefore, a tendency for many series episodes to appear as a basic blueprint of narrative with stock situations, as illustrated by their recourse to the same stock music cues at similar moments. In other words, stock music can reveal just how stock the dramatic situation might be. Indeed, it can tend towards stylisation, as illustrated by *Twin Peaks*, where the repeated repertoire of musical cues played an absolutely central role in defining the character of the programme and its unsettling processes.[53] Angelo Badalamenti's music was written as distinct pieces with their own internal musical logic and then simply cut in to the action of the programme. The album of cues was released part of the way through the first series, while a handful of cues was added for the second series, much of which was tracked from the first.

In the 1960s, musical pieces from purpose-produced stock music albums such as Trevor Duncan's *Synchro Stings* were cut into dramatic programmes as a commonplace dramatic device. For example, British science-fiction serial *Doctor Who* included one completely self-enclosed 25-minute episode that functioned as a taster for a later story. 'Mission to the Unknown' (tx. 1965) had no sustained music, and simply utilised a few bursts of stock music as 'stingers' to underline shock and add dramatic sound flourishes to match the on-screen action. All of these were taken from the *Synchro Stings* album. During the 1960s, *Doctor Who* used stock music in many episodes, although a fair proportion had music written especially for them. 'Inferno' (1970) was the last story in the show's history to be tracked with stock music.[54] Two of the most significant pieces among those used were 'Blue Veils and Golden Sands' and 'The Delian Mode' (which appeared twice), both of which were composed and realised by Delia Derbyshire. They are both *musique concrète* pieces, in which a prominent element of the former was treated taped cymbal sounds. Derbyshire was a pioneer of electronic and experimental music in the context of broadcasting, notably at the BBC Radiophonic Workshop, and the pieces had been created some time before the production of 'Inferno'. Indeed, 'The Delian Mode' had appeared on an internal BBC disc called *BBC Radiophonic Workshop* some two years earlier.[55] Another programme that ran concurrently, the bizarre and surreal television serial *The Prisoner*, not only shared some of these music practices, but also some of the composers of stock music. For example, different stock pieces written by Paul Bonneau appear in the *Doctor Who* story 'Tomb of the Cybermen' (tx. 1967) and *The Prisoner* stories 'The Chimes of Big Ben' and 'Dance of the Dead', both of which used the Chappell music library despite being produced by different television channels (the BBC, and ITC for commercial television).

All stock music in *The Prisoner* was from the Chappell library. 'The Chimes of Big Ben' used Jack Beaver's 'Spaceways' as Nadia escapes by swimming (the same piece was used in the episode 'Checkmate'), Beaver's 'Ionosphere' for the crate journey, Robert Farnon's 'Zero Minus Sixty' as a dinghy is used for escape, Paul Bonneau's 'Tropical Forest' as Number Six cuts down a tree, Bonneau's 'A Child's Lullaby' for a late-night drink and Philip Green's 'Awkward Squad' as the tune that Number Six says he hates (and which I discuss in this book's introduction).

Along with original compositions by Ron Grainer, Wilfred Josephs and Albert Elms, music editor Eric Mival (and on some, Robert Dearburg) chose the music, and it was cut in by John S. Smith.[56] According to Robert Langley, Mival was made music editor when Dearburg left the project. He familiarised himself with the Chappell library. He first worked on the penultimate episode, and procured the use of The Beatles's 'All You Need Is Love' for £48 for the final episode.[57] The programme was dominated by bizarre fairground music, humorous and playful music, ironic music, nursery rhyme-inspired and childish music (such as the musical box-style 'Art Class' written by Elms for *The General*), etc. The music for *The Prisoner* was hardly a commonplace dramatic score, a reflection that it was far from a normal dramatic television series.

Tough British copshow *The Sweeney* (1975–8, Euston Films) used a selection of music from different libraries: KPM (Keith Prowse Music), DeWolfe, Regency, Bruton and Chappell. *The Sweeney* not only bought tracks from their existing libraries, but also commissioned them to produce new pieces of music for the programme. A few of these library pieces became regulars on the show, such as 'Flying Squad' (by Brian Bennett), which was used for car chases, and 'The Big Fuzz' (by Johnny Pearson), which regularly accompanied the fist fights. Despite the disparate origins of some of the music, the tendency towards a homogeneous style in the cues – funky bass riffs, jazz/big band brass, synthesizer loops, organs, flutes and electric guitars – gave a sense of unity to the music that seemed to match the distinctive character of the programme.[58]

In relation to composition of music for television advertisements, Nicholas Cook notes that

> Traditionally, musicians compose with notes, rhythms, and perhaps timbres. Only with post-modernism has the idea of 'composing with styles' or 'composing with genres' emerged, at least as a consciously adopted procedure. But composing with styles or genres is one of the most basic musical techniques found in television commercials. . . . Musical styles and genres offer unsurpassed opportunities for communicating complex social or attitudinal messages practically

instantaneously. . . . Commercials often contain music that almost completely lacks 'content' as a music theorist would generally define it – that is, distinctive melodic, harmonic, or rhythmic shaping – but incorporates a musical logic based on style.[59]

Certainly, television composition has called for composers who are able to invoke a number of different styles and sounds that might be seen as more important than the actual melodies, harmonies and rhythmic schemes involved. Indeed, with stock music, where this process is most apparent, adding music to the screen could be performed by non-trained musicians (or even 'non-musicians'), wielding pre-existing blocks of music that may be stock, composed not to match screen action or derived from elsewhere.

Conclusion

During the late 1990s, soundtrack CDs for television dramas became widely available, even if they were unlikely to prove massively successful. In 1999, a BBC production of Robert McLiam Wilson's novel *Eureka Street* was screened with a simultaneous CD release. The conclusion of the three-part miniseries was an extraordinary audiovisual stylistic flourish. Jake, the drama's protagonist, stands on the roof of his house and surveys Belfast. The camera makes a slow 360-degree long-take pan, accompanied by a startling piece of music that is based on droning Celtic-style electric guitars, and builds to a dynamic climax with the entry of a guitar rhythm over the programme's end titles. The music is accompanied by Jake's poetic extra-diegetic voiceover, and an impressive shot that starts with a crane shot leaving a downstairs window and alighting on the roof of the building for the circular vista, and then ends with the appearance of Jake's face in shot. It was a jamboree of audiovisual style with which to conclude the drama, and contrasted markedly with the styles of contiguous television programmes. But did it reflect television aesthetics or aesthetics derived more from the cinema? Rather than the influence of film style, its richness might be explained more by the fact that this startling set piece was readily usable as an advertisement for the programme (and presumably as a selling point to overseas television broadcasters). The distinctive character of the music was indispensable to the sequence.

On certain occasions, television has required more expensive (and more expensive-sounding) music. In the late 1950s, Southern Television commissioned Richard Addinsell, the well-known composer of *The Warsaw Concerto*, to write the 'Southern Rhapsody'. This piece was used daily to signal the start of broadcasting, and represented a fairly substantial, 'classical' high-class opening for a commercial television station that seemed, at the time, downmarket in relation to the BBC. More recently, the most obvious examples of this trend would be British costume dramas and natural history programmes, both of which have exploited expensive orchestral scores to attain 'quality' status. Increasingly, the production of more expensive television drama, inspired by the possibility of higher financial returns through overseas sales and sell-through on video and DVD, has led to an infiltration of the more traditional styles of television by the more upmarket modes of film. This development of 'film style' on television is most evident in the increasing aestheticisation of television visuals, through more expensive-looking camerawork, lighting and especially music. The previously dominant natural-ism, with its aim for an unspectacular and thus 'invisible' audiovisual style, increasingly has been displaced by an aesthetic derived more from the cinema, with high produc-tion values, camerawork that is more than merely functional and opulent music.

It is possible to trace a historical trajectory over the last fifty years or so. In the 1950s, technological limitations kept most television (drama included) a live prop-osition. The increasing use of videotape from the late 1950s onwards led to a record-ing ethos, which allowed for a massive increase in the possibilities for the use of music in programmes. As we have seen, it also meant that productions began more closely to resemble film productions, which was compounded later by the develop-ment of international markets in film and television. This allowed for more expens-ive television productions, which often used their high production values as an important selling point. Starting in the 1980s, television drama production began to move almost wholesale into film production. In Britain, this was evidenced by Channel Four's 'Film on Four' slot and BBC 2's 'Screen 2'. Hardly a British film was released that was not a co-production with Channel Four, and many of them evince a tangible mixture of television traditions with film style.[60]

The use of blocks and stock music underlines the importance of the music editor at the expense of the composers of the music. On the other hand, the type of musi-cal underscore that is constructed by a composer to fit the specificities of television drama derives more from the sort of blueprint offered by film music. While television and cinema are superficially similar, actually they present very different contexts. Per-haps some of the aesthetic strategies (music included) are the same, and, indeed, people tend to watch (and hear) films more on television sets than in the cinema, but the contexts' radical difference means that some film music sounds overwhelming and perhaps even a little ridiculous in a home environment. The fact that televisions were almost always equipped with a very small speaker set clear limitations on the ambi-tions of music on television, and indeed on television sound more generally. The grad-ual proliferation of home-cinema set-ups with multiple speakers including woofers (specialist bass speakers) means that television, to a certain extent, will catch up with the sort of sonic experience offered by cinema (and for which many of the films on television were designed). This is inevitable, in that the cheap, rough-and-ready live-inspired immediacy that has been a traditional and remarkable attribute of television increasingly has been displaced by an aesthetic of 'quality', derived from the higher audiovisual standards of cinema, and enabled by the continuing convergence of tele-vision with the film and DVD industries, not to mention with the music industries. This will mean louder and more powerful, as well as more subtle, music in the future. According to Philip Tagg, television programmes account for over a quarter of all the music we hear.[61] This is a startling statistic, and emphasises that while television music may often appear facile, commonplace and everyday, it is extraordinarily per-vasive, compounding its status as music that aspires to influence its listeners.

Notes

1 Bernadette Casey, *et al.*, *Television Studies: The Key Concepts* (London: Arnold, 2001); John Corner, *Critical Ideas in Television Studies* (Oxford: Oxford University Press, 1999).

2 John Ellis, *Visible Fictions: Film, Television, Video* (London: Routledge, 1982); John Fiske, *Television Culture* (London: Routledge, 1987).

3 A key aspect of television, which provided the title for Jason Jacobs, *The Intimate Screen: Early British Television Drama* (Oxford: Oxford University Press, 2000).

4 Raymond Williams, *Television: Technology and Cultural Form* (London: Fontana, 1974); John Caughie, 'The Rush of the Real: An Aesthetic of Immediacy' in *Television Drama: Realism, Modernism and British Culture* (Oxford: Oxford University Press, 2000), pp. 88–125; Jane Feuer, 'The Concept of Live Television: Ontology as Ideology' in E. Ann Kaplan, ed., *Regarding Television. Critical Approaches – An Anthology* (New York: AFI, 1983).

5 John Ellis refers to the key televisual structure of 'segmentation', where it is constantly divided into smaller units. *Visible Fictions*, p. 112.

6 Robin Nelson, *TV Drama in Transition: Forms, Values and Cultural Change* (Basingstoke, Hants: Macmillan, 1997), p. 24.

7 Williams, *Television: Technology and Cultural Form*, p. 78.

8 John Fiske, *Television Culture* (London: Routledge, 1987), p. 74.

9 Ellis, *Visible Fictions*, p. 128.

10 Rick Altman, 'Television/Sound' in Tania Modleski, ed., *Studies in Entertainment: Critical Approaches to Mass Culture* (Bloomington: Indiana University Press, 1986), p. 42.

11 Yet we should always remember that large tracts of television schedules are made up of feature films made for cinematic exhibition.

12 For a further discussion, see Philip Tagg, *Kojak – 50 Seconds of Television Music: Toward the Analysis of Affect in Popular Music* (Gothenberg: Musikvetenskapliga Institute, University of Gothenberg, 1979).

13 Jeff Bond, *The Music of Star Trek: Profiles in Style* (Los Angeles: Lone Eagle, 1999), p. 36.

14 Jeff Berkwits, 'Graeme Revell – Journeys to *Dune*' [interview], *Soundtrack*, vol. 19, no. 76, Winter 2000, p. 5.

15 Jeremy G. Butler notes that an organ was the common accompaniment for soap operas, much like it had been for their radio forerunners. *Television: Critical Methods and Applications* (Belmont, CA: Wadsworth, 1994), p. 211.

16 In other cases, single musicians record and perform more complex music, such as Mark Snow's individual scores for each episode of the *X-Files*, which used electronic keyboards to produce subtle and acclaimed non-diegetic accompaniment, and was also made available on CD as *The Truth and the Light: Music from the X-Files* (Warner Bros. 46279). Yet Snow developed this music through improvising at the keyboard to the video images. Richard Davies, *Complete Guide to Film Scoring* (Boston, MA: Berklee Press, 1999), p. 351.

17 See, for example, Neil Postman, *Amusing Ourselves to Death: Public Discourse in the Age of Show Business* (London: Viking, 1986).

18 Tagg, *Kojak – 50 Seconds of Television Music*. Excerpt available at <www.mediamusicstudies.net/tagg/udem/musimgmot/filmfunx.html> (accessed 27 March 2004).

19 Butler, *Television: Critical Methods and Applications*, pp. 191–2.

20 Music was not central to the 'sense of the real world' that film-makers such as John Grierson wished to bring to cinema documentaries. Brian MacFarlane, *An Autobiography of British Cinema: By the Actors and Filmmakers Who Made It* (London: Methuen, 1997), p. 251.

21 On special occasions, and when more money is spent on such episodes, musical strategies change. *EastEnders* included interludes in Spain, when Peggy attended ex-husband Frank's funeral (28–9 January 2002), and in the Christmas episodes when Jamie was dying in a hospital bed (24–5 December 2002). On these occasions, the programme's usual documentary realist origins were eclipsed by the drama of tension drones and Christmas carols used as sound bridges.

22 It is interesting to note that a year later, Pink Floyd's experimental soundscape/song-cycle album *Dark Side of the Moon* was embraced by popular record buyers, making it one of the best-selling records of all time.

23 David J. Howe, Mark Stammers and Stephen James Walker, *Doctor Who: The Seventies* (London: Virgin, 1994), p. 51.

24 David J. Howe and Stephen James Walker, *Doctor Who: The Television Companion* (London: BBC, 1999), p. 226.

25 Unidentified radio interview, BBC Radio 3, *c.* 1985.

26 It might even be compared to the mock-classicism of the theme music to *Dynasty*. The melody is strangely reminiscent of John Williams's main theme for *Jurassic Park* (1994).

27 K. J. Donnelly, 'A Ramble through the Margins of the Cityscape: The Postmodern as the Return of Nature' in Michael Dear and Steven Flusty, eds., *Spaces of Postmodernity: Readings in Human Geography* (Oxford: Blackwell, 2002), p. 33.

28 Cf. K. J. Donnelly, 'Walking with Dinosaurs' in Glen Creeber, ed., *100 Television Programmes* (London: Arnold, 2003).

29 Including individual musical pieces assigned to some of the main characters, and an exciting jazz-rock edge to the music, most memorably the percussion and brass-led title theme in 5/4 time.

30 Simon Archer and Stan Nicholls, *Gerry Anderson: The Authorised Biography* (London: Legend, 1996), p. 34.

31 Ibid., p. 66.

32 David Hirsch, 'CD Microbreweries Part 1: Fanderson Records', *Soundtrack*, vol. 10, no. 76, Winter 2000, p. 17.

33 Ibid, p. 17.

34 Archer and Nicholls, *Gerry Anderson*, p. 55.

35 Interestingly, in 1975 an Italian film *Spazio 1999* was released on video. It comprised 'Breakaway', 'Ring around the Moon' and 'Another Time, Another Place' edited into an 88-minute feature, and with music by Ennio Morricone.

36 Elmes recorded the guitar, bass guitar and drums of the title theme with John McCoy and Liam Genockey (later in the group Gillan with the ex-Deep Purple singer). 'The Vic Elmes Interview', <www.geocities.com/Area51/Jupiter/1630/vhelms.html> (accessed 20 April 2003).

37 Hirsch, 'CD Microbreweries', p. 18.

38 The combination of the images of space and existing classical music makes it reminiscent of *2001: A Space Odyssey.*

39 'Five episodes out of 24 were again scored for the second series, though Wadsworth wrote considerably more music, some tracks going unused or partially used until later episodes. Farnon's "How Tender is the Night" was tracked into episode "New Adam New Eve".' Hirsch, 'CD Microbreweries', p. 18. ('How Tender Is the Night' was not originally written for *Space 1999*.)

40 Ibid., p. 17.

41 As is quite common with television series music, *Twin Peaks* was tracked from the scored first couple of episodes, although Badalamenti also wrote 'new' additional music for later episodes. Kathryn Kalinak, ' "Disturbing the Guests with This Racket": Music and *Twin Peaks*' in David Lavery, ed., *Full of Secrets: Critical Approaches to Twin Peaks* (Detroit: Wayne State University Press, 1994), pp. 90ff.

42 Bond, *Music of Star Trek*, p. 34.

43 Fred Steiner, 'Music for *Star Trek*: Scoring a Television Show in the Sixties' in Iris Newsom, ed., *Wonderful Inventions: Motion Pictures, Broadcasting and Recorded Sound at the Museum of Congress* (Washington: Museum of Congress, 1985) [no page number supplied], quoted in Bond, *Music of Star Trek*, pp. 34–5.

44 Ibid., p. 36.

45 Ibid., pp. 54–5.

46 This technique has been used in cinema serials of the 1930s, such as *Flash Gordon*, which used tracked music, some from *Bride of Frankenstein*. Franz Waxman's organ waltz that accompanied the monster's meeting with Pretorius in the crypt was used for the clay men section of the serial. His music for the episode in which the bride is 'charged up' to life is used for the sequence of the demonstration of the 'death dust' to Emperor Ming in *Flash Gordon Conquers the Universe* (1940). Both were produced by Universal.

47 For example, the documentary *It Shouldn't Happen to a Children's Television Presenter* (1999, LWT) simply credited DeWolfe for the programme's music.

48 Upon the DVD release of the 1963 production *Doctor Who: The Aztecs* in 2002, I was intrigued to find that it included an extra episode with a totally new soundtrack in Arabic, including different music. To my great surprise, the first piece of incidental music that appeared on the soundtrack was the same stock mystery cue used prominently in *The Singing Detective* in 1986.

49 *The Avengers* mixed newly written underscore with library music, as well as repeating cues regularly, as, most obviously, in the use of the same piece of epilogue music in each episode.

50 Almost all of these pieces were recorded outside the USA in order to avoid reuse fees, to be paid to the musicians' union. Bernard Herrmann's *Twilight Zone* episodes include small ensembles: for example, 'Living Doll' was for two harps, celesta and bass clarinet; 'Ninety Years without Slumbering' was for seven musicians (two clarinets, bass clarinet, oboe, flute, vibraphone and harp); yet the opening episode 'Where Is Everybody' was scored for a 33-piece small orchestra. Christopher Husted, sleeve notes to Bernard Herrmann, *The Twilight Zone*, conducted by Joel McNeely (Varese Sarabande VSD2 6087, released 1999).

51 Bond, *Music of Star Trek*, p. 34.

52 Nelson, *TV Drama in Transition*, p. 1.

53 Kalinak, 'Disturbing the Guests with This Racket', p. 90.

54 Andrew Pixley, 'DWM Archive: Inferno', *Doctor Who Magazine*, no. 305, 2001, p. 41.

55 Ibid.

56 Karen Langley, sleeve notes to *The Prisoner, Volume 3* (Silva Screen CD FILMCD126, released 1992).

57 Robert Langley, sleeve notes to *The Prisoner File #1* (Silva Screen CD FILMCD601, released 2002).

58 The title theme, for example, has a jazz-rock edge to it, mixing wah wah guitar with a jazz-based brass-dominated ensemble. It was written by Joe South and performed by the Joe South Orchestra.

59 Nicholas Cook, 'Music and Meaning in the Commercials', *Popular Music*, vol. 13, no. 1, 1994, p. 35.

60 An example is the film *Rita, Sue and Bob Too* (1986), which was directed by Alan Clarke, who had made his reputation in television dramas. Although filmic in scale, it was based on the small ensemble acting, location shooting and fluid documentary camerawork evident in social realist television drama in slots like the BBC's *Play for Today* in the 1970s. It contained a minimal amount of music.

61 Philip Tagg, 'TV Music: Quick Fixes, Semiotics and the Democratic Right to Know', paper presented at the Stockholm 'Music and Manipulation' conference in 1999, p. 3. Available on <www.tagg.org/texts.html> (accessed 20 April 2003).

Chapter 7

Music on Television 2: Pop Music's Colonisation of Television

Not only has the use of music under dialogue proliferated on television in recent years, but it also happens to be pop music rather than the sort of incidental music traditional to television. Indeed, pop music is now the dominant form of stock music used on British television. In fact, it is often the more esoteric edge of pop/rock music that has proved itself well suited to continuity sections and as incidental music. Increasingly, it has filled expanding continuity and advertising spaces. Production companies have their own music libraries, and some record companies use 'song sourcers' to place songs on television and in these libraries for repeated use.[1] The licensing of pop music for screen use is increasingly important for the music industry, spawning a form of 'multipurpose music' that, as well as being music in its own right, can also be resold as stock music (also known as library music) for television. While in the 1980s there was a rush to tie in pop music with films, from the late 1990s, increasingly this strategy has moved to television.

As noted in the previous chapter, television is dominated by moments of climactic drama among its fragmentation within a continuous 'flow'.[2] This requires that certain moments are emphasised, noted as significant, monumentalised and aestheticised. Pop music has proved adept at all of these, although its principal usage in recent years has been as an aestheticisation, adding depth and colour to information-laden continuity sections between programmes and aiding moments of reflection in news programmes and documentaries. Pop music is now dominant as stock music on television, filling the expansion of continuity and advertising spaces, and indicating the degree of industrial integration and collaboration between the television and music industries. It also appears regularly in the title spaces of television programmes, and, indeed, there are few areas it has not colonised. This process provides a particular dynamic, as pop songs are readymades, already existing pieces that might be known already.

Banzai (2001, Channel Four/Radar), a pseudo-oriental betting show that used regular excerpts from pop/rock music to accompany its fragmented visuals, also had a soundtrack album. In the episode transmitted on 14 February 2002, I noted music that included: Minnie Ripperton's 'Loving You', Sweet's 'Love Is Like Oxygen', UFO's 'Doctor Doctor', Sparks's 'Number One Song in Heaven', John Miles's 'Music', Visage's 'Fade to Grey', Genesis's 'Deep in the Motherlode', Jeff Wayne's *War of the Worlds* and Sky's 'Toccata' (an arrangement of Bach's *Toccata and Fugue* in D minor, BWV 565). The episode also included film and television theme music such as Stanley Myers's 'Cavatina' from *The Deer Hunter*, John Carpenter's 'Assault on Precinct 13', Dudley Simpson's theme for *Blake's Seven* and Edwin Astley's for *Return of the Saint*. This selection not only clearly demonstrates the pop literacy of those who choose the music for television programmes, but also betrays the eclecticism and cut-and-paste mentality that has been associated with dance music culture and promoted by computer software.

In situations where there is an absence or paucity of diegetic sound, music has become the norm. This was illustrated by television prank show *Trigger Happy TV* (2000–1, Channel Four/Absolutely). Each piece of footage from a hidden camera would be coupled with excerpts from a pop song. This included accompanying similar situations with the same song excerpt, such as the regular appearance of a non-painting portrait painter in Trafalgar Square to the sound of the opening of Gordon Lightfoot's 'If You Could Read My Mind'. The success of using pop music as stock music for the programme led to three best-selling *Trigger Happy TV* compilation CDs. The first one contained a broad selection of songs, none of which appear on any of the *Now That's What I Call Music* series of mainstream chart-hit compilation albums, instead comprising a slightly esoteric selection, running from the Television Personalities's 'I Know Where Syd Barrett Lives' to the Beta Band's 'Dr Baker'. It was released on a record label that had recently been formed to exploit stock pop music as tie-ins: a subsidiary of Channel Four television called Channel Four Music.

Television and Pop Music

Popular music has always been important for television, and since the 1960s, pop and rock music have gradually asserted themselves on a medium that never fully embraced their possibilities. Pop music's significance for television was demonstrated in two key British television dramas of the 1960s, *Up the Junction* (1965, BBC) and *Cathy Come Home* (1966, BBC), both of which were broadcast in the

Wednesday Play slot and directed by Ken Loach. These use pop songs to engage with a 'real', contemporary and rough and ready social space, as well as an emotional and modal space. In *Cathy Come Home*, Tony Garnett and Ken Loach's acclaimed drama, pop songs appear consistently as non-diegetic music, as a way of establishing a sense of the everyday to the action and complementing the drama-documentary techniques used by the programme.[3] Near the start, Ben E. King's hit record 'Stand by Me', released a few years earlier, accompanies footage of the young couple, Cathy and Reg, kissing. Some of this is obscured by tree foliage, giving the impression that this is an actual event shot secretly. The inclusion of a romantic pop song rather than orchestral music suggests something of the everyday character of the couple and the normality of their love, rather than portraying them as something special.[4]

In a way, this technique might be construed as bearing more resemblance to film aesthetics than the traditions of television drama, particularly as pop songs were starting to be used as non-diegetic music accompanying action in films at the time.[5] At this point, however, it was still something of a rarity in British television to use pop music in this manner. *Cathy Come Home* used a significant number of pop songs, firmly embedding the drama in the materiality of contemporaneous Britain, where pop music was becoming an increasingly prominent part of popular culture. One of the avatars of this development, The Beatles, had already made their own films, starting with *A Hard Day's Night* (1964). Later in the decade, they moved into television. The Beatles's *Magical Mystery Tour* (first tx. 26 December 1967, BBC 1) is premised upon the group performing a selection of new songs.[6] In this way, it is like a musical film, a style that is emphasised in the staging of 'Your Mother Should Know', in which the group perform in suits in a choreographed line and descend a staircase. The instrumental piece 'Flying' is more of an excuse for abstract accompanying images, including tinted landscapes that reputedly were originally shot for *2001: A Space Odyssey*. This makes it seem less of a set-piece song sequence. In terms of incidental music, the programme used an instrumental arrangement of The Beatles's song 'All My Loving' as non-diegetic accompaniment to the romantic sequence between Aunt Jessica and tour compère Buster Bloodvessel. Later, at what appears to be a fair, where a tug-of-war is taking place, the mechanical organ plays an arrangement of another of the group's hits, 'She Loves You'. Background music, in these cases, plays upon the audience's knowledge of the group's hits from previous years. The Beatles illustrated vividly how film and television could be subordinated to another cultural aspect – music. *Magical Mystery Tour*, while something of an aesthetic *mélange*, demonstrated how easily film aesthetics could be imported to television aesthetics. Without the pop songs, it surely would never have been considered for broadcast, as it received an extremely negative response from reviewers at the time.[7]

Apart from television shows that featured pop music performances, the appearance of songs usually meant rearranged and re-recorded versions by studio musicians. A drama series about a radio station, *WKRP in Cincinnati* (1978–82, MTM), was one of the first programmes to feature music by original artists rather than soundalikes.[8] Television producers discovered that utilising pop music was not the expense they had imagined. This was also at a time when record companies were starting to look for other arenas in which to make money (with MTV and widespread film tie-ins developing over the next few years), and a time when the desire was awakening to make money from old back catalogues (realised later with the coming of CDs).[9]

In the early 1980s, *Miami Vice* (1984–9, Universal TV) set a precedent of having stylish visuals accompanied by contemporary pop music, and it succeeded in moving pop music from a television ghetto of its own making. *Miami Vice* was a show that was not simply pop music-based, as had been *The Monkees* (1966–8, NBC) (and more recently has been the case with British pop group series S Club 7, in *Miami 7* [1999, BBC], *L.A. 7* [2000, BBC] and *S Club 7 in Hollywood* [2001, BBC]), but included pop music as an integrated element of mainstream television, be it drama, documentary or advertisement. *Ally McBeal* (1997– , Fox Television/David E. Kelley) has made a feature of its 'musical' sequences, where characters dance to music only they (and the audience) can hear. If they are interrupted by anyone, the music ceases with the sound of a vinyl record having the arm scratchily ripped away. This music has become an important and defining aspect of the show, perhaps most notably the non-diegetic and subjective appearance of Barry White's 'You're the First, the Last, My Everything' for the John Cage character. This clearly demonstrates pop music's social and iconic status, while illustrating the common elision of its historical status (it was released in 1974). *Ally McBeal* also featured what was meant to be live music in a bar at the end of the show. These songs were performed diegetically by Vonda Shepard, and were made available on CDs tied to the programme. The featured status of pop music in programmes like this is underlined by the production of special 'musical' episodes of series such as *Xena, Warrior Princess* (1995–2001, Universal/MCA), *Lexx* (1997, TiMe/Salter Street/Silverlight) and *Buffy the Vampire Slayer* (1997–2003, Mutant Enemy/Fox). Robin Nelson notes that recently there has been a

> discernible shift in the soundscape. Popular music on radio has become a dominant feature of (post)modern life. Correspondingly music soundtrack features more in television drama than in the past when a stricter naturalism precluded non-diegetic sound. Traditionally music is used, as in film, to mask visual edits by sustaining a rhythmic structure of sound or to create atmosphere or underscore the mood of the action. As TV drama has drifted away from sense-making narrative structures, to looser compilations reflecting new patterns of production and consumption, however, music is increasingly used for the sake of its own appeal and only loosely related to the dramatic action.[10]

Music doubtless has become more prominent in British television drama, bringing it stylistically more in line with US television. This development is as much to do with the rise in screen music as an elevated cultural item as increased budgets.

On current British television, it is the norm to hear pop music being used in the place of what would likely have been traditional stock music even a decade ago. On the evening of Saturday 2 February 2002, during a fifteen-minute viewing of the most popular terrestrial television channel (ITV 1, Midlands-Carlton), I heard 'Flawless' by The Ones used to accompany images and voiceover in the programme *It Shouldn't Happen to a . . . Soap Star*. This had only been in the pop charts a month earlier. At the end of the programme, during a short commercial break, the *Sunday Times* had placed an advertisement for the following day's issue, which included a guide to cars, to the accompaniment of The Stereophonics's 'Have a Nice Day'. This was followed by a preview of the new series of police show *The Vice*, which was a montage of dramatic images accompanied by an instrumental section of Death in Vegas's 'Soul Auctioneer' from *The Contino Sessions*. After this break, at 10.30, the evening's football coverage *The Premiership* started, with a montage of football action accompanied by U2's 'Beautiful Day'.

Over the past few years, pop music – and in many cases pop music of a very distinct kind – has been sprinkled liberally across continuity segments on British television. These sections provide a bridge between television programmes, offering preview tasters of forthcoming programmes and supplying other information. While on independent (commercial) television, these are part of the commercial break, on the BBC, with its direct licence-fee funding, these segments have taken on something of a character of their own, although they are modelled upon the advertising break of commercial television. From late 2001 into 2002, the BBC used The Dandy Warhols's contemporaneous single 'Bohemian Like You' in some of its previews. The song had already gained some prominence on a television advertisement for a mobile phone company, a fact that was indicated on a sticker attached to the single cover informing buyers that it was the music from that specific ad. Despite its very distinct temporal structure (a classic song form) and words that reference an elsewhere, the song could be decontextualised enough to fit into a different television requirement. The exploitation of pop songs in this manner is relatively cheap for television production, and can provide priceless exposure and publicity for the recordings in question. In the wake of this, Royksopp's single 'So Easy' was also used for a mobile phone advertisement and had a similar sticker on the record cover, both of which doubtless helped it to become a hit.

Advertising on commercial television also has proven more than amenable to the use of pop music. Traditionally, pop songs have been used as 'jingles', where the song's original words or context are altered, such as in the advertisement for a deodorant that uses a version of The Police's 'Don't Stand So Close to Me'. However, Levi's jeans have made it a policy to use pop songs that can become hits and synergetically retain product profile. Examples include the successful re-release of Marvin Gaye's 'I Heard It through the Grapevine', Stiltskin's 'Inside' and Mr Oizo's 'Flat Beat' (a surprise UK no. 1). Other instances of pop music in contemporary advertising abound, including, for example, Morcheeba's 'World Looking In' for the Ford Mondeo car, Leftfield's 'Phat Planet' for the celebrated Guinness surfer advertisement and Rob D's 'Clubbed to Death' for Caffrey's stout, which replaced an instrumental mix of Cornershop's 'Brimful of Asha'. Indeed, instrumental pop music has proven more versatile than songs. Recently, Kinobe's 'Slip into Something More Comfortable', a mixture of easy beat and sumptuous strings, accompanied a Kronenbourg beer advertisement, where a femme fatale's presence causes a number of accidents. Similarly, David Holmes's 'Rodney Yates' (from his album *lets get killed*) was used on an advertisement for Nat West insurance in 1999, accompanied by animated characters. This same piece was also much in evidence in *The Holiday Show* in June 1999 on BBC 1, and has proved to be very profitable as a piece of stock music. More recently, in May 2001, Holmes's '69 Police' has been used by the BBC under their advertisements for BBC Education's Revision service. Indeed, this new zone of popular music has rapidly colonised the stock music market, fuelled by the proliferation of television channels and aesthetic developments that required more in the way of music as continuity and as background in programmes.

Much instrumental music appears to fit the visuals effortlessly and thus has filled television's extensive continuity sections. Indeed, some pop/rock music appears almost to be crying out for use as incidental music on television and in films. A good example was DJ Shadow's album *Endtroducing . . .* (1996), which consisted largely of samples and fragments plundered from other recordings, adding up to a *mélange* of speaking voices, instrumental pieces and atmospheres. It was not too long before some was employed as incidental music in the cinema, with Welsh-set film *Twin Town* (1997) using the piece 'Stem'. Shortly afterwards, the same piece was used by the BBC in its continuity bridges between programmes. Although it is unlikely that the inspiration to use this DJ Shadow piece came from watching *Twin Town*, it is beyond doubt that the BBC's employment, at the turn of the millennium, of the energetic instrumental opening of Iggy Pop's 'Lust for Life', was inspired by the piece's prominent and memorable position at the beginning of *Trainspotting* (1996).

Television continuity segments and montage sequences within programmes have opened up opportunities for instrumental music that has the capacity to become an atmospheric or energetic underscore. For example, a report on BBC 2's *Newsnight* on 12 February 2001, concerning new revelations after the publication of the human genome, prominently used 'Horizons' by LTJ Bukem, a maverick British drum and bass producer. A perennial favourite as stock television music, this piece was also used extensively in *Celebrity Detox Camp* (Channel Five/Ginger TV, tx. 22 May 2003). During August 2001, cable channel FilmFour screened a series of fill-ins, where various minor celebrities were asked about their favourite films. This used 'Soon Forward', an atmospheric experimental piece of ambient dance music by DJ Spooky, in the background and under the dialogue to unify the small segment. In June 2001, Boards of Canada's 'Happy Cycling' was used in continuity segments to advertise a Channel Four series about drugs. This Scottish duo, who produce highly individual ambient music emanating from a dance music background, create precisely the kind of music that is highly effective when coupled with an image. This is exactly the sort of product that film and television producers want, and consequently a number of their pieces have graced British television sets, both in previews and as incidental music in drama. On the other hand, some music that was never conceived as anything but absolute music also has proved suitable for television continuity sequences. In September 1999, BBC 2 began advertising a new science series, *Living Proof*, with an obscure piece of avant-garde pop music from the early 1980s, 23 Skidoo's 'The Gospel Comes to New Guinea'. Perhaps it was no coincidence that this immediately preceded 23 Skidoo's unexpected comeback, fifteen or so years after the group's original demise. Indeed, the past decade has seen an acceleration in the rediscovery of old music, especially as the rights for its use can often be bought reasonably cheaply. With this has come the discovery of qualities in earlier music that can be utilised as an accompaniment to the moving image. This has been partially determined by the growing demand for pop as stock music during the 1990s. Jeremy Butler noted that a

> principally aesthetic, reason that some TV genres have shifted away from popular music in the past is because rock music during the 1950s and 1960s was associated with subversive or countercultural elements. Soap operas and sports programs, for instance, avoided rock music until the 1980s because it was perceived as too decadent for those historically conservative genres. The fact that both sports and soaps now regularly incorporate rock tunes indicates both a change in rock's position in U.S. culture (it has now become mainstream) and a change in the genres themselves – an attempt on their part to attract younger viewers.[11]

As younger viewers have grown older – the inexorable movement of the demographic bulge of the baby boom – pop/rock has become culturally acceptable; indeed, it has become dominant. ITV's *The Premiership*'s use of U2 is clear confirmation of this. We can identify the point in British television where this started to change. In the early 1990s, football show *Match of the Day* (BBC 1) began to accompany its 'Goal of the Month' competition with an instrumental mix of the Lightning Seeds's 'The Life of Riley'. This would suggest that pop/rock is now fully acceptable, losing any connotation of sedition that it might have had. Interestingly, on 16 October 2001, the main theme from the film *The Virgin Suicides* by French group Air was used in ITV football show *The Big Match: Champions League Highlights*, playing over a montage sequence of on-pitch action and footage of football managers. While the connotations for those familiar with the piece might have proven bizarre, clearly the physical properties of such instrumental pop/rock music can win a prime place both in cinema and on television, as well as in the record charts.

As I have noted, instrumental music, or instrumental passages from songs, have proven particularly suited to use as stock music. Ambient music clearly offers a variety of possibilities, one of which is as soundtrack for television or film. Brian Eno's pioneering work in this sphere merged a sonic environmental awareness with the functional aspects of film soundtrack music.[12] In fact, the more accessible end of ambient music owes much to film music, or at least to the concept of the 'cinematic'. It is premised upon 'atmosphere' and the construction of soundscapes in a similar manner to the way film composers and sound designers construct film soundtracks. This is often 'image-friendly music'. It can thus easily be used in television programmes or films, and so provides the opportunity to be sold twice over. Notably, the sort of music that has become popular in 'chill-out rooms' at dance clubs seems popular with television producers. This brand of ambient music, sometimes called 'intelligent dance music' (or 'braindance', among other things) or seen as part of a broader 'electronica', was a development from electronic dance music in the wake of House music.[13] It embraces a broad church of sounds, embodied by albums such as Green Jelly's *KY* (2000) (which brings together *The Bath EP*, *The Yellow EP* and *The Midnight EP*). A number of tracks from this album have been cut into television programmes. For example, in November 2001, the Channel Five documentary that discussed whether the moon landings were a hoax used Green Jelly's 'In the Bath'. Excerpts from albums such as the aforementioned Boards of Canada's *Music Has the Right to Children* (1998) and Moby's *Play* (1999) have been endemic on British television continuity sections over the last couple of years.

Moby's *Play* is a very distinctive set, owing more to an ethic of eclecticism than to any specific musical genre. Despite the singularity of this album's music, it has been used with great regularity on television continuity sections. In fact, it was noted in the media that it was the first album that had licensed all its tracks to appear on television and in films, whether as incidental music, continuity music or for advertisements.[14] 'Find My Baby' advertised a Nissan car, while 'Run On' was used to sell a Renault car and 'The Sky Is Broken' advertised Galaxy chocolate. It was possible to hear the whole album in fragments on television, demonstrating the durability and versatility of the music. In a similar manner to Moby, music by Boards of Canada has proven itself particularly effective as accompaniment to television images, with tracks taken from both the *Music Has the Right to Children* album and the EP *In a Beautiful Place Out in the Country* (2000). 'Kid for Today', from the latter, appeared on a BMW car advertisement in 2002, while 'Roygbiv', from the former, sounded like a television programme theme waiting to happen. Other television favourites include Death in Vegas's *The Contino Sessions* album (1999), which has seen the tracks 'Flying' and 'Dirge' used in multiple contexts on television, and instrumental sections of Massive Attack's *Mezzanine* (1998).

One of the most discussed albums of its year of release was U.N.K.L.E's *Psyence Fiction* (1998). One of its tracks, 'Celestial Annihilation', a piece that marries orchestral strings and dance beats, has appeared as incidental music on different television programmes. One such case was the dramatised documentary *The Crime Squad*, where it was used to accompany reconstructed (dramatised) images of burglary and fraud (tx. Monday 4 October 1999 on BBC 1). Another appeared on Saturday 22 February 2002 on Channel Four, where it was used under a montage of film images advertising the cable channel FilmFour. Craig Armstrong has also produced music that joins orchestral forces with pop music beats, as well as having been much in demand for his string arrangements for groups such as Massive Attack and Texas. He regularly crosses the thin permeable membrane that now separates pop music and film music, having co-scored films such as Baz Luhrmann's *Romeo and Juliet* (1996) and *Plunkett and Maclaine*. Indeed, his debut album, *The Space Between Us* (1998), includes pieces from films along with songs and other instrumental pieces. During May and June 1999, a television advertisement appeared starring Claudia Schiffer, in which she disrobed gradually as she descended a staircase, approached and then drove off in a car. This was accompanied memorably by Craig Armstrong's 'Rise'. His single 'This Love' (1998) had a sticker attached to the cover that read: 'Includes *Rise* as used in the Citroen Xsara TV ad starring Claudia Schiffer'. After this advert had been running for some time, the BBC began using the same Craig Armstrong strings and beats track to advertise the programme *Living Proof* (in October 1999). Something of a television continuity favourite, 'Rise' also was used by the BBC in 2002 to advertise *Of Apes and Men* on digital channel BBC 4. Another track that is heard with startling regularity on television is 'Bentley's Gonna Sort You Out' by Bentley Rhythm Ace. This track was used on a Lynx deodorant advertisement, and more recently on the BBC to publicise their 'Pure Soap' website, as well as accompanying astonishing images of hands with small human heads to advertise BBCi (an interactive digital channel). Not only has the use of pop music on television reached saturation point, but also a number of pieces of pop music are starting to acquire an iconic status as stock music.

The BBC's self-publicising adverts screened on its own television channels have become a quite expensive but aesthetically interesting reminder for viewers about what their licence fee pays for. In 1997, the most prominent was a performance-based video of a re-recorded version of Lou Reed's 'Perfect Day' by a constellation of star singers. This pop video, advertising the BBC's quality and value, appeared regularly in between programmes and then was released as a single, which reached the top of the charts in the same year. At the turn of 2002–3, the BBC's advertisement for its own digital channels was accompanied by the introduction to Coldplay's 'Clocks'. This advertisement, fronted by Steven Berkoff (and a host of other television characters), made effective use of the instrumental, piano-led opening of the album track from Coldplay's hit album *A Rush of Blood to the Head* (2002). The process of synergy became particularly apparent when Room 5 (featuring Oliver Cheatham) had a big British hit single with 'Make Luv' in early 2003 on the back of its use in a Lynx deodorant advertisement. Tellingly, the promo video copied closely the movements of the dancer in the advert.

Songs in Television Dramas and Tied-in Commerce

In documentaries, it is now commonplace to hear pop music used as accompaniment to montage sequences, or sequences that contain many images and a voiceover. This is partially due to the preponderance of dramatised material with music in contemporary documentaries (or 'docudramas'[15]), in opposition to the cinéma vérité style of television documentary,[16] which tends to eschew the use of incidental music.

Miami Vice

However, television drama has found pop music as amenable to use as stock music in its many different scenarios. In the wake of *WKRP in Cincinnati* and, more significantly, *Miami Vice*, pop music has been a crucial option in the construction of drama on television. British television drama has included a spate of programmes that have regularly employed excerpts from pop songs as a featured aspect of their style. Over the past few years, this has included series and serials, such as *Heartbeat* (1992–, Yorkshire Television), *Our Friends in the North* (1996, BBC), *The Lakes* (1997, BBC) and *The Lakes 2* (1999, BBC), *The Young Person's Guide to Becoming a Rock Star* (1998, Channel Four/Company Television), *Queer as Folk* (1999–2000, Channel Four/Red) and *Queer as Folk 2* (2000, Channel Four/Red), *As If* (2001–4, Channel Four/Carnival) and *Teachers* (2001–, Channel Four/Tiger Aspect). While programmes such as these obviate the need for more traditional dramatic underscores through their use of music imported from another context, their status as part of pop culture and sellable commodities in their own right cements the aesthetic strategies and marketing synergy. Of course, there are exceptional cases where not cheap, but 'expensive', featured music is required, such as in nature blockbusters like the *Blue Planet* and *Walking with Dinosaurs*, as discussed in the previous chapter. The distinction of their orchestral music might be seen as a self-conscious contrast to the prevalence of cheap and vernacular pop music. A similar comment might be made about some of television's many opulent car advertisements.

The bold ITV soap opera, *Night and Day*, made a point of utilising a regular succession of excerpts from pop songs as part of its very distinctive stylistic character. The programme owes a fair amount to the distinctiveness of David Lynch's

Twin Peaks, not only aiming for stylistic individuality, but also borrowing the format of a central mystery around which more traditional soap opera elements could be built. It uses excerpts from pop songs, not only as diegetic and non-diegetic music, but also ambiguously. While this might leave the audience uncertain of the music's status, it points to the increasing irrelevance of this in relation to the world constructed on the television screen. Furthermore, the music in *Night and Day* is regularly unceremoniously cut off to emphasise a narrative event (such as a revelation). Sometimes, the music even simulates the scratching noise of a vinyl disc having the arm pulled off while it is playing – an audiovisual icon derived, as we have seen, from *Ally McBeal*. In an episode screened in January 2002, Coldplay's 'Trouble' appeared in a scene where teenager Tom is looking at some books and finds his parents' marriage guidance appointment card. The same character recites some of the song's lyrics in class as a poem he is supposed to have written, and impresses his teacher. Later, she hears the same Coldplay song and realises his deception. *Night and Day*'s title song is sung by Kylie Minogue, yet has not been made available as a single and is credited only in small print at the programme's conclusion. Perhaps the programme is trying to make a point about the proliferation of tied-in music on television. Another soap, aimed at a youth audience and premised upon youth characters, *As If*, contained almost continuous dance music. An important location in the drama was a bar, where the music appeared to be diegetic, until it becomes evident that each sequence compresses time around the beat of the music, making music the defining aspect for time in the programme.

    Heartbeat illustrates the extreme possibilities of product-placing music in television drama. During the show's conception, music was seen as one of the main potential audience attractions.[17] This is clearly evident in the vast number of tied-in albums available, including *Heartbeat Volume One*, *Heartbeat Volume Two*, *Heartbeat Moments* and *The Official Heartbeat Tenth Anniversary Double Album*. Each album is simply a collection of classic songs, with the only modern recording being the programme's first star Nick Berry's cover of Buddy Holly's 'Heartbeat'. In fact, *Heartbeat* is almost as much a franchise for old songs as it is a television drama. The process of recycling 'Golden Oldies' for the nostalgia market was endemic across culture in the 1980s, with record companies milking back catalogues for the cinema screen. Denisoff and Plasketes described the industrial strategy of music and screen synergy, involving the co-ordination of record releases from a film soundtrack as mutual publicity,[18] while Jean Rosenbluth pointed to the accommodation where 'Studios and record companies began to work together regularly to maximise their products' financial potential.'[19] A similar sort of synergy has clearly now moved into television. British dramas that have had tied-in CDs include *Queer as Folk* (two albums), *The Lakes*, *Spaced* (including artists such as Cornelius, David Holmes, Fluke and Nightmares on Wax) and *Hollyoaks* (1995– , Channel Four/Mersey Television) (an album entitled *40 Hits for the Hollyoaks Generation*).

    Some television dramas have made more of music for dramatic purposes. Stephen King's *Sleepwalkers* (1992, Columbia/Ion) is bookended by Enya's

'Boadicea' (on its opening and end titles), while also employing incidental music by Nicholas Pike. It also uses pop music as a narrative device. The murderous shapeshifters repeatedly play and dance to a record of Santo and Johnny's 'Sleepwalk'. Television playwright Dennis Potter's serials were replete with music and thus allowed for best-selling tied-in records. Both *Pennies from Heaven* and *The Singing Detective* included tied-in albums of popular songs largely from the 1930s and 1940s. *Lipstick on Your Collar* (1993, Channel Four/Whistling Gypsy) included a large number of rock'n'roll songs from the late 1950s and early 1960s. However, Potter's use of popular music was far more complex than the simple adornment evident in programmes like *Heartbeat*. Anodyne popular songs such as 'The Umbrella Man' were imbued with sinister undertones in *The Singing Detective*, while in *Lipstick on Your Collar*, rough and noisy sex was memorably matched to Gene Vincent's 'Lotta Lovin''.

Pop Songs as Title Themes

Title themes provide product differentiation within a crowded arena of competing television programmes. They provide essential branding, providing audiences with instant recognition of the forthcoming programme. In this respect, title themes are clearly a relation of the advertising jingle, which is often a shorter and rather downmarket relation. Historically, these theme tunes might be seen as an inheritance from radio drama, although they are now a perfect space for pop songs. Theme tunes have to be remarkably enduring and hard-wearing. They must stand up to repeated listenings without upsetting television viewers. For example, Granada Television's *Coronation Street* has been on British commercial television since 1960, appearing up to four times a week (as of 2002), including omnibus editions. The theme music, a jazz lament by Eric Spear,[20] appears twice each time, along with a small variation for each cut to and from the advertisements. This adds up to a breathtaking number of appearances that far exceeds the durability of classical music or the short-term but mass distribution of pop songs. As such, it is a phenomenon that deserves some serious research. This example illustrates how musical material that is apparently alien to the programme subject matter can be assimilated by television. Pop songs have proven themselves easily assigned as television programme themes.

It is not as if television theme tunes are specifically concocted to serve these functions of longevity, endurability and instant identification. One would expect music to be written to fit a television programme's distinct character. Yet in many cases, themes are not necessarily written for the programme at all. For example, *Charmed* (1998– , Spelling/Northshore) uses an arrangement of a mid-1980s pop song by The Smiths called 'How Soon Is Now?', performed by Love Spit Love. The song's words seem to say little of pertinence to the programme, but the music provides a good identifier. Similarly, *CSI: Crime Scene Investigation* (2000– , CBS/Touchstone/Jerry Bruckheimer/Alliance Atlantis) uses The Who's song 'Who Are You?' from the late 1970s as its theme, in what appears to be a reference to the narrative's search for killers. There does not need to be a direct connection between the theme music and the programme, merely a learned connection that will cement their association for audiences.[21] Even such prominent musical theme tunes as the music for *The Avengers* was not written especially to suit the distinctive character of the programme: 'The Shake', by Laurie Johnson, had already appeared on a record before being chosen as the show's theme music.[22]

Police show *The Vice* (1999–2003, Carlton Television) used the song 'Sour Times' by Portishead as its title music, despite having a very characteristic sounding score by Peter Salem. Portishead's song uses samples from, and is very closely based on, a Lalo Schifrin cue from *Mission: Impossible* called 'Danube Incident'.[23] The original cue used the very distinctive sound of the Hungarian gypsy cimbalom (like a hammered dulcimer) and bass guitar to delineate exotic location for *Mission: Impossible*. Portishead's version adds singing, but ends up back on the screen, albeit now the repeated theme music for a hard-hitting complex police programme.

Generally speaking, musical style and genre, the coding of cultural ideas in music, furnish viewer expectation of the programme. For example, the theme music to *Buffy the Vampire Slayer*, by Nerf Herder, provides a good idea of the character of the programme. It is fast, exciting rock, which suggests youth, energy and action, a programme that is hip to modern youth culture. (The music changed slightly part of the way through the programme's run, although this was not significant enough to warrant much notice.) This example tells us much about the way that cultural coding works with music (while simultaneously defining those very cultural codes). It is premised upon simple ideas and associations, following stereotypical notions about certain musical genres, and certain individual timbres.

Synergy with respect to television theme music is certainly nothing new. Many shows have used title music that became hit singles, such as *Friends* (1994– , Warners) with The Rembrandts's 'I'll Be There for You' (2001). In Britain, there were Simon May's soap themes/songs in *EastEnders* (Nick Berry's 'Every Loser Wins' [a UK no. 1, 1986] and Anita Dobson's 'Anyone Can Fall in Love', [UK top 5, 1986]), *Howard's Way* (1985–90, BBC; Marti Webb's 'Always There' [UK top 10, 1986]) and *Crossroads* (1964–88, ATV, then Central TV), with Kate Robbins's 'More Than in Love' (UK no. 2, 1981) and 'Summer of My Life' (UK top 10, 1976). However, in recent years, pop/rock music increasingly can be heard as incidental music in programmes, and not necessarily simply as a commercial tie-in with the programme. Other examples include current affairs programme *Weekend World* (1972–88, LWT) using an instrumental section of Mountain's 'Nantucket Sleighride' for its titles, and the employment of old songs in *The Wonder Years* (1988–93, New World Television/Black-Marlens) – Joe Cocker's 'I'll Get by with a Little Help from My Friends' – and *Absolutely Fabulous* (1992– , BBC) – Julie Driscoll's 'Wheel's on Fire'. These reveal the use of pop music as a vernacular, with historical as well as significatory and musical connotations.

Soap operas *Dallas* and *Crossroads* both updated their themes using the styles of pop music. *Dallas* originally had a brass-dominated big band theme with a backbeat, written by Jerrold Immel. The later version reflected much more of an influence from disco music, with prominent slap bass guitar, a slower beat and less of a 'big band' sound. *Crossroads*'s original theme was written by Tony Hatch, but later updated with electronic instruments in the 1970s by Paul McCartney and Wings.[24] This was fairly short-lived, however, although other attempts to replace the original theme were even more fleeting. Two pop songs mentioned earlier, 'Summer of My Life' (by Simon May) and 'More Than in Love' (by Kate Robbins), enjoyed a very short tenure on the programme's end titles in the mid-1970s. Since its return, the programme has sported two different versions of the original music written by Tony Hatch. Simon May's theme for *EastEnders* did not sound like promising hit material in its television form, with its pub piano mixed with chiming that included 'Bow bells' peals. Yet the structure followed song form, used a backbeat and had a song-like melody, which was transformed into the aforementioned hit single 'Anyone Can Fall in Love', sung by Anita Dobson, one of the show's lead characters. Like Mike Post in the USA, Simon May has become one of the consummate television theme composers.[25] Yet ultimately, theme music works almost solely on conditioned association. While some tunes are relevant to the programme's material, it is hardly a necessity.

Conclusion

There are those who might argue that pop music has been the consensual stock music of everyday life for some time. It is incontrovertible that popular music and television have an increasingly close relationship. This is not only testified to by the success of primetime search-for-a-star programmes *Pop Stars* (2001, LWT) and *Pop Idol* (2001– , LWT/19TV), first in the UK and then the USA, but also by the mutual influence and cross-pollination between television and music. Moby's 'Go' was derived from Angelo Badalamenti's incidental music for David Lynch's television serial *Twin Peaks*, while White Town's 1997 UK no. 1 'Your Woman' was covertly a reply to (and based on a sample from) a substantially older Al Bowlly song from the 1930s called 'My Woman' that had been repackaged in Dennis Potter's *Pennies from Heaven* and made available as part of a tied-in record release.

Pop music has become endemic as the new stock music on television, being simply 'cut in' to the action. The motivation for this is both aesthetic and financial. The proliferation of pop/rock music is a testament to its pervasive status more generally. It provides energy and atmosphere, and allows for recycling and cross-promotion. This partly has been enabled by its adoption of a less confrontational aspect, together with the phenomenon of an ageing population who see little that is culturally unacceptable about pop music. The pop singles charts are now dominated by anodyne boy bands, manufactured pop, polite rock and anonymous club fodder. In contrast, screen music has become an appealing prospect for pop musicians, not only financially, but also aesthetically. This situation – the convergence of pop music and screen culture – has led to the development of a seemingly new burgeoning zone of pop music. While David Toop noted that the work of artists like David Bowie in the late 1970s was on a trajectory towards becoming film music,[26] a new generation of musical artists have grown up influenced directly by film music and with a desire for their music to be married to the screen.

At the same time, the dominant 'recycling culture' of the 1990s has led to the wholesale reselling of back catalogues on CD. The licensing of pop music for screen use is an increasingly important part of this process. Recontextualised music is now a prime cultural logic, spawning a form of 'multipurpose music' that, as well as being music in its own right, can also be resold as temp track 'readymades' or stock music for television. In 1997, Sony Classical was inspired to branch out into film music by the fact that sales of soundtrack albums had quadrupled in ten years.[27] While a key development in the 1980s was the rush to tie in pop music with films, in the 1990s, the trend has been increasingly to tie in pop music with television, a move reflected by the sheer weight of television 'soundtrack' CDs currently available.

Notes

1 Dave Simpson, 'Plug and Play', *Guardian*, 5 May 2000, p. 14.

2 Robin Nelson, *TV Drama in Transition: Forms, Values and Cultural Change* (Basingstoke, Hants: Macmillan, 1997), p. 24; Raymond Williams, *Television: Technology and Cultural Form* (London: Fontana, 1974), p. 78.

3 Lez Cooke, *British Television Drama: A History* (London: BFI, 2003), p. 52.

4 One might also argue that it equates American popular culture (the song) with the British working class, as a reaction to the association of 'high culture' with the ruling classes.

5 K. J. Donnelly, *Pop Music in British Cinema: A Chronicle* (London: BFI, 2001), p. 16.

6 Cf. The Rolling Stones's television programme *Rock'n'Roll Circus* (1969).

7 Robert Neaverson, *The Beatles Movies* (London: Cassell, 1997), p. 71.

8 Jeremy G. Butler, *Television: Critical Methods and Applications* (Belmont, CA: Wadsworth, 1994), p. 190.

9 Jeremy Eckstein, ed., *Cultural Trends 19*, vol. 3, no. 3 (London: Policy Studies Institute, 1993), p. 45.

10 Nelson, *TV Drama in Transition*, p. 25.

11 Butler, *Television*, p. 190.

12 Mark Prendergast, *The Ambient Century: From Mahler to Moby – the Evolution of Sound in the Electronic Age* (London: Bloomsbury, 2000); David Toop, *Ocean of Sound: Aether Talk, Ambient Sounds and Imaginary Worlds* (London: Serpent's Tail, 1995), p. 8.

13 Prendergast, *Ambient Century*, pp. 52–3.

14 Simpson, 'Plug and Play', p. 14.

15 John Corner, *The Art of Record: An Introduction to Documentary* (Manchester: Manchester University Press, 1996), p. 183.

16 Brian Winston, *Lies, Damn Lies and Documentaries* (London: BFI, 2000), p. 2.

17 Nelson, *TV Drama in Transition*, p. 79.

18 R.Serge Denisoff and George Plasketes, 'Synergy in 1980s Film and Music: Formula for Success or Industry Mythology?', *Film History*, vol. 4, no. 3, 1990, p. 257.

19 Jean Rosenbluth, 'Soundtrack Specialists: Maximizing Cross-Market Connections', *Billboard*, 16 July 1988, p. S-4.

20 Spear had scored low-budget British films, including *Ghost Ship* (1953), *Shadow Man* (1953), *The Stranger from Venus* (1954), *The Golden Link* (1954) and *The Vulture* (1966).

21 Similarly, the Friday evening live entertainment programme on Channel Four, *TFI Friday* (1996–2000, Channel Four/Ginger Television), employed theme music that had originally been used for 1960s television spy drama *Man in a Suitcase* (1967, ITC). These were profoundly different types of programme. A more ironic use of a television theme was the adoption of *Danger Man*'s (1960–1, 1964–6, ITC) theme for the Mark Radcliffe (evening) show on BBC Radio 1 in the early to mid-1990s. These two illustrations demonstrate the extended life that is possible for old television music, indeed much in the way of old music more generally, where people are simply waiting to sell it to us again.

22 Similarly, the BBC's long-running snooker programme, *Pot Black* (1969–84), used a Scott Joplin piano rag, while its costume drama about a steamship company, *The Onedin Line* (1971–80), employed the same romantic big orchestral theme from Khachaturian's *Spartacus* that later was used as the main theme for *The Hudsucker Proxy* (1994).

23 In fact, the Portishead song adds only a couple of elements to Schifrin's original cue.

24 It followed in the wake of *Z Cars* (1962–78, BBC), which had also updated its theme with electric instruments and used the folk rock group Steeleye Span.

25 May has composed themes for *El Dorado*, a song for *Crossroads*, *Pet Rescue* (Channel Four/Bazal), *Food and Drink* (BBC 2/Bazal), *The Holiday Programme* (BBC), *EastEnders*, *Howard's Way* and *Trainer*.

26 David Toop, 'Rock Musicians and Film Soundtracks' in Jonathan Romney and Adrian Wootton, eds, *Celluloid Jukebox: Popular Music and the Movies since the 50s* (London: BFI, 1995), p. 179.

27 Jeff Smith, 'Selling My Heart: Music and Cross-Promotion in *Titanic*' in Kevin S. Sandler and Gaylyn Studlar, eds., *Titanic: Anatomy of a Blockbuster* (New Brunswick, NJ: Rutgers University Press, 1999), p. 47.

Chapter 8

Soundtracks without Films

While films and film music have become an increasingly significant influence on pop music, pop music has exerted a steadily increasing influence on film music. We can now go to record shops and buy pop music CDs without visiting a 'pop music' section. Instead, among the specialist genres, like dance music or heavy metal, or indeed the film soundtracks section, we can find copious amounts of pop music mixed with CDs of more traditional film scores. Pop music and film music increasingly have converged. It is a regular occurrence to find mainstream films 'fitted up' with a succession of pop songs and have music composed by pop musicians; it is also common to hear sound samples cut from films and pasted into pop music, and to hear pop musicians talk about the influence of film music upon their craft.

Since the 1960s, a distinct zone of pop music has emerged that is looking for accompanying images, marking out an intermediate territory, an 'interzone', between film music and pop music. This area of music might be dubbed the 'soundtracks without films' sector.[1] In a reciprocal relationship, pop music techniques have infiltrated the modes of film scoring, to match the marked influence film soundtracks have had on pop music, and stemming most obviously from the increasing number of pop musicians producing music for films.

The 'soundtracks without films' phenomenon has become more prominent in recent years. There are many so-called 'soundtrack' albums that have no film – that do not appear in any film – or have lost their connection with their film, to the point where they are almost fully autonomous. The term 'soundtrack' has changed its meaning over the past decade or so. Indeed, for a long time, it has not been used exclusively for describing music from films. The term also applied to television and to the music accompanying computer games. A music periodical such as *The Wire* will regularly employ the term to describe music of a certain character, although not necessarily tied to a film. Best-selling group Doves referred to their new material as having 'quite a filmic quality',[2] while Leeds-based club Up Yer Ronson have released a number of CDs of dance music called 'soundtracks'. Indeed, a particular type of dance music has requisitioned the whole notion of film soundtracks. Some seem completely unrelated to the notion of film soundtracks, while others reference the idea most explicitly. A double CD of continuous dance music was released in 2000 called *Soundtrack for the Weekend* (on Global Records), while the front cover of DJ Dave Seaman's *Back to Mine* (1999) album stated: 'A soundtrack without a film. Lie back. Close your eyes. And watch the in-flight movie on the inside of your eyelids.'[3] Such is the attraction of cinema and film music that some pop musicians even erroneously identify their product with the cinema, such as Caustic Soda's *Music from the Motion Picture* (1996), The Cinematic Orchestra's *Motion* (1999) and Spleen's *Soundtrack to Spleen* (1996) – and much earlier, 10cc's *Original Soundtrack*, released in 1975. Record purchasers might easily be fooled into thinking that they contain music from films. In the case of Spleen, the extensive narratives in the song lyrics at times even suggest the possibility that the music is an accompaniment to a visual object of some sort.

Hot on the heels of the international success of Hollywood film *American Beauty* (1999), Thomas Newman's haunting and distinctive film music was converted into a club dance record, Jakatta's 'American Dream', becoming an international hit as well as a piece of music that could be easily utilised for television continuity sections and advertisements. The record used Newman's main theme unchanged, with the addition of a dance beat and a sample from another record. It is an eloquent testament to how close pop music and film music have become in recent years. Beyond this, there is a more definite intermediate area between the more traditional formats of film music and pop music, where musical techniques (not to mention imagery) have cross-bred to foster and develop what might be construed as a new form of music.

Music Looking for Images

Aesthetic convergence between music and images is hardly anything new. If we peruse musical history, we can see that among nineteenth-century orchestral music there was a marked tendency toward visualisation. Examples include Alexander Scriabin's wish to accompany his music with light shows, and Beethoven's Sixth Symphony, with its sketching of pastoral images in sound. This proliferated later in the 19th century and became known as 'programme music'. Further examples of this are Mendelssohn's 'Fingel's Cave' ('The Hebrides', Overture in B minor, Op. 26, 1830) and Berlioz's *Symphonie fantastique* (Op. 14),[4] in both of which the 'programme' of images was painted by the music. Claude Debussy took this 'impressionism' one step further into metaphorical representation with pieces like *La Mer* (from 3 Symphonic Sketches, 1903) and *Images*,[5] and later works such as *La Cathédrale engloutie* (the sunken cathedral) from the *Préludes* (Book 1) of 1910. This last piece acquired different images much later, in an electronic arrangement in John Carpenter's film *Escape from New York*. With the advent of modernism in art music, the 'representational' receded in favour of a concept of 'pure music', music that was not related to specific images or connected with other media. However, the more austere sounds of the second Viennese school spawned a bizarre singular piece,

Schoenberg's *Begleitung zu einer Lichtspielszene* (*Accompaniment to a Cinematic Scene*, for orchestra, Op. 34, 1930), which I touched upon in an earlier chapter. It was written without a specific film in mind, and indeed was lacking in any narrative or cinematic features. Schoenberg famously told Hollywood producers that he would only consider writing film music if he could control the film and adapt it to the music's requirements, which meant, not surprisingly, that no film projects were forthcoming. Until the 1970s that is, when avant-garde film-makers Jean-Marie Straub and Daniele Huillet made a film to accompany Schoenberg's piece of film music without a film: *Enleitung zu Arnold Schoenbergs 'Begleitung zu einer Lichtspielszene'* (*Introduction to Arnold Schoenberg's 'Accompaniment to a Cinematic Scene'*). Despite the image painted in Hollywood of Schoenberg as an unreasonable figure, it is worth noting that this initial foray into music for images was written before his arrival in Hollywood and prior to the establishment of the classical film score in the later 1930s.

Perhaps film music owes more to this more autonomous tradition than to the functional music accompanying theatre productions, which has often been identified as the parent of film music. If we look at the more populist orchestral music of the Victorian period, one of the most successful pieces, Albert Ketèlbey's *In a Persian Market*, fulfilled the criteria for image-conjuring yet manifests a divergence from the 'legit' music tradition I have just described. Popular music has always been connected to films. The Fats Waller song 'The Sheik of Araby' was tied to and sold through Rudolph Valentino's film *Son of the Sheik* (1926). In classical Hollywood, songs appeared with some regularity in films that were not musicals. Perhaps the most famous example was *Casablanca*, while in *To Have and Have Not* (1944), Hoagy Carmichael sang a number of his songs, including a duet with Lauren Bacall. Westerns presented a more obvious site of interaction between popular music and cinema, with the singing cowboys of B-pictures and Dimitri Tiomkin's title songs, often sung by Tex Ritter. Additional instances include perennially popular pieces from established film music composers, such as Max Steiner's composition for *A Summer Place* (1959), 'Unchained Melody' by Alex North from the prison film *Unchained* (1955) and Henry Mancini's 'Moon River' from *Breakfast at Tiffany's* (1960). This process accelerated in the 1980s, emblematised by Giorgio Moroder's version of Fritz Lang's 1927 film *Metropolis* (1984), which was replete with pop songs as well as reserving a small space for Moroder's electronic score.[6] In reality, there never has been a barrier between popular music and film scores. Film music underscores were sometimes made into popular music, as was the case with Victor Young's love theme from the RKO war film *One Minute to Zero* (1952), which later had words added to become the perennial 'When I Fall in Love (It Will Be Forever)'. Young had also written the music for 'Stella by Starlight' for the film *The Uninvited* (1944) and later had a massive hit with the 'Around the World in 80 Days' from the film of the same title, released in 1956.

The advent of rock'n'roll threatened the established popular music industry. In terms of films, it was shunted into a specialist movie ghetto, although gradually, as pop music's cultural status rose and its styles developed, it became fully integrated with cinema, now almost on a genetic level. Since the 1960s and the expansion of pop music, there has been an increased 'visualisation' of music, where pop music 'implies' images, places, subjectivities – in both lyrics and music. This is a point where pop music and cinema have converged – pop becoming more 'cinematic' and cinema increasingly integrating pop music. This has been aided more recently by changes in cinema. In addition to this, the destruction of musical counterculture and the increasing untenability of an art music 'avant-garde', has led to the appearance of a 'pop avant-garde', which has broken free from the three-minute song format and in certain ways looks towards films for inspiration. Clearly, cinema has been a major influence on the imagery of pop music, as well as on its sound. However, it should be noted that the influence has by no means been all one way, and that, in musical terms at least, a convergence between film scores and pop music has always been a possibility and in recent years has become a very obvious reality.[7]

The term 'pop music' fails to describe anything specific; the same goes for 'popular music' and what some see as the more 'serious' end of pop music, what is customarily called 'rock'. At the very least, the term 'pop music' is appallingly imprecise. It seems to embrace a whole spectrum of music from industrial noise like Scorn and Throbbing Gristle to teenage sugarpop like the Cheeky Girls or Take That. Encompassing such a fragmented zone of musical culture, maybe it has become a less useful term. While 'pop music' might still describe chart-oriented songs, its use as a marketing genre is increasingly being superseded by a number of more meaningful subgenres. Record shops not only have a (mainstream) 'pop' section, but also regularly subdivide it into such categories as 'rap', 'metal', 'r and b', 'soul', 'alternative', etc.[8] Although I will use the term 'pop' here, I wish to register its problematic status.[9] I have even located recordings of ambiguous genre such as Walter/Wendy Carlos's *Switched on Bach* and electronic music by Isao Tomita in the popular music sections of record shops. This is compounded by the confusion of 'popular' 'classical' music, which regularly appears in the album charts. The categories of 'pop music' and 'popular music' have been challenged since the late 1960s, and the development of more 'serious' (or, rather, more self-serious) rock music and some of its extreme forms of differentiation, such as progressive rock. Concept albums tested the boundary of 'pop music', rupturing its traditional conception with their pretensions and referencing of high art.[10]

For the purposes of analysis here, it is possible to distinguish two types of concept albums. On the one hand, there is the 'story' type, as embodied by The Pretty Things's *S.F. Sorrow* (1968), The Who's *Tommy* (1969) and other song cycles like the Small Faces's *Ogden's Nut Gone Flake* (1968) and Pink Floyd's *The Wall* (1979). On the other hand, there is the 'conceptual unity' concept album that lacks any story, such as The Beatles's *Sergeant Pepper's Lonely Hearts Club Band* (1967). In many cases, both types of concept album include instrumental pieces, which sometimes take inspiration from films and sometimes are described as 'cinematic' in reviews. In general, the use of 'narrative' tends to destroy any limited sense of pop

LPs, while these recordings are, in effect, 'programme music', music with a pro-gramme, as in art music. Arguably, they resemble song cycles and modern sym-phonies in their two respective forms. Pink Floyd's *The Wall* even had a later feature film made to accompany it, directed by Alan Parker and released in 1982. Instru-mental concept albums that enjoy a unity in themselves but are based on a looser concept include Terry Riley's work like *A Rainbow in Curved Air* (1967), which clearly inspired Mike Oldfield's *Tubular Bells*, which was in turn used as underscore in *The Exorcist* in the same year, and Brian Eno's work, including *Music for Films* (1978), which, while not written for specific films, was used later in films and tele-vision programmes. The type of instrumental electronic music purveyed by Tanger-ine Dream found its way easily into films, with the German group providing the whole score for *Sorcerer* (aka *Wages of Fear*, 1977), *Thief* (1981), *Legend* (1985, US version only) and *Near Dark* (1987).

The instrumental excesses and desire to transcend the 32-bar, three-minute pop song meant that progressive rock was open to a fruitful two-way interaction with films. In 1969, *Melody Maker* declared that their yearly poll results 'were proof of the tastes of the vast majority of young people in Britain today – they want pop that is progressive played by musicians who are honest. And they don't want old-style showbiz type pop.'[11] Progressive rock originated in the American west coast music scene of the late 1960s and the British rock music that was initially inspired by its instrumental trends as well as its drug-orientation.[12] The primary concerns of this musical substratum were instrumental virtuosity combined with a differentiation of this form from mainstream pop music. These aims were achieved largely through playing extended songs rather than the three-minute format that characterised the charts. They consequently became patronised through album sales, the format allowing for long and unfolding musical pieces that attracted a more mature audi-ence.[13] In the 1970s, LPs rather than singles became the principal means of pop and rock song dissemination. The development of an LP market meant more income generated from sales, although this was in parallel to, rather than directly replacing, the singles market. The growth of LP sales in the late 1960s, consolidated through the expansion of the market in terms of age range and crystallised by the 1970s music genre and marketing category of AOR ('adult oriented rock'), was aimed almost entirely at the demographic bulge of the baby boom.

'Progressive rock' blossomed during the early 1970s, with groups accelerating to excess, particularly in terms of song length, instrumental complexity and references to high art. Concept albums were loftily conceived narrative song cycles, sometimes consciously similar to art music, and their production values became conspicuously high. The emblematic album for this form of pop music production is probably Pink Floyd's *Dark Side of the Moon* (released in 1973), which included both songs and instrumental pieces, special sound effects, brand new synthesizer technology, snatches of film-like dialogue, a gatefold sleeve with lyrics and posters and a vague overall unifying concept. *Dark Side of the Moon* sold by the million, breaking the record for time spent in the LP charts.[14] While it was not a particularly visual album that had no explicit unity across the songs, it resembled a film soundtrack in many ways, including sound effects, disembodied speaking voices, as well as instrumental 'mood pieces'. *Dark Side of the Moon* was a pioneering aural cultural item, something like a sound sculpture for a stereo set, exploiting new 'hi-fi' systems and standards. It was also a soundtrack LP without a film, constructing something that approximates a cinematic experience within domestic space. Another concept album from roughly the same time was the Genesis double album *The Lamb Lies Down on Broadway* (1975). This was unified by a narrative that was anchored by a written story on the gatefold sleeve, which also included photographs from the story depicting the characters and activities. These could almost have been stills from a film to which the album was a soundtrack. Released in 1978, Jeff Wayne's *War of the Worlds* was a narrative concept album. The cover tells the story, characters appear and sing roles and animated pictures on the sleeve suggest a film soundtrack more than anything else.[15]

The advent of punk in the late 1970s targeted concept albums as indicative of how remote, pretentious and overblown rock music had become. Despite punk and new wave's antipathy towards pop and rock traditions, or at least their established modes of operation, there was nevertheless a continuing interest in films as cultural objects and as artistic possibilities. In an interview following the release of the Public Image Limited album *The Flowers of Romance* in 1981, John Lydon (previously punk *bête noire* Johnny Rotten) declared that the music on the LP was better understood as 'film themes rather than songs'.[16] The group had proclaimed their intention to make a film soundtrack, and one piece in particular, 'The Order of Death', used in *Hardware* (1990), suggests a return to the medium that was its prime influence if not a direct inspiration for its existence.[17] This is a testament to the degree of mutual interaction and influence that has taken place between pop music and film music, while pop music, in its variety of forms, has insinuated itself firmly in films in its own right as a replacement for more traditional film music, namely the orchestral score.

Other artists on the verges of pop music made bold recordings. Barry Adamson, previously the bass guitar player with Magazine and Nick Cave, recorded an album called *Moss Side Story* in 1989. As well as its reference to the film *West Side Story* (1961) in its title, it was a concept album that included a story, narration and many instrumentals, all of which fostered the impression that it was an accompaniment to a film. It also included versions of Elmer Bernstein's film theme 'The Man with the Golden Arm' and Gounod's 'Portrait of Hitch', the iconic music for *Alfred Hitchcock Presents*.[18] Of course, a similar process had occurred in radio drama, which, in the 1960s and 1970s, led to a range of LPs that, in their use of dramas with narration and music, almost resembled 'talking books'. A good example of this is *Hammer Presents Dracula with Christopher Lee* (1974), in which Christopher Lee provided a voiceover narration across James Bernard's music from a number of Hammer horror films.

Similar things began to happen in pop music in the early 1980s, enabled by developments in recording and sampling technology. For example, *My Life in the*

Bush of Ghosts (1981), a collaboration between Brian Eno and Talking Heads singer David Byrne, eschewed singing in the traditional sense, to replace it with 'found voices', including a telephone exorcist and a recording of a Lebanese mountain singer. Recordings like this challenge the notion of 'pop music' in a fundamental way. A similar technique was evident in *Abba Pater* (1999), a best-selling album of Pope John Paul II singing and speaking, which had been put to music and released by Sony with endorsement from the Vatican.[19] The practice of accompanying voices with music may owe much to radio drama, but both might be construed as having been inspired more by the cinema. David Holmes has made music that combines dramatic 'score' with what sounds like film dialogue. Starting as a club DJ, he has ploughed a furrow directly from dance music into film music. *Mixmag* commented on his second album: 'It's 30 years' worth of music cast on [*lets get killed*], as a cine-matic shuffle through the mean streets of New York.'[20] The record not only includes dance and mood pieces, but also recordings of voices in between the tracks, giving a sense of place and a notable sense of purpose to the album. *lets get killed* (1997) also includes Holmes's version of Monty Norman and John Barry's famous James Bond theme, entitled 'Radio 7'. Holmes's first album, *this films crap lets slash the seats*,[21] had also been inaugurated in a very 'cinematic' fashion. According to one review:

> nothing could have prepared the listener for the epic cinematic sweep displayed here. Inspired by the movie *In the Name of the Father*, opening track *No Man's Land* somehow makes stock sounds – church bells, footsteps, slamming doors, even breathy string sweeps – sound compelling … [The rest of *this films crap lets slash the seats* contains] more movie-inspired madness. 'People picked up on the fact that my music sounded cinematic before I did. It's just something that seems to come out,' shrugs David.[22]

'No Man's Land' is strikingly similar to Holmes's opening music for his score to *Resurrection Man*. Holmes's comments above underline the stylistic convergence that has occurred between film music and some areas of pop music, although Holmes's discography suggests that films and film music have become a more per-vasive influence on pop music. His first single, a collaboration with Ashley Beedle in 1993 under the name of The Disco Evangelists, bore the cinematically inspired title 'De Niro', and used a musical sample from Ennio Morricone's musical score for *Once Upon a Time in America* (1984). His first two albums, *this films crap lets slash the seats* and *lets get killed*, led directly to work for film and television, such as Linda La Plante's television serial *Supply and Demand* (1997, ITV), Steven Soderbergh's *Out of Sight* (1998) and *Buffalo Soldiers* (2001). Holmes's third album aimed to go fur-ther in the direction of cinema,[23] including an unrealised film script, entitled 'Living Room', on which the album's narrative was based. *Bow Down to the Exit Sign* (2000) contained dialogue performed by actor Sean Gullette and songs seemingly pertinent to the story sung by guest vocalists. Holmes noted that it was partly inspired by the *mélange* of a soundtrack to the film *Performance*,[24] and went on to say:

> The reason why I'm doing movies is because of my perseverance with my own music, wanting to take it further in that direction. . . . I always wanted to avoid sampling films on my records, so *Bow Down* was the next step – let's make our own film.[25]

This was certainly an extreme step.[26] Many groups have been content simply to reference films, either by writing about cinematic subjects or using samples of sounds, music or dialogue from films. The outlying edges of popular music have certainly been accustomed to incorporating film dialogue samples. For example, Ministry's 'Jesus Built My Hotrod' includes a sample of Dennis Hopper as Frank shouting 'Let's hit the fuckin' road', from David Lynch's *Blue Velvet*, and appears prominently in the extended mix version (the 'Redline/Whiteline' version). The same sample was used in Mr Bungle's 'Squeeze Me Macaroni'. Indeed, a whole sector of pop music has incorporated samples of film dialogue into their music. Canadian group Skinny Puppy, active during the 1980s and 1990s, are an excellent example. 'Draining Faces', on the album *Cleanse, Fold and Manipulate* (1987), includes a dialogue sample from David Cronenberg's *Videodrome* (1983) of Barry Convex saying, 'Forgive me if I don't stay around to watch. I just can't cope with the freaky stuff.' On 'Fritter (Stella's Home)' on *VIVIsectVI* (1988), there is a dialogue sample from Stanley Kubrick's *The Shining* of Jack Torrance (Jack Nicholson) saying, 'It's OK. He saw it on the television.'[27] Another memorable voice sample is that of war criminal dentist Szell (Laurence Olivier) asking, 'Is it safe?', from *Marathon Man* (1976), which appears on 'Assimilate' from the album *Bites* (1985). These are just a few examples from the group's output, which is replete with dialogue samples gleaned from films. Similarly, Rob Zombie, one-time singer in the group White Zombie, released the album *Rob Zombie Presents Words and Music from Frankenstein* (Uni/Hip-O records, 1999). The CD includes music and dialogue from *Frankenstein* (1931), *Bride of Frankenstein* and *Ghost of Frankenstein* (1942), and, indeed, Zombie has also used many film samples on his music before this point. The majority of groups using samples are more left field, although some chart acts have used prominent samples. Big Audio Dynamite, for example, have wielded samples from *Performance* (on 'E=MC2') and the spaghetti Westerns *The Good, the Bad and the Ugly* and *Duck You Sucker!* (1971) (on 'The Medicine Show'). La Tour's only big hit, 'People Are Still Having Sex', from 1991, used a sample of a demonic voice saying 'Hello Lover' from the film *Evil Dead 2* (1987).[28]

Music has not simply used film dialogue, though. The Beastie Boys used samples from Bernard Herrmann's music for the shower scene in *Psycho* in the song 'Egg Man' from *Paul's Boutique* (1989), while the Sneaker Pimps's '6 Underground' (from *Becoming X* [1996]) was based on a short repeated five-note harp motif from John Barry's score for *Goldfinger* (1964), where Bond (Sean Connery) finds the dead body of Jill Matheson (Shirley Eaton) covered in gold paint. Going further than simply short musical samples, in the summer of 2001, an extraordinary album called *The Director's Cut* was released by Fantomas (a fringe rock supergroup featuring ex-members of Faith No More, the Melvins and Slayer). The album consisted of raucous but compelling versions of film and television music, including Bernard Herrmann's *Cape Fear*, James Bernard's *The Devil Rides Out* and Krzysztoph Komeda's theme music for *Rosemary's Baby*. This was not only a unique reworking of film and television themes, but was also sold in record shops alongside best-selling pop albums.

The Influence of Films

Films and film music have exerted a significant influence on pop music, while, equally, pop music has had an increasing influence on film music. Perhaps one of the most obvious examples of film music as pop music was the succession of title songs for the series of James Bond films. The majority were co-written by John Barry, and each was sung by a special featured artist. They appeared over sumptuous, elegant title sequences, apart from Louis Armstrong's 'All the Time in the World', from *On Her Majesty's Secret Service* (1969), which appears as non-diegetic music rather than in the film's title sequence. More recently, film composer David Arnold completed a project to record a number of James Bond title songs with a selection of contemporary singers. The album, *Shaken and Stirred* (1997), included artists such as David McAlmont and the Propellerheads.[29] The influence of Bond music is evident in Robbie Williams's song 'Millennium', released in 1998, which is based on a loop of two very distinctive and identifiable bars taken from the main theme to *You Only Live Twice* (1967), a connection underlined by the promo video casting Williams in a Bond-style role.[30]

A film music influence was apparent in the early 1980s in pop groups like Adam and the Ants, who owed a clear debt to Ennio Morricone's spaghetti Western scores, with their trebly guitar lines and wordless vocal chants. His Italian compatriot, Nino Rota, had a most singular tribute album to his film music performed by various pop acts, including Debbie Harry from Blondie. *Amarcord Nino Rota* (1981) was overseen by Hal Willner, a record producer who later went on to be musical director on Robert Altman's *Short Cuts* (1993).[31] Some film music was reissued on CD and became part of a renewed interest in 'easy listening' music in the mid-1990s. This was not the Bert Kaempfert-Klaus Wunderlich-Mantovani brand of 'easy listening', but more attuned to exotic club music from the 1960s, and was more aptly called 'Lounge' or, more floridly, 'Loungecore'. This revival brought back to prominence the music of bands and small orchestras from the 1950s and 1960s, and by luminaries of exotica such as Martin Denny. An album that provides something of the flavour of this sort of music was *Easy Project: 20 Loungecore Favourites* (2000), which included music by artists such as Laurie Johnson, Johnny Hawksworth, Alan Tew and John Schroeder, mixing electronic space music with television crime show themes. It also allowed the rediscovery of the pop music capacities of some film music, such as Manfred Huebler's music for Jess Franco's film *Vampiros lesbos* (1970) and Gerd Wilden's music for films like the *Schoolgirl Report* series in the 1970s and *El bikini rojo* (1966). John Carpenter's music from his own films made an impression on pop/rock musicians. His theme to his film *Assault on Precinct 13*

(1976) has been recorded by Afrika Bambaataa (as 'Bambaataa's Theme') and by gothic punk group Blood and Roses in the early 1980s.[32] Carpenter's film themes, particularly the one for *Halloween*, exerted an unacknowledged influence on the electronic pop music that burgeoned in the early 1980s using preset synthesizers, instruments that needed minimal programming and no traditional musical training to play. More recently, Mortiis, a purveyor of medieval-sounding Norwegian black ambient music, who was once bass player in satanic black metal group Emperor, has created a whole persona and world fabricated under at least the partial influence of science-fantasy film. He stated: I'm influenced by the soundtrack to the Conan movies . . .',[33] and noted the influence of film scores generally.[34] Mortiis's music clearly owes far more to film music than to the traditions of heavy metal, although this is precisely where you will find his CDs in the shops. I was once passing a 'Games Workshop' outlet, and was bemused to hear that as an accompaniment for their 'dungeons and dragons' type role-playing games, the people in the shop had chosen Basil Poledouris's incidental music from *Conan the Barbarian* (1982).

Mortiis's music is often referred to as 'black ambient', and indeed it has more in common with the ambient music genre than it does with heavy metal. Ambient music is probably the genre that owes most to film music, or at least to the concept of the 'cinematic'. It is premised upon 'atmosphere' and the construction of sound-scapes, in much the same way as film composers and sound designers construct film soundtracks. Often 'image-friendly music', it can thus easily be used in television programmes or films, and so has the capacity to be sold twice over. The modern 'pop' version of ambient music was a development, on the one hand, from Brian Eno's electronic experiments in the 1970s and, on the other, from post-House dance music.[35] Current ambient music has fragmented into experimental music ('electroacoustic music'), relaxed dance music (for the 'chill-out' zone in clubs) and new age music (merging with 'easy listening' and 'relaxation music'). As Eno noted on the cover of *Ambient 4: On Land* (1982): 'cluster all disparate sounds into one aural frame: they become music', echoing Erik Satie's desire for unassuming *musique d'ameublement*, music to mix with the sounds of knives and forks at dinner, and expensively produced Muzak to seduce shoppers into increased purchasing.

The late 1970s and early 1980s, around the time of Eno's most ground-breaking work, was a period of crisis for the music industry. As one journalist put it in 1982: 'With the British record industry now in the depths of the severest decline it has ever known, there are real fears that rock music will never regain the lion's share of the entertainment market it held in the mid-seventies.'[36] The mood of the record industry was demonstrated vividly by their overriding concern in the early and mid-1980s: namely, piracy. The industry's campaign, which united behind the slogan 'Home taping is killing music', put pressure on the British government to levy a charge on blank recording tapes to 'compensate' record companies for revenue lost by the illegal but endemic home taping of records. One corollary of this industrial contraction was that pop music's past glories became the basis for future sales, which is why the conservatism of the July 1985 Live Aid roster was so striking: Eric

Clapton, Status Quo, even Led Zeppelin re-formed in order to appear. This meant that the focus of the music lay more in the 1970s than the 1980s, looking to the past more than to the future, and reflecting marketing rather than aesthetic develop-ments. The atmosphere of apparently lost revenues, heaped upon dwindling profits, led to a retrenchment of the international music and recording industry, which towards the end of the decade was boosted by the arrival of compact discs as a new standard format.[37] This was the conclusion of a strategy that allowed record companies to reanimate and resell all their back catalogues as much as, if not more than, selling contemporary artists. Record companies could thus concentrate on AOR, aiming at adult audiences rather than the poorer youth market. Cultural recy-cling became the order of the day in the mid-1980s,[38] with record companies gut-ting their back catalogues for the screen, the buzzword 'synergy' describing the co-ordination of record releases from a film soundtrack as mutual publicity.[39]

Music, along with other culture, is often now seen as 'multipurpose'. It can be used in a number of different formats, of which film is only one of the most obvi-ous outlets.[40] Yet we should never forget that the motivation for recycling is aes-thetic as well as financial. Kubrick replaced Alex North's score for *2001: A Space Odyssey* with its existing temp track of orchestral recordings for aesthetic reasons rather than financial considerations, and the same goes for Dennis Hopper and Peter Fonda's decision to use rock songs as accompaniment to *Easy Rider* (1968).

Pop songs have, for some time, been used as 'stock' music for films, and are increasingly used on television in this capacity (as discussed in Chapter 7). They are easy to 'cut in' to films. Yet some 'pop music' is crying out to be used as incidental music in films and on television.

The compilation score for recent films has been well-established since the 1970s. Jeff Smith notes that

> The development of this 'machinery' [to create hit songs in films] came in response to a number
> of industrial, historical, and sociological factors in the 1950s and early 1960s, including the trend
> towards diversification and conglomeration in film distribution, the emergence of studio-owned
> record labels, the establishment of radio and records as important ancillary markets, and changes
> in popular music tastes and consumption patterns.[41]

Yet films such as *Natural Born Killers* (1994) have used music as a central part of the film's aesthetics and, rather than simply release a tied-in album, the film has what might almost be seen as a parallel object album, produced by Nine Inch Nails's Trent Reznor, mixing the songs that appeared as part of the film's non-diegetic music (and diegetic music) with dialogue to create a 'cinematic' experience.

Song tie-ins have led to films being named after songs, such as *That'll Be the Day* (1973), *Blue Velvet, Jumpin' Jack Flash* (1986), *Stand by Me* (1986), *Pretty Woman* (1990) and *In Dreams* (1999).[42] However, the classical musicals had already set a precedent here, with such obvious examples as *Top Hat* (1935), *Singin' in the Rain* (1952) and *White Christmas* (1954). Indeed, it is not difficult to make a case that the aesthetic impetus of the musical has migrated to mainstream, non-musical films (as much as has the desire to sell tied-in songs).[43] A notable and seemingly incongruous example is the concluding shoot-out in John Woo's *Face/Off*, which is shot in balletic slow motion accompanied by 'Somewhere over the Rainbow' (performed by Olivia Newton John). Indeed, the marginalisation of diegetic sound in favour of music recalls Rick Altman's description of the audio dissolve that inaugurates song sequences in the classical musical.[44]

On isolated occasions, pop groups have provided the musical score for films. Perhaps the most obvious examples are Goblin (including *Profondo rosso, Suspiria* [1977] and *Dawn of the Dead* [1978]), Popol Vuh (including *Aguirre: The Wrath of God* [1973], *Nosferatu the Vampyre, Fitzcarraldo* [1982])[45] and Tangerine Dream (*Sorcerer, Thief, Fright Night* and *Near Dark* [1987]). Admittedly, these were extraordinary groups that were hardly very 'pop' at all. Other examples include Ashton, Gardner and Dyke performing Jon Lord (Deep Purple's keyboard player) and Tony Ashton's score for *The Last Rebel* (1970), or the score provided by chart act Wang Chung for William Friedkin's *To Live and Die in LA* (1985).

In recent years, individual pop musicians have increasingly been composing and, in some cases, performing film scores. Apart from those already mentioned, there is John Barry (from the John Barry Seven), Hans Zimmer (once in the Buggles), James Newton Howard (who played with Elton John), Carter Burwell (who collaborated with members of New Order in Thick Pigeon), Clint Mansell (Pop Will Eat Itself), George Clinton (Parliament/Funkadelic), Keith Emerson (Emerson, Lake and Palmer and The Nice), Danny Elfman (Oingo Boingo), Graeme Revell (SPK), John Murphy (SPK), Colin Towns (Gillan), David Arnold and songwriters Randy Newman and Randy Edelman. This is by no means an exhaustive list. While keyboard players are well represented (Howard, Towns, Hans Zimmer, Mark Mancina, Stanislas Syrewicz, Giorgio Moroder, Mark Mothersbaugh, Vangelis, Ryuichi Sakamoto and Nick Glennie-Smith[46]), guitar players are less so. However, over the past two decades, scores have been written (and often performed) by guitarists such as Ry Cooder, Trevor Rabin, Eric Clapton, Mark Knopfler, David Arnold, W. G. 'Snuffy' Walden, David A. Stewart and Neil Young.[47] Bass guitarists are perhaps more rare. Apart from Barry Adamson, Marcus Miller and John Cale, jazz-rock bassist Stanley Clarke has produced some startling incidental music for *Romeo Must Die!* (2000), which mixes rap songs with Clarke's funky groove-based underscore.[48] Drummers are rarer still, with only Brian Bennett and Stewart Copeland immediately coming to mind.[49] This suggests, if only obliquely, that rhythmic impetus is still of less importance to screen music than texture and melody.

Simon Boswell had previously been involved as much, or perhaps more, in pop music than in film scoring, providing the music for a number of Italian films, such as *Demons 2* (1986), *The Church* (1991) and Dario Argento's *Phenomena* (1984).[50] Boswell also had a significant background in pop music, originally as a solo artist, then in the group Live Wire. Subsequently, in the early 1980s, he produced artists like Amii Stewart, Nik Kershaw, Nine Below Zero, Sex Gang Children and experimental pop group 23 Skidoo. His score for *Hardware* (1990) is almost completely electronic, utilising predominantly synthetic timbres that have become commonplace since the widespread availability of easily programmed keyboard synthesizers and MIDI equipment in the mid-1980s.[51]

By the 1970s, many film scores had incorporated significant aspects from pop music – usually via jazz-rock – into their fabric, with films as diverse as *The Omega Man* (1971), *Get Carter* (1971) and *Magnum Force* (1973), using loud bass guitars and drum backbeats along with jazzy brass and traditional string arrangements. In the 1970s, the desire for legitimate status fostered by progressive rock was one reason why pop music became increasingly hybridised.[52] Just as there was an art music crossover, so there was a crossover between film music and pop music. A number of pop music-oriented LPs were like soundtrack recordings without films. Pink Floyd's *Dark Side of the Moon* sounded like a film, with its mixture of music, dialogue and sound effects, while Tangerine Dream's electronic, instrumental (voiceless) and programmatic albums evoked imagery through sounds. In contrast to the main melody, simple harmonies and rhythm of the vast majority of pop songs, their work resembled art music more than pop music. It was a logical step for the German group to move very effectively into the area of film soundtrack production, providing wholly electronic scores for films from the late 1970s onwards.

In the 1970s, a number of pop stars from the 1960s, in a desire to show how they had matured as musicians, consistently told the press that they were writing film soundtracks.[53] Translocation from pop music to films was a 'natural progression' for some 'mood producing' musicians.[54] Paul McCartney had been the first pop musician to turn feature film composer, with *The Family Way* (1966). He later returned briefly to the field, providing the song and main theme for the James Bond film *Live and Let Die* (1973). One of McCartney's pop star predecessors from the 1960s, the Shadows's drummer Brian Bennett, built a career providing music for television,[55] a path that was followed by many others. A logical conclusion of the trajectory of legitimisation for pop musicians, this offered another way of promoting themselves as artists, and presented an increasingly attractive and viable option for ageing musicians. Bill Wyman, the Rolling Stones bass player, declared, 'I think it's a natural progression from playing popular music. You can experiment more.'[56] Ironically, his score for *Green Ice* (1981) was not only his first, but would prove to be his last. Yet there was a concerted move from the pop music world into film scoring, increasing the degree of pop music techniques evident in contemporary film music, as well as giving further impetus to the use of pop music as non-diegetic music. David Toop suggests that the move into film scoring is the result of the adventurousness of pop musicians themselves,[57] and, indeed, the bounds of pop music had become very wide since the late 1960s, if not altogether untenable as a distinct musical genre. Pop and rock music embraced a thriving underground, which might be called an avant-garde and which never aimed directly at high recordings sales, although much of the progressive rock underground arguably constituted the mainstream album market itself. David Bowie's career in the late 1970s was heavily influenced by more left-field music, inspired largely by his collaboration with Brian Eno. Eno was a significant influence on much of the more 'serious' end of pop and rock from the 1970s onwards and had written some stock music for film, released as *Music for Films* in 1978. Bowie's albums *Low* (1977) and *Heroes* (1978) demonstrated the influence of film music and ambient music in their instrumental pieces on side two of each LP.[58]

The 'pop avant-garde' has been more than willing to move into writing film music, while simultaneously many of the same groups were attempting to move into film and video production. For example, Download (ex-Skinny Puppy) provided the music for Jim Bebber's *Charlie's Family* (1997), a documentary about Charles Manson. Coil provided the music for Derek Jarman's *The Angelic Conversation* (1985) and *Blue* (1993) and had a score rejected for *Hellraiser*. The instrumental music produced by groups such as these already evinced 'cinematic' elements, and was certainly suited to use in films. It is not difficult to see some of this music as following the impetus of film music to allow the creation of 'film scores' outside of films. The artist Lustmord, now more commonly and prosaically known as Brian Williams, in partnership with film composer Graeme Revell (both were in SPK at one point), has worked on the sound design for *The Crow* (1994), *Mighty Morphin Power Rangers* (1995) and *Spawn* (1997), among others. Before this, his albums sounded remarkably like film atmospheres, with *The Place Where the Black Stars Hang* (1994) being effectively spatial sound design, while *The Monstrous Soul* (1992) included some very prominent samples from British horror film *The Night of the Demon* (aka *Curse of the Demon* in the USA). These 'atmospheres' are soundtracks that precede films and are testament to the intermediate area between atmospheric film music and certain more experimental areas of pop music.

Stylistic Convergence

I would argue that pop music style has changed recent orchestral film music, adding significant aesthetic developments to Kathryn Kalinak's description of the established classical film score of traditional mainstream cinema.[59] It is not the only development that has overtaken the classical film score. Both modernist classical music, inspiration for the music in the *Alien* films, and jazz, as in *Lift to the Scaffold* (*Ascenseur pour l'échafaud*, 1958), performed and written by Miles Davis, and *The Man with the Golden Arm*, evince significant stylistic development from the traditions of Hollywood (and other mainstream) film music. Other developments have also made their mark, such as the desire to use 'featured' sounds, exotic instruments that provide instant 'flavour'. More identifiable musical timbres include the shakuhachi (Japanese bamboo flute), the zither in *The Third Man* (1949) or James Horner's use of uillean pipes in his scores for *Braveheart*, *Titanic* and *The Devil's Own*. Nicholas Cook discusses the dominant musical strategies used in advertisements, which bear out the increased use of generic style and sound in compositions:

Traditionally, musicians compose with notes, rhythms, and perhaps timbres. Only with post-modernism has the idea of 'composing with styles' or 'composing with genres' emerged, at least as a consciously adopted procedure. But composing with styles or genres is one of the most basic musical techniques found in television commercials. . . . Musical styles and genres offer unsurpassed opportunities for communicating complex social or attitudinal messages practically instantaneously. . . . Commercials often contain music that almost completely lacks 'content' as a music theorist would generally define it – that is, distinctive melodic, harmonic, or rhythmic shaping – but incorporates a musical logic based on style.[60]

This is a widespread feature of film music, and can be illustrated with recourse to any film that uses a generic cast in its underscore. Examples would include the 'rock' of Danny Elfman's score for *Midnight Run* (1988) or the hillbilly country music of Carter Burwell's score for *Raising Arizona* (1987). The style and techniques of music for advertisements was, at least partially, derived from cinema, but these strategies have since permeated screen music more generally.

As part of this process, the influence of pop music has led to a notable preponderance of more simple and lyrical (in the sense of possessing a song-like structure) melodies, as exhibited by the 'mature' scores of John Williams. Indeed, Williams's main themes for *Superman*, *Star Wars* and *E.T.* (1982) became hit singles, and also could be easily adapted for 'pop' versions, such as Meco's (Meco Monardo) hit disco version of the *Star Wars* theme. Jeff Smith notes that the traditional classical film score crossbred with popular music influences, to create the pop score, which

often adapted popular musical forms to the particular needs of the film it accompanied. Traditional devices such as ostinatos, pedal points and sustained chords, were written in pop idioms and combined with sixteen- and thirty-two-bar song forms. Through this process of adaptation, pop song forms were sometimes shortened, fragmented, and varied to fit the temporal constraints of the scenes they accompanied. This adaptation enabled the pop score to serve both dramatic functions within the film and commercial functions within the record industry in the somewhat different format of the soundtrack album.[61]

Stronger beats also became evident, as in, for example, John Barry's score for the James Bond films, which included some elements apparent in earlier John Barry Seven hit records, such as Vic Flick's trebly lead guitar. As pop music became more influential, and pop musicians began to score films, more in the way of 32-bar structures and four-bar strophes became discernible. In Danny Elfman's score for *Batman*, the music often maintains a busy pulse that remains almost solidly in 4/4 time. Such techniques betray a certain autonomy of film scores in relation to the films they accompany, where the specific dynamics of action are less important than was typically the case with the subordinated music in classical Hollywood cinema. Arguably, this is down to the fragmentation of cinema into a number of attractions, where music can be a featured element as much as any other, and, indeed, often becomes a foregrounded component of cinema's effects.

Film and television music composer Graeme Revell observes that 'With a few exceptions, producers and directors no longer want the old-style film scoring.'[62] As the basic blueprint of film music established by the Hollywood studio system, the classical film score is a heavily dated language. Film studies students are only too ready to laugh at the unsubtle underscore in romances such as *Now, Voyager*. Pop music speaks in a very current and direct emotional language, allowing films to register an emotional impact with audiences accustomed to pop music rather than orchestral art music. This cannot be underestimated. In the past couple of decades, the two languages have been mixing increasingly. For example, Bill Conti's music for the James Bond film *For Your Eyes Only* (1981) includes drum backbeats for car chase sequences. Similarly, David Arnold's incidental music for the underwater action and the Hamburg break-in in *Tomorrow Never Dies* (1997) constantly exhibits the direct mixing of pop music and traditional film music aspects. In fact, an obvious example of this is the way more generally that the James Bond theme itself is cut into films without being matched to screen dynamics.

In another Bond film, *Goldeneye* (1995), Eric Serra uses large amounts of pop backbeats. The car chase near the start of the film begins with an obvious funky dance style on synthesizers, but then, as the chase and the piece develop, the beat and rhythm track remain as orchestral strings enter and then come to dominate. This mixture of pop beat and film music's traditional orchestral forces has become more prominent in recent film music. A good example of the stylistic convergence of the two is *The Boxer*, which has a musical score by pop musicians Gavin Friday and Maurice Seezer that mixes the techniques of traditional film music and pop music, embodying the interzone between the two. Cinema is now a grab bag of effects, in which film music is regularly foregrounded and aspects such as pop music's regulated musical rhythm have become prominent. This aligns increasingly autonomous film music with the 'absolute' music championed by art music, moving it away from its perceived functional status and producing music that is less geared towards the dictates and dynamics of individual films.

Gavin Friday was originally a member of the Virgin Prunes, an art performance-inspired post-punk group from Dublin. He then went on to sing solo, forging a parodic cabaret singer persona, and later became involved in making film music. Friday and regular collaborator Maurice Seezer had worked together on Friday's solo albums and then on the score for *In the Name of the Father*. They supplied a number of songs, working with Sinéad O'Connor and Bono from U2. The underscore for the film was written by Trevor Jones, although part of the melody of the end titles song 'You Made Me the Thief of My Heart' appeared within the film's underscore. The opening of *The Boxer* combines a number of sonic elements. It also includes a tolling bell on each first beat of a two-bar loop that goes along with the drum backbeat, after which the main theme enters on strings. It includes voice samples, without any notable tune, while using a simple volume control and halting as dynamics. The visual track appears to be cut directly to the structure of the music, rather than vice versa. However, despite being orchestral, the music's influences are more from film music and some pop music than from orchestral classical music.

The mix of strings and beats is very evident in the music of Craig Armstrong. He trained at the Royal Academy of Music, but then went on to work in both art music and pop music, being involved with the groups Texas and Massive Attack, among others. Armstrong's debut album, *The Space between Us* (1998), is very strange for a pop album, as it contains only a few songs and is otherwise dominated by Armstrong's trademark string orchestra sound but incorporating more straight-forward melodies, in which pop elements such as drum beats are prominent. It also includes some material from his film work, notably from Baz Luhrmann's *Romeo and Juliet*. Armstrong also scored Peter Mullan's *Orphans* (1997), *The Bone Collector* (1999), *Moulin Rouge* (2001) and *The Quiet American* (2002), along with the icon-oclastic historical costume film *Plunkett and Maclaine*. It was an audacious score that showed the ability of the pop music sensibility to make dynamic incidental music for films. Armstrong's score not only included the sort of string writing that might not seem out of place in a film score, but at times also showed some inspiration from contemporary electronic dance music, notably in the extreme of exciting kinesis during the film's party sequence.

The rediscovery of easy listening and lounge music allowed for the increased use of a mixture of beats and strings, much of which was performed by band-type ensembles or small orchestras. At the same time, the mixture of strings and beats was more evident in mainstream pop music and its more experimental edges. One of the most discussed albums of the last decade, U.N.K.L.E's *Psyence Fiction*, which I touched upon in a previous chapter, bears a heavy film influence. It includes a notable piece called 'Celestial Annihilation', which is based on string arrangements of the type that adorned films, and represented a development by Wil Malone from his *Concerto for Strings and Beats*. Malone has a substantial track record of arrang-ing for pop musicians, but also wrote the music for the British film *Death Line* (1972).[63] Along similar lines, some hit singles in the 1990s mixed a body of strings with a strong spine of a beat, such as Massive Attack's 'Unfinished Sympathy' and The Verve's 'Bittersweet Symphony', which was a British number one record. How-ever, in each case it is difficult to see a direct influence from classical orchestral music, and they might be better explained with recourse to the influence of film music. The endemic use of a combination of strings and beats is testament to the increasing aesthetic alliance between cinema and pop music,[64] as illustrated not only by such pop music, but also by film music, such as the opening title theme for *Unbreakable* (2000) by James Newton Howard.

Conclusion

Traditionally, there has been a close relationship between popular music and film, as exemplified first by Hollywood musicals, and later in films starring the likes of rock'n'roll singers Elvis Presley and Tommy Steele, who went from a singing career straight into the cinema.[65] Many commentators have only dealt with pop and cinema on a level of 'addition', noting the insertion of pop songs into films, whereas perhaps we should begin to conceive the situation more on a level of genetic fusion.

A central component of this chapter addressed a strand of music that has always crossed over between the zones of film music and 'pure' popular music, music seemingly not allied to the image or other activity. Recent developments, I would suggest, where the two forms have converged more explicitly, are not fully explicable with reference to the concentration of industries in multinational corporations, but are also the logical extension of an aesthetic and social trajectory that has its origins in the 19th century and in developments in music's wider use. The work of someone like David Holmes embodies this occurrence, bridging not only dance and ambient music, but also concept albums and film soundtracks.

The soundtrack album industry has become one of the main ways to repackage existing music, and the expansion of the film soundtrack market has matched the contraction of the pop music market since the early 1970s. This has siphoned pop music back catalogues into the domain of 'film music' in much the same way as silent film music cannibalised music from the classical concert hall. Cinema is now often a grab bag of effects, in which music is regularly foregrounded and aspects such as pop music's regulated musical rhythm become critical. The surprising net effect of this has been to align increasingly autonomous forms of film music with the 'absolute' music championed by art music aficionados, moving it away from its perceived status as simply functional.

In terms of cultural status, film music has steadily advanced to take on something of the mantle of 'legit'/'classical' or 'art' music (call it what you will) for generations of pop musicians and audiences more generally. Modernist music became remote during the 20th century, no longer operating as a zone of expansive arrangement and melodic and harmonic invention and scope. That function has been displaced by orchestral film music. Outside of university music departments and high-art bastions, film music can attain a fairly high cultural status, perhaps partly due to its typical orchestral basis but more likely because of its significant emotional effect and the regular enormity of its sound.

Certainly, pop and rock musicians have tended to be charmed by films and film music. A number of writers have pointed to pop music's obsession with the cinema, yet none have accounted for it convincingly. I think it is because cinema appears like popular 'art'. It seemingly has the possibility of a transcendent status while lacking the remoteness of more lofty 'art', and thus functions as aspirational for some areas of pop music and popular culture more generally. It should be noted that the visualisation of music has involved a reciprocal musicalisation of vision. Changes in the cinema's modes of production, the apparent collapse of a strong musical counter-culture and the increasing untenability of the art 'avant-garde' has encouraged a pop music 'avant-garde', which has wrested itself free of the constraints of the three-minute song format and the pop charts and forced its way into films.

Notes

1 Indeed, one might be able to trace a direct trajectory from Pink Floyd's music written for the Barbet Schroeder film *More* (1969) to their best-selling album *Dark Side of the Moon*, which includes certain soundtrack-like elements.

2 Gal Detourn, 'Lost Souls Take Flight', *Making Music*, issue 177, January 2001, p. 12.

3 Both this and the album's sleeve notes were written by Alexis Petridis. The album includes Craig Armstrong and 'trip hop' group Lamb.

4 Interestingly, both pieces premiered in 1830, nearly a hundred years before the establishment of sound cinema.

5 *Images* was written for piano in 1905–7, and included *Reflets dans l'eau* and *Et la lune descend sur le temple qui fût*.

6 Over the past decade, there has also been a boom in live accompaniment to silent films, both by orchestras and rock groups. See further discussion in this book's final chapter.

7 Of course, the scores for classical musicals were a mixture of wall-to-wall dramatic scoring and songs, blending the melodies of the numbers with the score.

8 This fragmentation is reflected in the proliferation of different generic sales charts.

9 The same goes for the term 'classical music'.

10 In a way, rock operas should be seen as the cinematic equivalent or manifestation of the concept album.

11 Quoted in Simon Frith, 'Youth Culture/Youth Cults' in Charlie Gillett and Simon Frith, eds., *The Beat Goes On: The Rock File Reader* (London: Pluto, 1996), p. 147. (The article originally appeared in 1978.)

12 Sheila Whiteley, *The Space between the Notes: Rock and the Counterculture* (London: Routledge, 1992), pp. 6, 3; Steve Chapple and Reebee Garofalo, *Rock'n'Roll Is Here to Pay: The History and Politics of the Music Industry* (Chicago: Nelson Hall, 1977), p. 72.

13 Long playing records (LPs) had become widely known as 'albums' (in the manner of art folios) since the advent of *Sergeant Pepper's Lonely Hearts Club Band*. It was the first LP to include a lyric sheet and have a gatefold sleeve, and arguably was the first concept album.

14 *Dark Side of the Moon* remained in the charts for 294 weeks, first appearing in March 1973.

15 At least I thought so. As a youngster, I was hoping to see this 'film' at some point! The album can still be found in the 'film soundtracks' sections of some shops.

16 Gavin Martin, 'Company Lore and Public Disorder' [interview with PiL], *New Musical Express*, 14 March 1981, p. 32.

17 K. J. Donnelly, 'Constructing the Future through Music of the Past: The Software in *Hardware*' in Ian Inglis, ed., *Popular Music and Film* (London: Wallflower, 2003), p. 140.

18 Barry Adamson went on to work in films, composing music for British–French co-production *Shuttlecock* (1991) and David Lynch's *Lost Highway*, as discussed in Chapter 2.

19 A bizarre doppelgänger album that also included images and sounds of the Pope was Laibach's *Also Sprach John Paul II* (1998).

20 Rob Fearn, 'Scary Tales of New York', *Mixmag*, no. 76, September 1997, p. 119.

21 Which to some degree inspired the collection *This Film's Crap Let's Sample the Soundtrack* (North South FLMCRP007).

22 <http://www.futurenet.com/musiciansnet/hitech/People/Holmes/Holmes.html> (accessed 18 December 1998).

23 Michael Bonner, 'Primal Screen' [review of David Holmes's CD *Bow Down to the Exit Sign*], *Uncut*, no. 37, June 2000, p. 102.

24 For an analysis of *Performance*'s remarkable music, see K. J. Donnelly, '*Performance* and the Composite Film Score' in K. J. Donnelly, ed., *Film Music: Critical Approaches* (Edinburgh: Edinburgh University Press, 2001), pp. 152–66.

25 David Holmes, 'Inside Track' [about his latest album], *Uncut*, no. 37, June 2000, p. 102.

26 Some pop musicians have been inspired to make their own films, such as Bauhaus's *Shadow of Light* (1981) and Prince's *Under the Cherry Moon* (1986). Both of these lacked success or acclaim, but certainly not ambition. David Byrne's *True Stories* (1986) was unique in gaining all three.

27 This very same sound sample was also used on Brutal Truth's 'Perpetual Larceny'.

28 Despite being a one-hit wonder, La Tour went on to provide a song for *Basic Instinct* (1992).

29 Another Arnold collaboration, with Vic Reeves on 'Don't Put Your Daughter on the Stage' (from *Twentieth Century Blues* [1998], an album of Noel Coward songs), included sumptuous strings that were strikingly reminiscent of Bernard Herrmann's score for *Vertigo*.

30 In June 2001, ITV's advertisements for their forthcoming screening of *You Only Live Twice* used Williams's 'Millennium'.

31 Willner also went on to produce Gavin Friday's albums.

32 We perhaps should not underestimate the influence of his synthesizer work on electronic music of the late 1970s and early 1980s, such as Gary Numan, the Human League and Soft Cell.

33 Steven Wells, 'Boy, I'm Really Nervous', *New Musical Express*, 25 September 1999, p. 25.

34 Satpal Kalsi, '*The Stargate*', *Terrorizer*, issue 70, September 1999, p. 50.

35 Mark Prendergast, *The Ambient Century: From Mahler to Moby – the Evolution of Sound in the Electronic Age* (London: Bloomsbury, 2000), pp. 131, 52–3.

36 News article, *Sounds*, 17 July 1982, p. 2.

37 Jeremy Eckstein, ed., *Cultural Trends 19*, vol. 3, no. 3 (London: Policy Studies Institute, 1993), p. 45.

38 Realigning pop record sales with the age trajectory of the baby-boom generation.

39 R. Serge Denisoff and George Plasketes, 'Synergy in 1980s Film and Music: Formula for Success or Industry Mythology?', *Film History*, vol. 4, no. 3, 1990, p. 257.

40 In the 1990s, Ted Turner bought MGM and immediately released old movies on videos and film musical soundtracks on CD.

41 Jeff Smith, *The Sounds of Commerce: Marketing Popular Film Music* (New York: Columbia University Press, 1998), p. 2.

42 Noted by Jeff Smith, 'Popular Song and Comic Allusion in Contemporary Cinema' in Pamela Robertson Wojcik and Arthur Knight, eds., *Soundtrack Available: Essays on Film and Popular Music* (Durham, NC: Duke University Press, 2001), p. 413.

43 Indeed, Ian Garwood suggests that the romantic comedy might be approached as an 'incomplete' musical, 'Must You Remember This?: Orchestrating the "Standard" Pop Song in *Sleepless in Seattle*' in Kay Dickinson, ed., *Movie Music: The Film Reader* (London: Routledge, 2003), p. 114.

44 Rick Altman, *The American Film Musical* (London: BFI, 1989), p. 110.

45 See further discussion in K. J. Donnelly, 'Angel of the Air: Popol Vuh's Music for Werner Herzog's Films' in Miguel Mera and David Burnand, eds., *European Film Music* (Aldershot, Hants: Ashgate, 2005).

46 James Newton Howard has worked with Elton John, Earth, Wind and Fire, Chaka Khan, Olivia Newton John and Leo Sayer, among others; Mark Mancina has played with Yes and Seal, while Nick Glennie-Smith has played with Pink Floyd, Phil Collins, Tina Turner and Paul McCartney.

47 It is interesting to note that among top creative rock guitar players, Robert Fripp has not written film music. He was involved with ambient music along with Brian Eno but appears to have resisted the pull toward film music (although some of his music was used in Amos Poe's *Subway Riders* [1981]).

48 Another was Roger Waters, the bassist in Pink Floyd, who provided the music (collaborating with Ron Geesin) for *The Body* (1970), a documentary about René Magritte and for the animated film *When the Wind Blows* (1987), as well as writing the music and script for *Pink Floyd: The Wall*.

49 Mark Snow once drummed for the New York Rock'n'Roll Ensemble, which also featured Michael Kamen. He is famed for composing and performing the music for the *X-Files* and is known primarily for television music.

50 Maitland McDonagh notes, erroneously, that Boswell had been in Goblin, the experimental rock group that provided the music for many of Dario Argento's films. *Broken Mirrors, Broken Minds: The Dark Dreams of Dario Argento* (London: Sun Tavern Fields, 1991), pp. 9–10.

51 MIDI (musical instrument digital interface) was central to the development of integrated digital synthesis and studios built around personal computers.

52 Some progressive rock 'crossed over' and became mainstream successes like Mike Oldfield's *Tubular Bells*, which had massive worldwide sales. Progressive rock was also crossing over with art music, as two years later a new version of *Tubular Bells* was released as an orchestral arrangement conducted by David Bedford. The late 1970s also saw the appearance of *Classic Rock* LPs, which entailed orchestral arrangements of rock songs.

53 Mark Sinker, 'Music as Film' in Jonathan Romney and Adrian Wootton, eds., *Celluloid Jukebox: Popular Music and the Movies Since the 50s* (London: BFI, 1995), p. 111.

54 David Toop, 'Rock Musicians and Film Soundtracks' in Jonathan Romney and Adrian Wootton, eds., *Celluloid Jukebox: Popular Music and the Movies since the 50s* (London: BFI, 1995), p. 73.

55 He provided music for the *Ruth Rendell Mysteries* (1990–, TVS) and *The Knock* (1994, LWT), among other programmes.

56 Neil Norman, 'Green Ice for a Grey Stone' [interview with Bill Wyman], *New Musical Express*, 30 May 1981, p. 11.

57 Toop, 'Rock Musicians and Film Soundtracks', p. 79.

58 Indeed, Mark Sinker notes that the cover of *Low* was a photograph taken during the shooting of *The Man Who Fell to Earth* (1976), in which Bowie starred but provided none of the soundtrack. 'Music as Film', p. 111.

59 Kathryn Kalinak, *Settling the Score: Music and the Classical Hollywood Film* (Madison: University of Wisconsin Press, 1992), pp. xv–xvi.

60 Nicholas Cook, 'Music and Meaning in the Commercials', in *Popular Music*, vol. 13, no. 1, 1994, p. 35.

61 Smith, 'The Sounds of Commerce', p. 6.

62 Graeme Revell, quoted in Jeff Berkwits, 'Graeme Revell – Journeys to *Dune*' [interview], *Soundtrack*, vol. 19, no. 76, Winter 2000, p. 6.

63 Wil(son) Malone has been an arranger in the British pop music industry since the 1960s, working for groups like Massive Attack and Simple Minds, after originally being in the group Orange Bicycle.

64 However, earlier songs have similarities. Genesis's 'Can Utility and the Coastliners' from *Foxtrot* (1972) uses a superficially similar configuration of strings (the keyboard Mellotron) and beats in its middle section.

65 K. J. Donnelly, *Pop Music in British Cinema: A Chronicle* (London: BFI, 2001), p. 1.

Chapter 9

Loose Ends and Last Words

> The isle is full of noises,
> Sounds and sweet airs, that give delight and hurt not;
> Sometimes a thousand twangling instruments,
> Will hum about mine ears, and sometimes voices
> That, if I then had waked after long sleep,
> Will make me sleep again.
>
> (Caliban in *The Tempest*, Act III, Scene 2)

This sounds remarkably like a description of film music, and adumbrates a magical sound space that predated cinema. Music's aural bath of affect and essentially emotional character make it a potent aspect of film and television. Non-diegetic music might be seen as manifesting an unconscious level of the film, as well as a level of unconscious within the film. Indeed, the soundscape itself might be conceived as an analogue to the virtual space of mental processes, as a repository of half-memories, primal emotion and the seemingly illogical. 'Ghosts' inhabiting a film are often little more than shapes, momentary musical configurations or half-remembered sounds. Music can suggest, or even can lead directly to, an elsewhere, like a footnote. Sometimes, when you look at a library book, the scrawled notes and comments written in the margins not only reorientate your view towards the hallowed text itself, sometimes they can prove to be far more interesting. 'Annotated versions' of books can be intriguing precisely because of their footnotes. This approach allows us to see cinema as fully intertextual and paradigmatic, rather than simply a linear and progressive communicational discourse. Music can implicate an elsewhere, particularly when the music in question is recontextualised, and may often carry a myriad of associational baggage. Developments since the 1960s, with both industrial and aesthetic determinants, have increasingly involved the insertion of existing music into film and television, as well as promoting a 'featured' status for incidental music in some films.

Film music is not what it once was. It is consumed more widely and in a different manner than it was even a few years ago. The expansion of the soundtrack market has matched the contraction of the pop record market since the 1970s. Jeff Smith describes Sony Classical's immense sales of their CDs of James Horner's score for James Cameron's *Titanic*, which not only outsold other soundtrack albums, but also the rest of Sony's classical music catalogue, demonstrating the popularity of orchestral film music in the face of orchestral 'classical' music.[1] This is part of a piecemeal music industry strategy to reinvigorate 'classical music' through associating it with orchestral music in films. *Titanic* was a musical event as well as a cinematic event. The film spawned a massive hit single, Celine Dion's 'My Heart Will Go On', which emanated from the film's underscore themes and graced the film's end titles. Two soundtrack CDs were made available: *Music from Titanic* and *Back to Titanic*, which later were combined into a double CD package. The first outsold all other instrumental scores ever produced, the success and subject matter of the film stimulating the record industry to an astonishing degree. I have come across a startling twenty-four CD albums that were tied in some way to the film. Apart from the two official soundtrack albums already noted, these include: *The Ultimate Titanic Experience*, *My Heart Will Go On*, Ronan Magill's *Titanic, 10–15 April 1912: Five Pieces for Solo Piano* (a 1998 re-recording of a 1988 piece), *Music Inspired by the Titanic and Other Hits of the Time*, *Titanic – Melodies from the White Star Music Book*, Ian Whitcomb and the White Star Line Orchestra's *Titanic: Music as Heard on the Fateful Voyage*, *Music Aboard the Titanic*, *Titanic Serenade: Music from an Age of Elegance*, *Celtic Love Collection: Songs Inspired by Titanic* (by the Countdown Orchestra), *Titanic: Music from the Era*, *The Ultimate Collection* (themes from the film and the stage musical), Steve Cameron's *Titanic Suite* (written in 1988, and which, after the initial re-release, was repackaged as part of *Titanic Trilogy*), *Spirit of the Titanic, Volume 1*, *Spirit of the Titanic, Volume 2*, *A Romantic Tribute to the Titanic* (by the New Millennium Chorus and Symphony), *Titanic & Other Movie Hits* (by the American Film Orchestra), *Joan Plays . . . Themes from Titanic* (by pianist Joan Matey Mallory), *Titanic Tunes: A Sing-a-Long in Steerage* (old music-hall songs performed by Ian Whitcomb), *Titanic – My Heart Will Go On: Music from Titanic*, *Titanic Ship of Dreams*, *Titanic: Epic Songs of the Sea*, *Great Titanic* (by the Transatlantic Orchestra & Singers) and finally, *Titanic* (by the Movie Sounds Unlimited Orchestra). While a handful of the CDs included pieces of Horner's film music, many of them comprised polite period pieces for palm court orchestras, the rights to which could be acquired reasonably cheaply.

Increasingly, music from films is prominent enough to elicit special events, such as the 'Film Music Prom', part of the annual Henry Wood promenade concert series at the Albert Hall, London. It was broadcast live on BBC radio in the summer of 2002. A second 'Film Music Prom' was staged as part of the following year's Prom concert series, and broadcast not only live on BBC radio, but also on BBC television. There has also been a proliferation of live music as accompaniment to silent films. Carl Davis has held a virtual monopoly on this in Britain during the last couple of decades, including conducting a live performance of the music for Charlie Chaplin's *City Lights* (1931) in 1995, which necessitated masking the original recorded version of the score on the film's print. *Sight and Sound* magazine commissioned new soundtracks for films by Maya Deren (*Meshes of the Afternoon* [1943]) and Norman McLaren among others, as part of the 'Score' touring event in October and November 1996. The music was composed by 'today's electronic innovators', including Slab and DJ Andrew Weatherall. German group Faust provided music for F. W. Murnau's silent film *Nosferatu: eine Symphonie des Grauens*, which was released as the album *Faust Wakes Nosferatu* (1998), while there was a subsequent screening with a live musical performance at the Royal Festival Hall, London, on 25 October 2000. On 20 July of the following year, London's National Film Theatre screened Vsevolod Pudovkin's *Storm over Asia – The Heir of Genghis Khan* (1928) with live music by Yat-Kha (a group that mix traditional Tuvan throat singing with western rock). Other 'film music' events have included Turner Prize-winning artist Douglas Gordon's installation entitled 'Feature Film', which used Bernard Herrmann's score for *Vertigo* as an accompaniment to mostly close-up images of Paris Opera Orchestra conductor James Conlon's hands as he conducts the music.[2] A new print of *E.T.* was premiered at The Shrine, Los Angeles, on 16 March 2002, and projected on a fifty-foot screen, with music performed live by a hundred-piece orchestra, and conducted by John Williams. It included a new quasi-overture, based on *E.T.*'s musical themes, which was accompanied by colourful images of space and some shots of the orchestra in action.[3] The proliferation of isolated scores on DVD releases is an eloquent testament to the way that screen music is being consumed in a different manner from the way it had been, and furthermore in a manner that differs from that which was intended.

Scores that were never used in films have been re-recorded, such as Bernard Herrmann's *Torn Curtain* and Alex North's *2001: A Space Odyssey*. Such works are thus reconceived as 'listening' music rather than 'accompanying' music. The sales of orchestral soundtrack albums is solid evidence that film music functions as more than 'incidental' to its film. Some successful films, such as *Braveheart* and *Gladiator*, have produced two different soundtrack albums of orchestral music, realising their full commercial potential. In terms of song compilation scores, many mainstream films release song albums that often contain only a few of the songs, if that, featured in the film itself. These albums resemble – indeed, to some degree have replaced – the compilation albums of yore, such as the series of *Rock Machine Turns You On* albums of the early 1970s. In the UK, albums of songs can be found in record shops when the film is still far from release here or, in some cases, never reaches these shores.

If some music in films never actually appears in the films, the principal of musical accompaniment developed and solidified in the classical film score has not only moved partially across to television, but also to other electronic media, such as computer games,[4] and arguably to life itself. Joseph Lanza noted that 'Mood music, production music, and stock music libraries have adapted movie soundtrack principles to other media.'[5] Ambient music and the ethos of using music as a background sound is endemic. We can visit expensive restaurants that play classical music such as Vivaldi or Schubert in the background as we eat, reconfiguring it as cheap but upmarket wallpaper furnishing the cultural distinction required by high-class eateries. This recontextualisation of art music would not only most likely have upset the music's composer greatly, but also indicates the monumental cultural changes that have arisen relatively recently. The same goes for the music's appearance in films. Recontextualised music is a commodity that can be resold, and this has become one of the central cultural logics in play where recorded music is concerned. The proliferation of personal stereos in the 1980s led to a whole new aesthetic associated with the way that people use music as a soundtrack to their lives. Kissing couples could listen to the score from *Now, Voyager*, joggers can listen to Vangelis's score from *Chariots of Fire*, while I imagine that somewhere a dentist's waiting room is surreptitiously playing the music from *Marathon Man* (1976). While this seems an innocent enough activity, it retains the logic of film music, underscoring events, articulating activities and creating emotional effects.

Music is used more generally for its engaging qualities and manipulative potential. In John Carpenter's *In the Mouth of Madness* (1995), the beleaguered Trent (Sam Neill) has been incarcerated in a padded cell in a mental hospital where the other patients groan appallingly. A doctor switches on a recording of a popular song. The inmates calm down and then begin singing along. Trent shouts, 'Oh No! Not the Carpenters too!' Of course, the depiction of the use of music in mental hospitals (and elsewhere) as a pacification device and as a counterpart to a regime of drug sedation is hardly a new invention. But it does suggest something of its similarity with screen music's character, as a palliative, aimed at encouraging certain behaviour and making us more accepting of the status quo, both in life and on screen. Discussing the uses recorded music is put to, Tia DeNora notes: 'Using music as a resource for creating and sustaining ontological security, and for entraining and modulating mood and levels of distress, is by no means unique to the purview of the professional music therapeutic encounter.'[6] As consumers, we may use recorded music to create our world, but the music is also configuring us. We may use it to fulfil certain desires, but it is the material character of the music itself that offers the promise of fulfilment. Somatic music can 'soothe the savage beast', and, to paraphrase the *Mary Poppins* (1964) song, it can be the spoonful of sugar that helps the medicine go down, allowing us to consume tragedy and morbidity more easily in films such as *Titanic* and *Schindler's List*.

There appears to be unequivocal evidence that small influences upon the mind are commonplace, but no solid evidence for strong subliminal persuasion.[7] The whole media furore about 'backmasking', where backwards messages or entreaties are hidden in musical recordings, tells us more about the fears concerning the power of music and imperceptible control than it does about anything else. Indeed, backmasking appears almost to have been forged to embody the so-called 'hypodermic' model of effect, where the audience is given an impetus of which it is unaware and totally unable to resist. Prominent court cases in the 1980s, such as the action taken against Ozzy Osbourne's 'Suicide Solution' (from the album *Blizzard of Ozz*) and

Judas Priest's 'Better by You, Better than Me' (from the album *Stained Class*),[8] both concerned teen suicides that were allegedly carried out at the behest of the music. Both prosecutions failed outright. However, despite the seeming hysteria,[9] backmasking exists. On Pink Floyd's album *The Wall*, the track 'Empty Spaces', when played backwards, reveals Roger Waters intoning, 'Congratulations. You have just discovered the secret message. Send your answer to Old Pink in care of the funny farm.' This may not have the insidious intention accorded to some rock music, but it certainly illustrates the unapparent and ephemeral aspects of music. This 'message' reappeared without remark in the film *Pink Floyd: The Wall*, and the covert status of such backmasking rhymes with the transient and subliminal character of screen music, while engaging a potential that might be related to effect, however unlikely.

Screen music is a social and cultural phenomenon; in fact, it might be seen as a philosophy. Aesthetic systems are systems of thought. This includes the denial of epistemologies and ontologies as well as their validation.[10] Adorno suggests as much. His description of audiences as 'marching in line' to music with a regular pulse implies that marching is not simply an activity, and marching music is not simply a reaction to military desires and needs,[11] but that marching is a *whole philosophy* – and so is film music, particularly non-diegetic music, the underscore.[12] Screen music sees the world as articulated by and understandable through music – it constitutes a way of looking at the world that was perhaps most clearly defined in the Hollywood film musical, but is evident in all walks of film and television where music is involved.

Notes

1 Jeff Smith, 'Selling My Heart: Music and Cross-Promotion in *Titanic*' in Kevin S. Sandler and Gaylyn Studlar, eds., *Titanic: Anatomy of a Blockbuster* (New Brunswick, NJ: Rutgers University Press, 1999), pp. 47, 54.

2 At the Atlantis Gallery, Brick Lane, London, 1 April–3 May 1999.

3 This event is documented on 'John Williams Live at the Shrine Auditorium 2002 Premiere', *E.T.* DVD extra (Universal B00003CX9Q).

4 Cf. David Bessell, 'What's That Funny Noise? An Examination of the Role of Music in *Cool Boarders 2*, *Alien Trilogy* and *Medieval 2*' in Geoff King and Tanya Krzywinska, eds., *ScreenPlay: Cinema/Videogames/Interfaces* (London: Wallflower, 2002), pp. 136–44.

5 Joseph Lanza, *Elevator Music: A Surreal History of Muzak, Easy-Listening and Other Moodsong* (London: Quartet, 1995), p. 63.

6 Tia DeNora, *Music in Everyday Life* (Cambridge: Cambridge University Press, 2000), p. 16.

7 Norman F. Dixon, *Subliminal Perception: The Nature of Controversy* (London: McGraw-Hill, 1971), p. 27.

8 The Judas Priest case was discussed in detail in *Time*, 30 July 1990, p. 65.

9 Cf. John R. Vokey and J. Don Read, 'Subliminal Messages: Between the Devil and the Media', *American Psychologist*, vol. 40, no. 11, 1985, pp. 1231–9.

10 'Structural standardization aims at standard reactions. Listening to popular music is manipulated not only by its promoters but, as it were, by the inherent nature of this music

itself, into a system of response mechanisms wholly *antagonistic to the ideal of individuality in a free, liberal society* [my italics].' Theodor Adorno, 'On Popular Music' in Simon Frith and Andrew Goodwin, eds, *On Record: Rock, Pop and the Written Word* (London: Routledge, 1990), p. 305.

11 'This obedient type is the rhythmic type . . .' who is happy to conform and to march in line. '. . . the standardized meter of dance music and of marching suggests the coordinated battalions of a mechanical collectivity.' Adorno, 'On Popular Music', p. 312.

12 Film music is not a philosophy in the sense of being a fully integrated system that thinks of itself as a philosophy – but as an aesthetic worldview.

Bibliography

Adorno, T. W., and Max Horkheimer, *The Dialectic of Enlightenment* (London: Verso, 1979).

Adorno, T. W., *Introduction to the Sociology of Music* (New York: Seabury, 1976).

Adorno, T. W., 'On Popular Music' in Simon Frith and Andrew Goodwin, eds., *On Record: Rock, Pop and the Written Word* (London: Routledge, 1990).

Adorno, T. W., *Philosophy of Modern Music* (New York: Seabury, 1973).

Altman, Rick, *The American Film Musical* (London: BFI, 1989).

Altman, Rick, 'Cinema and Popular Song: The Lost Tradition' in Pamela Robertson Wojcik and Arthur Knight, eds., *Soundtrack Available: Film and Popular Music* (Durham, NC: Duke University Press, 2001).

Altman, Rick, ed., *Sound Theory, Sound Practice* (London: Routledge, 1992).

Altman, Rick, 'Television/Sound' in Tania Modleski, ed., *Studies in Entertainment: Critical Approaches to Mass Culture* (Bloomington: Indiana Univ. Press, 1986).

Archer, Simon, and Stan Nicholls, *Gerry Anderson: The Authorised Biography* (London: Legend, 1996).

Arnold, Dennis, ed., *The New Oxford Companion to Music* (Oxford: Oxford University Press, 1983).

Barker, Martin, Jane Arthurs and Ramaswami Harindranath, *The Crash Controversy: Censorship Campaigns and Film Reception* (London: Wallflower, 2001).

Barron, Lee, ' "Music Inspired by . . .": The Curious Case of the Missing Soundtrack' in Ian Inglis, ed., *Popular Music and Film* (London: Wallflower, 2003).

Barthes, Roland, *Mythologies*, translated by Annette Lavers (New York: Hill and Wang, 1972).

Baudrillard, Jean, *The Evil Demon of Images* (Sydney: Power Institute, 1994).

Baudrillard, Jean, *The Revenge of the Crystal: Selected Writings on the Modern Object and Its Destiny, 1968–1983* (London: Pluto, 1999).

Bazelon, Irwin, *Knowing the Score: Notes on Film Music* (New York: Van Nostrand Reinhold, 1975).

Bennington, Geoffrey, 'Postal Politics and the Institution of the Nation' in Homi K. Bhaba, ed., *Nation and Narration* (London: Routledge, 1990).

Berg, Chuck, 'Fade Out in the West: The Western's Last Stand' in Wheeler Winston Dixon, ed., *Film Genre 2000: New Critical Essays* (Albany, NY: SUNY Press, 2000).

Berkwits, Jeff, 'Graeme Revell – Journeys to *Dune*' [interview], *Soundtrack*, vol. 19, no. 76, Winter 2000.

Bessell, David, 'What's That Funny Noise?: An Examination of the Role of Music in *Cool Boarders 2*, *Alien Trilogy* and *Medieval 2*' in Geoff King and Tanya Krzywinska, eds., *ScreenPlay: Cinema/Videogames/ Interfaces* (London: Wallflower, 2002).

Billington, Monroe Lee, and Roger D. Hardaway, eds., *African Americans on the Western Frontier* (Boulder: University of Colorado Press, 1998).

Bond, Jeff, *The Music of Star Trek* (Los Angeles: Lone Eagle, 1999).

Bondanella, Peter, *Italian Cinema: From Neorealism to the Present* (New York: Continuum, 1996).

Bonner, Michael, 'Primal Screen' [review of David Holmes's CD *Bow Down to the Exit Sign*], *Uncut*, no. 37, June 2000.

Bordwell, David, *Making Meaning: Inference and Rhetoric in the Interpretation of Cinema* (Cambridge, MA: Harvard University Press, 1991).

Born, Georgina, and David Hesmondhalgh, 'Introduction' in Georgina Born and David Hesmondhalgh, eds., *Western Music and Its Others: Difference, Representation and Appropriation in Music* (Berkeley: University of California Press, 2000).

Bourdieu, Pierre, *Language and Symbolic Power*, edited by John B. Thompson, translated by Gino Raymond and Matthew Adamson (Oxford: Polity, 1991).

Brown, Mick, *Performance, Bloomsbury Movie Guide, No. 6* (London: Bloomsbury, 1999).

Brown, Royal S., *Overtones and Undertones: Reading Film Music* (Berkeley and Los Angeles: University of California Press, 1994).

Buhler, James, Caryl Flinn and David Neumeyer, eds., *Music and Cinema* (Hanover, NH: Wesleyan University Press, 2000).

Burke, Edmund, *A Philosophical Inquiry into the Origins of Our Ideas of the Sublime and Beautiful* (Oxford: Oxford University Press, 1990).

Burnand, David, and Benedict Sarnaker, 'The Articulation of National Identity through Film Music', *National Identities*, vol. 1, no. 1, 1999.

Burt, George, *The Art of Film Music* (Boston, MA: Northeastern University Press, 1994).

Buscombe, Edward, *The Making of Legend of the Werewolf* (London: BFI, 1976).

Butler, Jeremy G., *Television: Critical Methods and Applications* (Belmont, CA: Wadsworth, 1994).

Carlsson, Mikael, 'Interview with the Composer' on *Music from the Movies* website <www.musicfromthemovies.com/ pages/goldenthal_interview.html> (accessed 10 October 2000) (previously published in *Moviescore*, no. 2, 1995, and *Music from the Movies*, no. 10, 1995–6).

Carroll, Noel, *Theorising the Moving Image* (Cambridge: Cambridge University Press, 1996).

Carson, Ciaran, *Irish Traditional Music* (Belfast: Appletree, 1999).

Casey, Bernadette, Neil Casey, Ben Calvert, Liam French and Justin Lewis, *Television Studies: The Key Concepts* (London: Arnold, 2001).

Caughie, John, 'The Rush of the Real: An Aesthetic of Immediacy' in *Television Drama: Realism, Modernism and British Culture* (Oxford: Oxford University Press, 2000).

Celeste, Reni, '*Lost Highway*: Unveiling Cinema's Yellow Brick Road', *Cineaction*, no. 43, Summer 1997.

Chapple, Steve, and Reebee Garofalo, *Rock'n'Roll Is Here to Pay: The History and Politics of the Music Industry* (Chicago: Nelson Hall, 1977).

Chion, Michel, *Audio-Vision: Sound on Screen*, edited and translated by Claudia Gorbman (New York: Columbia University Press, 1994).

Chion, Michel, *David Lynch* (London: BFI, 1995).

Cinema Sounds (*Sight and Sound/The Wire* Supplement) (London, 1993).

Cohen, Annabel J., 'Film Music: Perspectives from Cognitive Psychology' in James Buhler, Caryl Flinn and David Neumeyer, eds., *Music and Cinema* (Hanover, NH: Wesleyan University Press, 2000).

Cook, David A., 'American Horror: *The Shining*', *Literature/Film Quarterly*, vol. 12, no. 1, 1984.

Cook, Nicholas, 'Music and Meaning in the Commercials', *Popular Music*, vol. 13, no. 1, 1994.

Cook, Pam, ed., *Gainsborough Pictures* (London: Cassell, 1997).

Cooke, Lez, *British Television Drama: A History* (London: BFI, 2003).

Copland, Aaron, 'Tip to the Moviegoers: Take Off Those Ear-Muffs', *The New York Times*, 6 November 1949.

Corner, John, *The Art of Record: An Introduction to Documentary* (Manchester: Manchester University Press, 1996).

Corner, John, *Critical Ideas in Television Studies* (Oxford: Oxford University Press, 1999).

Coyne, Michael, *The Crowded Prairie: American National Identity in the Hollywood Western* (London: I. B. Tauris, 1997).

Creeber, Glen, 'Banality with a Beat: Dennis Potter and the Paradox of Popular Culture', *Media, Culture and Society*, vol. 18, no. 3, 1996.

Dancyger, Ken, *The Technique of Film and Video Editing* (London: Focal Press, 1996).

Darby, William, and Jack Du Bois, *American Film Music: Major Composers, Techniques, Trends, 1915–1990* (Jefferson, NC: McFarland, 1990).

Davies, Richard, *Complete Guide to Film Scoring* (Boston, MA: Berklee Press, 1999).

DeNora, Tia, *Music in Everyday Life* (Cambridge: Cambridge University Press, 2000).

Denisoff, R. Serge, and George Plasketes, 'Synergy in 1980s Film and Music: Formula for Success or Industry Mythology?', *Film History*, vol. 4, no. 3, 1990.

Derrida, Jacques, *Specters of Marx: The State of the Debt, the Work of Mourning and the New International* (London: Routledge, 1994).

Descartes, René, *Meditations on First Philosophy*, translated by Ronald Rubin (Claremont, CA: Arete, 1986).

Detourn, Gal, 'Lost Souls Take Flight', *Making Music*, issue 177, January 2000.

Devereux, Paul, *Places of Power: Measuring the Secret Energy of Ancient Sites* (London: Blandford, 1999).

Dickinson, Kay, ed., *Music, The Film Reader* (London: Routledge, 2002).

Dixon, Norman F., *Subliminal Perception: The Nature of Controversy* (London: McGraw-Hill, 1971).

Donnelly, K. J., 'Angel of the Air: Popol Vuh's Music for Werner Herzog's Films' in Miguel Mera and David Burnand, eds., *European Film Music* (Aldershot, Hants: Ashgate, 2005).

Donnelly, K. J., 'The Classical Film Score Forever?: Music in the *Batman* Films' in Steve Neale and Murray Smith, eds., *Contemporary Hollywood Cinema* (London: Routledge, 1997).

Donnelly, K. J., 'Constructing the Future through Music of the Past: The Software in Hardware' in Ian Inglis, ed., *Popular Music and Film* (London: Wallflower, 2003).

Donnelly, K. J., ed., *Film Music: Critical Approaches* (Edinburgh: Edinburgh University Press, 2001).

Donnelly, K. J., 'The Hidden Heritage of Film Music: History and Scholarship' in K. J. Donnelly, ed., *Film Music: Critical Approaches* (Edinburgh: Edinburgh University Press, 2001).

Donnelly, K. J., '*Performance* and the Composite Film Score' in K. J. Donnelly, ed., *Film Music: Critical Approaches* (Edinburgh: Edinburgh University Press, 2001).

Donnelly, K. J., *Pop Music in British Cinema: A Chronicle* (London: BFI, 2001).

Donnelly, K. J., 'A Ramble through the Margins of the Cityscape: The Postmodern as the Return of Nature' in Michael Dear and Steven Flusty, eds., *Spaces of Postmodernity: Readings in Human Geography* (Oxford: Blackwell, 2002).

Donnelly, K. J., '*Walking with Dinosaurs*' in Glen Creeber, ed., *Fifty Key Television Programmes* (London: Arnold, 2003).

Donnelly, K. J., 'Wicked Sounds and Magic Melodies: Music in Gainsborough Melodramas' in Pam Cook, ed., *Gainsborough Pictures* (London: Cassell, 1997).

Dyer, Richard, *Only Entertainment* (London: Routledge, 1992).

Dyer, Richard, *White* (London: Routledge, 1997).

Eckstein, Jeremy, ed., *Cultural Trends 19*, vol. 3, no. 3 (London: Policy Studies Institute, 1993).

Eisler, Hanns, and Theodor Adorno, *Composing for the Films* (London: Athlone, 1994).

Ellis, John, *Visible Fictions: Film, Television, Video* (London: Routledge, 1982).

Elsaesser, Thomas, 'Tales of Sound and Fury: Observations on the Family Melodrama' in Christine Gledhill, ed., *Home Is Where the Heart Is: Studies in Melodrama and the Woman's Film* (London: BFI, 1987).

Fearn, Rob, 'Scary Tales of New York', *Mixmag*, no. 76, September 1997.

Feuer, Jane, 'The Concept of Live Television: Ontology as Ideology' in E. Ann Kaplan, ed., *Regarding Television: Critical Approaches – An Anthology* (New York: AFI, 1983).

Fiske, John, *Television Culture* (London: Routledge, 1987).

Fiske, John, 'Moments of Television: Neither the Text nor the Reader' in Ellen Seiter, Hans Borchers, Gabriele Kreutzner and Eva-Marie Warth, eds., *Remote Control: Television, Audiences and Cultural Power* (London: Routledge, 1989).

Fitzgerald, Thomas K., 'Media, Ethnicity and Identity' in Paddy Scannell, Philip Schlesinger and Colin Sparks, eds., *Culture and Power: A Media, Culture and Society Reader* (London: Sage, 1992).

Flinn, Caryl, *Strains of Utopia: Gender, Nostalgia and Hollywood Film Music* (Princeton: Princeton University Press, 1992).

Foucault, Michel, *Discipline and Punish: The Birth of the Prison* (New York: Vintage, 1995).

Friedson, Steven M., 'Dancing the Disease: Music and Trance in Tumbuka Healing' in Penelope Gouk, ed., *Musical Healing in Cultural Contexts* (Aldershot, Hants: Ashgate, 2000).

Frith, Simon, 'Mood Music: An Enquiry into Narrative Film Music', *Screen*, vol. 25, no. 3, May–June 1984.

Frith, Simon, 'Youth Culture/Youth Cults' in Charlie Gillett and Simon Frith, eds., *The Beat Goes On: The Rock File Reader* (London: Pluto, 1996).

Gallagher, Tag, *John Ford: The Man and His Films* (Berkeley: University of California Press, 1988).

Garwood, Ian, 'Must You Remember This?: Orchestrating the "Standard" Pop Song in *Sleepless in Seattle*' in Kay Dickinson, ed., *Movie Music: The Film Reader* (London: Routledge, 2003).

Gorbman, Claudia, *Unheard Melodies: Narrative Film Music* (London: BFI, 1987).

Gorbman, Claudia, 'Scoring the Indian: Music in the Liberal Western' in Georgina Born and David Hesmondhalgh, eds., *Western Music and Its Others: Difference, Representation and Appropriation in Music* (Berkeley: University of California Press, 2000).

Hamer, Mick, 'Silent Fright', *New Scientist*, 21–28 December 2002.

Hammer Horror Collectors' Special, no. 1, 1994.

Hennion, Antoine, 'The Production of Success: An Antimusicology of the Pop Song' in Simon Frith and Andrew Goodwin, eds., *On Record: Rock, Pop and the Written Word* (London: Routledge, 1990).

Henry, Michael, 'Le Ruban de Mobius' [interview with David Lynch], *Positif*, no. 432, January 1997.

Higson, Andrew, *Waving the Flag: Constructing a National Cinema in Britain* (Oxford: Oxford University Press, 1997).

Higson, Andrew, *English Heritage, English Cinema* (Oxford: Oxford University Press, 2003).

Hirsch, David, 'CD Microbreweries Part 1: Fanderson Records', *Soundtrack*, vol. 10, no. 76, Winter 2000.

Holmes, David, 'Inside Track' [about his latest album], *Uncut*, no. 37, June 2000.

Howe, David J., Mark Stammers and Stephen James Walker, *Doctor Who: The Seventies* (London: Virgin, 1994).

Howe, David J., and Stephen James Walker, *Doctor Who: The Television Companion* (London: BBC, 1999).

Huckvale, David, '*Twins of Evil*: An Investigation into the Aesthetics of Film Music', *Popular Music*, vol. 9, no. 1, 1990.

Hutchings, Peter, *Hammer and Beyond: The British Horror Film* (Manchester: Manchester University Press, 1993).

Inglis, Ian, ed., *Popular Music and Film* (London: Wallflower, 2003).

Jacobs, Jason, *The Intimate Screen: Early British Television Drama* (Oxford: Oxford University Press, 2000).

Jahn, Robert G., Paul Devereux and Michael Ibison, 'Acoustic Resonances of Assorted Ancient Structures', *Journal of the Acoustic Society of America*, vol. 99, no. 2, February 1996.

Jahn, Robert G., and Paul Devereux, 'Preliminary Investigations and Cognitive Considerations of the Acoustical Resonances of Selected Archaeological Sites', *Antiquity*, no. 70, 1996.

Kalinak, Kathryn, '"Disturbing the Guests with This Racket": Music and *Twin Peaks*' in David Lavery, ed., *Full of Secrets: Critical Approaches to Twin Peaks* (Detroit: Wayne State University Press, 1994).

Kalinak, Kathryn, 'The Language of Music: A Brief Analysis of *Vertigo*' in Kay Dickinson, ed., *Movie Music: The Film Reader* (London: Routledge, 2003).

Kalinak, Kathryn, *Settling the Score: Music and the Classical Hollywood Film* (Madison: University of Wisconsin Press, 1992).

Kalsi, Satpal, '*The Stargate*', *Terrorizer*, issue 70, September 1999.

Kant, Immanuel, *Critique of Judgement*, translated by Werner S. Pluhar (Indianapolis, IN: Hackett, 1987 [originally 1790]).

Kassabian, Anahid, *Hearing Film: Tracking Identifications in Contemporary Hollywood Film Music* (London: Routledge, 2001).

Kennedy, Barbara, *Deleuze and Cinema: The Aesthetics of Sensation* (Edinburgh: Edinburgh University Press, 2000).

Kitses, Jim, *Horizons West* (Bloomingtom: Indiana University Press, 1969).

Kracauer, Siegfried, *Theory of Film: The Redemption of Physical Reality* (Oxford: Oxford University Press, 1971).

Kramer, Lawrence, *Classical Music and Postmodern Knowledge* (Berkeley: University of California Press, 1996).

The Kubrick FAQ <www.visual-memory.co.uk/faq/html/shining/shining.html> (accessed 25 October 2002).

Lanza, Joseph, *Elevator Music: A Surreal History of Muzak, Easy-Listening and Other Moodsong* (London: Quartet, 1995).

Larson, Randall D., 'Fear and Laughter' [interview with John Frizell], *Soundtrack,* vol. 21, no. 83, 2002.

Larson, Randall D., *Music from the House of Hammer* (Metuchen, NJ: Scarecrow, 1996).

Lastra, James, *Sound Technology and the American Cinema: Perception, Representation, Modernity* (New York: Columbia University Press, 2000).

Lebow, Richard Ned, *White Britain and Black Ireland: The Influence of Stereotypes on Colonial Policy* (Philadelphia: Institute for the Study of Human Issues, 1976).

Levinson, Jerrold, 'Film Music and Narrative Agency' in David Bordwell and Noel Carroll, eds., *Post Theory: Reconstructing Film Studies* (Madison: University of Wisconsin Press, 1996).

Lipscomb, S. D., and R. A. Kendall, 'Perceptual Judgment of the Relationship between Musical and Visual Components in Film', *Psychomusicology*, vol. 13, Spring/Fall 1994.

Lissa, Zofia, *Asthetic der Filmmusik* (Berlin: Henschel, 1965).

LoBrutto, Vincent, *Sound-on-Film: Interviews with Creators of Film Sound* (London: Praeger, 1994).

'*Lost Highway* Soundtrack' <www.lynchnet.com/lh/lhst.html> (accessed 15 October 2003).

Lyons, Donald, 'La La Limbo', *Film Comment*, vol. 33, no. 1, January–February 1997.

MacFarlane, Brian, *An Autobiography of British Cinema: By the Actors and Filmmakers Who Made It* (London: Methuen, 1997).

Mackay, Robert, 'Leaving Out the Black Notes: The BBC and "Enemy Music" in the Second World War', *Media History*, vol. 6, no. 1, 2000.

MacRory, Pauline, 'Excusing the Violence of Hollywood Women: Music in *Nikita* and *Point of No Return*', *Screen*, vol. 40, no. 1, 1999.

Marcus, Greil, *The Dustbin of History* (London: Picador, 1997).

Martin, Gavin, 'Company Lore and Public Disorder' [interview with Public Image Limited], *New Musical Express*, 14 March 1981.

McArthur, Colin, 'Scotland and Cinema: The Iniquity of the Fathers' in Colin McArthur, ed., *Scotch Reels: Scotland in Cinema and Television* (London: BFI, 1982).

McClary, Susan, *George Bizet's Carmen* (Cambridge: Cambridge University Press, 1992).

McDonagh, Maitland, *Broken Mirrors, Broken Minds: The Dark Dreams of Dario Argento* (London: Sun Tavern Fields, 1991).

McLaughlin, Noel, and Martin McLoone, 'Hybridity and National Musics: The Case of Irish Rock Music', *Popular Music*, vol. 19, no. 2, 2000.

McLoone, Martin, *Irish Film: The Emergence of a Contemporary Cinema* (London: BFI, 2000).

Meyer, Leonard B., *Emotion and Meaning in Music* (Chicago: University of Chicago Press, 1956).

Middleton, Richard, *Studying Popular Music* (Maidenhead: Open University Press, 1990).

Moss, Robert F., *The Films of Carol Reed* (New York: Columbia University Press, 1987).

Motet, Dan, 'Music Therapy' in R. J. Corsini
and A. J. Auerbach, eds., *Concise
Encyclopedia of Psychology* (London: John
Wiley, 1996).

Narmour, Eugene, *Beyond Schenkerism: The
Need for Alternatives in Music Analysis*
(Chicago: University of Chicago Press,
1977).

Neaverson, Robert, *The Beatles Movies*
(London: Cassell, 1997).

Nelson, Robin, *TV Drama in Transition: Forms,
Values and Cultural Change* (Basingstoke,
Hants: Macmillan, 1997).

Norman, Neil, 'Green Ice for a Grey Stone'
[interview with Bill Wyman], *New Musical
Express*, 30 May 1981.

North, Adrian C., and David J. Hargreaves,
'Music and Consumer Behaviour' in Adrian
C. North and David J. Hargreaves, eds., *The
Social Psychology of Music* (Oxford: Oxford
University Press, 1999).

Nyman, Michael, *Experimental Music: Cage
and Beyond* (Cambridge: Cambridge
University Press, 1974).

Palmer, Christopher, *The Composer in
Hollywood* (London: Marion Boyars, 1990).

Pettit, Lance, *Screening Ireland: Film and
Television Representation* (Manchester:
Manchester University Press, 2000).

Pinder, David, 'Ghostly Footsteps: Voices,
Memories and Walks in the City', *Ecumene*,
vol. 8, no. 1, January 2001.

Pirie, David, *A Heritage of Horror: The English
Gothic Cinema, 1946–72* (London: Reynolds
and Hearn, 1973).

Pixley, Andrew, 'DWM Archive: Inferno',
Doctor Who Magazine, no. 305, 2001.

Pizzello, Stephen, 'Highway to Hell', *American
Cinematographer*, vol. 78, no. 3, March
1997.

Postman, Neil, *Amusing Ourselves to Death:
Public Discourse in the Age of Show Business*
(London: Viking, 1986).

Prendergast, Mark, *The Ambient Century: From
Mahler to Moby – the Evolution of Sound in
the Electronic Age* (London: Bloomsbury,
2000).

Prendergast, Roy M., *Film Music: A Neglected
Art* (New York: Norton, 1992).

Prys, Catrin, '*The Singing Detective*' in Glen
Creeber, ed., *Fifty Key Television
Programmes* (London: Arnold, 2004).

Punter, David, and Glennis Byron, eds., *Spectral
Readings: Towards a Gothic Geography* (New
York: St Martin's Press, 1999).

Raudive, Konstantin, *Breakthrough: An
Amazing Experiment in Electronic
Communication with the Dead* (New York:
Taplinger, 1971).

Reich, Willi, *Schoenberg: A Critical Biography*,
translated by Leo Black (London:
Longman, 1971).

Richards, Jeffrey, *Films and British National
Identity: From Dickens to Dad's Army*
(Manchester: Manchester University Press,
1997).

Rodley, Chris, 'David Lynch: Mr
Contradiction', *Sight and Sound*, vol. 6,
issue 7, August 1996.

Rodley, Chris, *Lynch on Lynch* (London: Faber
and Faber, 1997).

Rosar, William H., 'The *Dies Irae* in *Citizen
Kane*: Musical Hermeneutics Applied to
Film Music' in K. J. Donnelly, ed., *Film
Music: Critical Approaches* (Edinburgh:
Edinburgh University Press, 2001).

Rosar, William H., 'Film Music – What's in a
Name?', *Journal of Film Music*, vol. 1, no. 1,
Summer 2002.

Rosar, William H., 'Music for the Monsters:
Universal Pictures' Horror Film Scores of
the Thirties', *The Quarterly Journal of the
Library of Congress*, no. 40, Fall 1983.

Rosenbluth, Jean, 'Soundtrack Specialists:
Maximizing Cross-Market Connections',
Billboard, 16 July 1988.

Said, Edward, *Orientalism* (London: Random House, 1979).

Saunders, John, *The Western Genre: From Lordsburg to Big Whiskey* (London: Wallflower, 2001).

Sconce, Jeffrey, *Haunted Media: Electronic Presence from Telegraphy to Television* (Durham, NC: Duke University Press, 2000).

Simpson, Dave, 'Plug and Play', *Guardian*, 5 May 2000.

Sinker, Mark, 'Music as Film' in Jonathan Romney and Adrian Wootton, eds., *Celluloid Jukebox: Popular Music and the Movies since the 50s* (London: BFI, 1995).

Sirius, G., and E. F. Clarke, 'The Perception of Audiovisual Relationships: A Preliminary Study', *Psychomusicology*, vol. 13, Spring/Fall 1994.

Skal, David J., *The Monster Show: A Cultural History of Horror* (London: Plexus, 1993).

Slotkin, Richard, *Gunfighter Nation: The Myth of the Frontier in Twentieth Century America* (London: HarperCollins, 1992).

Smith, Jeff, 'Popular Song and Comic Allusion in Contemporary Cinema' in Pamela Robertson Wojcik and Arthur Knight, eds., *Soundtrack Available: Essays on Film and Popular Music* (London: Duke University Press, 2001).

Smith, Jeff, 'Selling My Heart: Music and Cross-Promotion in *Titanic*' in Kevin S. Sandler and Gaylyn Studlar, eds., *Titanic: Anatomy of a Blockbuster* (New Brunswick, NJ: Rutgers University Press, 1999).

Smith, Jeff, *The Sounds of Commerce: Marketing Popular Film Music* (New York: Columbia University Press, 1998).

Smith, Jeff, 'Unheard Melodies? A Critique of Psychoanalytic Theories of Film Music' in David Bordwell and Noel Carroll, eds., *Post Theory: Reconstructing Film Studies* (Madison: University of Wisconsin Press, 1996).

Sonnenschein, David, *Sound Design – The Expressive Power of Music, Voice, Sound* (Studio City, CA: Michael Wiese Productions, 2001).

Stanfield, Peter, *Horse Opera: The Strange History of the 1930s Singing Cowboy* (Chicago: University of Illinois Press, 2002).

Steiner, Fred, 'Music for *Star Trek*: Scoring a Television Show in the Sixties' in Iris Newsom, ed., *Wonderful Inventions: Motion Pictures, Broadcasting and Recorded Sound at the Museum of Congress* (Washington: Museum of Congress, 1985).

Steiner, Max, 'Scoring the Film' in Nancy Naumburg, ed., *We Make the Movies* (New York: Norton, 1937).

Stilwell, Robynn, 'Sound and Empathy: Subjectivity, Gender and the Cinematic Soundscape' in K. J. Donnelly, ed., *Film Music: Critical Approaches* (Edinburgh: Edinburgh University Press, 2001).

Stilwell, Robynn, ' "I Just Put a Drone under Him": Collage and Subversion in *Die Hard*', *Music and Letters*, no. 78, 1998.

Tagg, Philip, *Kojak – 50 Seconds of Television Music: Toward the Analysis of Affect in Popular Music* (Gothenberg: Musikvetenskapliga Institute, University of Gothenberg, 1979).

Tagg, Philip, 'TV Music: Quick Fixes, Semiotics and the Democratic Right to Know', paper presented at the Stockholm 'Music and Manipulation' conference in 1999 (available on <www.tagg.org/texts.html> accessed 20 April 2003).

Talbot-Smith, Michael, *Audio Explained* (London: Focal Press, 1997).

Tandy, Vic, 'The Ghost in the Machine', *Journal for Psychical Research*, vol. 62, no. 851, April 1998.

Taylor, Quintard, *In Search of the Racial Frontier: African American in the American West, 1528–1990* (New York: Norton, 1998).

Thompson, W. F., F. A. Russo and D. Sinclair, 'Effects of Underscoring on Closure in Filmed Events', *Psychomusicology*, vol. 13, Spring/Fall 1994.

Toop, David, *Ocean of Sound: Aether Talk, Ambient Sounds and Imaginary Worlds* (London: Serpent's Tail, 1995).

Toop, David, 'Rock Musicians and Film Soundtracks' in Jonathan Romney and Adrian Wootton, eds., *Celluloid Jukebox: Popular Music and the Movies since the 50s* (London: BFI, 1995).

van Leeuwen, Theo, *Speech, Music, Sound* (Basingstoke, Hants: Macmillan, 1999).

Vokey, John. R., and J. Don Read, 'Subliminal Messages: Between the Devil and the Media', *American Psychologist*, vol. 40, no. 11, 1985.

Warshow, Robert, *The Immediate Experience* (New York: Anchor, 1964).

Watson, Aaron, 'Hearing Again the Sound of the Neolithic', *British Archaeology*, no. 23, 1997.

Watson, Aaron, and David Keating, 'Architecture of Sound: An Acoustic Analysis of Megalithic Monuments in Prehistoric Britain', *Antiquity*, no. 73, 1999.

Weis, Elisabeth, and John Belton, eds., *Film Sound: Theory and Practice* (New York: Columbia University Press, 1985).

Wells, Paul, *The Horror Genre: From Beelzebub to Blair Witch* (London: Wallflower, 2000).

Wells, Steven, 'Boy, I'm Really Nervous', *New Musical Express*, 25 September 1999.

Whiteley, Sheila, *The Space between the Notes: Rock and the Counterculture* (London: Routledge, 1992).

Williams, Raymond, *Television: Technology and Cultural Form* (London: Fontana, 1974).

Winn, Denise, *The Manipulated Mind: Brainwashing, Conditioning and Indoctrination* (London: Octagon Press, 1983).

Winston, Brian, *Lies, Damn Lies and Documentaries* (London: BFI, 2000).

Wojcik, Pamela Robertson, and Arthur Knight, eds., *Soundtrack Available: Film and Popular Music* (Durham, NC: Duke University Press, 2001).

Woods, Paul A., *Weirdsville USA: The Obsessive Universe of David Lynch* (London: Plexus, 2000).

Wurtzler, Steve, ' "She Sang Live but the Microphone Was Switched Off": The Live, the Recorded and the Subject of Representation' in Rick Altman, ed., *Sound Theory, Sound Practice* (London: Routledge, 1992).

Index